OXFORD ENGLISH MONOGRAPHS

General Editors

CHRISTOPHER BUTLER   KATE FLINT

VINCENT GILLESPIE   HERMIONE LEE

ROGER LONSDALE   FIONA STAFFORD

Memories of a Lost War

American Poetic Responses to the Vietnam War

SUBARNO CHATTARJI

CLARENDON PRESS • OXFORD

OXFORD
UNIVERSITY PRESS

Great Clarendon Street, Oxford, OX2 6DP

Oxford University Press is a department of the University of Oxford.
It furthers the University's objective of excellence in research, scholarship,
and education by publishing worldwide in

Oxford New York

Athens Auckland Bangkok Bogotá Buenos Aires Cape Town
Chennai Dar es Salaam Delhi Florence Hong Kong Istanbul Karachi
Kolkata Kuala Lumpur Madrid Melbourne Mexico City Mumbai Nairobi
Paris São Paulo Shanghai Singapore Taipei Tokyo Toronto Warsaw

and associated companies in Berlin Ibadan

Oxford is a registered trade mark of Oxford University Press
in the UK and certain other countries

Published in the United States
by Oxford University Press Inc., New York

© Subarno Chattarji 2001

The moral rights of the author have been asserted

Database right Oxford University Press (maker)

First published 2001

All rights reserved. No part of this publication may be reproduced,
stored in a retrieval system, or transmitted, in any form or by any means,
without the prior permission in writing of Oxford University Press,
or as expressly permitted by law, or under terms agreed with the appropriate
reprographics rights organization. Enquiries concerning reproduction
outside the scope of the above should be sent to the Rights Department,
Oxford University Press, at the address above

You must not circulate this book in any other binding or cover
and you must impose the same condition on any acquirer

British Library Cataloguing in Publication Data

Data available

Library of Congress Cataloging in Publication Data

Data available

ISBN 0-19-818767-x
ISBN 0-19-924711-0 (Pbk.)

1 3 5 7 9 10 8 6 4 2

Typeset in Sabon
by Regent Typesetting, London
Printed in Great Britain
on acid-free paper by
Biddles Ltd,
Guildford and King's Lynn

For Neena

Foreword
by Jon Stallworthy

IN the Fall of 1977, two years after the fall of Saigon, I was teaching a course on War Poetry at Cornell University in up-state New York. I had led an articulate and lively company of English majors from the plains of Troy to the ford at Maldon, from Waterloo to Spionkip, from the Western Front in the First World War to the Western Desert in the Second.

'So far, I've done most of the talking', I told them, 'but today it's your turn to tell *me* about Vietnam.' They looked at me blankly and no one spoke.

'Did any of you have a father who fought there...? No? Or an uncle...? No? Well, which of you has met someone who went to Vietnam?' They stared at me and no one spoke.

'Who can tell me the name of a poet who wrote about that war? No one?' No one. The fall of Saigon seemed as much news to them as the fall of Troy, and rather less welcome. In England, I had been troubled by a school syllabus over-insistent (it seemed to me) on the importance of a knowledge of the First World War, but I found my American student's ignorance of *their* country's most recent war more troubling still. Could the explanation, I wondered, be simply that for English majors the literature of the Western Front seemed more deserving of study than that to have emerged from—and about—Vietnam? The American critic, Paul Fussell, author of *The Great War and Modern Memory*, the most searching and satisfactory study of the literature of that war, would later say: 'no one expects interesting poetry to emerge from that sad war. All we can expect is more of what we have, a few structureless free-verse dribbles of easy irony or easy sentiment or easy political anger.'[1]

In such matters, a foreigner will sometimes see things that locals overlook. As Professor Fussell saw patterns in British

---

[1] Paul Fussell, 'Killing, In Verse and Prose', *Thank God for the Atom Bomb and Other Essays* (New York and London: Summit Books, 1988) 135–6.

poetry of the First World War that British critics had overlooked, so Dr Chattarji has written a book that, in the depth of its research, the range of its sympathy, the acuity of its literary and political judgement, is worthy to stand beside *The Great War and Modern Memory* or such other classics of the genre as Edmund Wilson's *Patriotic Gore* and Malvern van Wyk's Smith's *Drummer Hodge: The Poetry of the Anglo-Boer War*.

All such studies focus on victims and witnesses. In 1918, Wilfred Owen told his mother: 'I came out in order to help these boys—directly by leading them as well as an officer can; indirectly, by watching their sufferings that I may speak of them as well as a pleader can.'[2] He called himself 'a conscientious objector with a very seared conscience'.[3] As a committed Christian, he respected the sixth commandment but was prepared to break it and suffer a seared conscience as the price of the testimony he felt called upon to make. History has justified his decision: his poems and those of his fellow veterans have done more to warn succeeding generations of the consequences of modern warfare than the novels and histories of the period;[4] while no conscientious-objector poems of 1914–18 are now remembered.

The first American poets to respond to the war in Vietnam were conscientious objectors and if, in their weaker poems, they 'adopted a stance of poetic and prophetic infallibility'[5]—bearing witness to events experienced only through the news media—their poems of witness to the impact of the war *in America* were important and effective. They, however, are not the heroes of Dr Chattarji's book. Those laurels are reserved for veterans of the war, whose poems are—by contrast — little known on either side of the Atlantic. The first of them, John Balaban, following the precedent of Walt Whitman in the American Civil War, went to Vietnam 'not to bear arms but to bear witness'.[6] He spent the years 1967–9 as a conscientious objector, working at a University

[2] *Wilfred Owen: Collected Letters*, edited by Harold Owen and John Bell (London and New York, Oxford University Press, 1967), 580.
[3] Ibid. 461.
[4] 'All a poet can do today is warn.' Wilfred Owen, 'Preface', *Wilfred Owen: The Complete Poems and Fragments*, ed. Jon Stallworthy (Chatto & Windus: The Hogarth Press and Oxford University Press, 1983), 535.
[5] See below, p. 196.
[6] John Balaban, *Remembering Heaven's Face: A Moral Witness in Vietnam* (New York, London: Poseidon Press, 1991), 17.

in the Mekong Delta, and then as a field representative for the Committee of Responsibility to Save War-Injured Children. His empathy with the Vietnamese, their culture and their language (which he speaks fluently), gives his poems of authentic witness a finer grain and greater moral force than are displayed in the earlier work of most 'stateside' protestors.

David Jones's modernist epic, *In Parenthesis*, regarded by many as the ultimate poetic expression of life and death on the Western Front, was published almost twenty years after the Armistice of 1918, and moving poems of the Vietnam War are still appearing. As, for the first time in American military history, poets on active service spoke out against the conduct of the war, so for the first time, American veterans have followed a course recommended by Balaban: 'Go visit Vietnam, I'd tell the troubled vets. Go visit, if you can, and do some good there, and your pain won't seem so private, your need for resentment so great.'[7] Several of these, notably W. D. Ehrhart, another of Dr Chattarji's heroes, have returned to Vietnam since the war and found the experience, their memoirs and poems suggest, in some ways a healing extension of the painful homecoming to the US recorded in their earlier poems.

David Jones dedicated *In Parenthesis* to his friends and fellow solders 'and to the enemy front-fighters who shared our pains against whom we found ourselves by misadventure'. In the same spirit of reconciliation, and even more poignantly, these American soldier-poets have returned to help the process of psychic recovery—their own, their country's, and that of their former enemies now in some cases their friends. In so doing, their courage, honesty, and generosity stand in stark contrast to qualities displayed in the Ramboesque 'returns' of some revisionist film-makers.

Poets may no longer be 'the unacknowledged legislator of mankind'[8] (if, indeed, they ever were), but Dr Chattarji shows them to be moving witnesses to what it felt like to be an American in America and in Vietnam during the Vietnam War and its painful aftermath. This is an important book that offers a salutary complement and corrective to much of the historical and

---

[7] Ibid. 333.
[8] Percy Bysshe Shelley, *A Defence of Poetry*, 1821.

political writing about the war. I wish it had been available to me and my Cornell class in 1977, and would have introduced it to them with the Harvard Professor's *caveat* that 'Those who cannot remember the past are condemned to repeat it.'[9]

[9] George Santayana, *Life of Reason*, 1905, vol. 1, ch. 10.

Preface

MORE than twenty years after the fall of Saigon, the Vietnam War continues to bedevil the American imagination and its foreign policy. Vietnam's effect on the former is evident in the large body of films, novels, memoirs, and poetry produced during and after the conflict. Its influence on the latter manifested itself during the presidency of Ronald Reagan and the Gulf War. Various modes of national and collective recuperation predicate the need to counteract the 'Vietnam syndrome', the moral outrage and defeatism that permeated sections of American society in the 1960s and 1970s. The aftermath, as Jean Elshtain writes, is often construed as one of 'universal victimization':

> Vietnam is even now in the process of being reconstructed as a story of universal victimization—of the Vietnamese by us; of our soldiers by the war—and by us when we didn't welcome them home; of our nation by the war at home and *the* war; of wives and girlfriends by disturbed veterans; of nurses by the war and later nonrecognition of *their* victimization.[1]

Such a construction conflates different experiences and thereby obliterates the distinctive and moral aspects inherent in each. In studying the poetry related to the period, I refer to contemporary historical and political contexts to highlight congruities and divergences from those milieux. Some poems are complicit with prevalent ideological assumptions, while others offer imaginative and moral critiques of those structures of justification. My contention is that poems in the latter category extend the boundaries of the debate in post-Vietnam America, introducing a human and moral context largely absent in the dominant discourse of politicians and military planners. The concerns manifested in the poems are not only aesthetic and formal but also ethical. Poetic truth is expressed and available not merely within an oppositional good–evil paradigm but posits values that expand the conceptual frameworks for understanding the

---

[1] Jean Bethke Elshtain, *Women and War* (New York: Basic Books, Inc., Publishers, 1987), 218.

Vietnam experience. There is a tendency in critical studies of this work either to valorize anti-war poetry, or to dismiss it on grounds of aesthetic poverty. My discussion of stateside and veteran poetry attempts to avoid the construction of too binary a critical perspective: between the wholly idealistic idea of 'good' poetry and that which may be claimed to be 'good' merely on the basis of the ideological position it articulates. I am conscious of the poor quality of some poems and do not wish to imply that all poems should be judged equally without aesthetic discrimination. However, the question of poetic value is not independent of context and this is particularly relevant for a body of poetry so closely tied to the war.

Combat poems by veterans dwell on the actuality and horror of the experience of war, but their obsession with that event does not end with the termination of the war. While stateside poets railed in laudably moral terms against America's involvement during the conflict and passed on to other subjects, veteran poets perceive Vietnam as a bedrock experience that has continuing personal, political, and moral consequences. This is evident in recent poems by John Balaban, W. D. Ehrhart, and Bruce Weigl, and is of crucial import within the larger political and cultural rewriting of the war. Poetry is a form of rewriting, but differs from reconstructions in the political sphere in its refusal to create justifying and ameliorative myths. The best poems articulate individual memories and trauma; they negotiate the complex terrain of poetry and politics, and raise questions regarding dissent and marginalization. In the words of Adrienne Rich, they 'Nam[e] and mourn damage, keeping pain vocal so it cannot become normalized and acceptable.'[2] In its marginal position within the dominant culture and its 'ineffectiveness' in the world of realpolitik, poetry is a paradoxical representation of truth and power. Unlike other cultural forms such as film and television that have been so influential in shaping perceptions about Vietnam, poetry does not occupy a dominant space in representations of the war experience. Some poets are troubled by their lack of instrumentality, their inability to influence politics, but that is an anxiety centred on a simplistic and propagandist model. Similar anxieties were expressed by poets of the Great War, yet the poems

[2] Adrienne Rich, 'What if?', *What Is Found There: Notebooks on Poetry and Politics* (London: Virago Press Limited, 1995), 242.

of Owen and Sassoon have been hugely influential in shaping British perceptions of warfare. It is the awareness of contradictions and complexities that creates the possibilities of a poetry of value and integrity. As Robert Pinsky writes, 'in some ways, having to do with expectation and need, poets are at the center of national life, where Whitman would have them; in other ways, they are at the fringes, supplanted by the overwhelming variety and power of a reckless national culture'.[3] My discussion of Vietnam War poetry is a literary exercise that examines individual poets and poems grappling with problems of language and representation, politics and power, memory and hope.

In the words of Edward Said: 'reading and writing texts are never neutral activities: there are interests, powers, passions, pleasures entailed no matter how aesthetic or entertaining the work.'[4] In subsequent chapters I outline various political contexts —ranging from American foreign policy imperatives to the anti-war protest movement—and analyse poems in relation to these 'outer' worlds. Of course the distinctive quality (or lack thereof) of the poems arises from the personal predilections of each poet, but the imbrication of poetry and politics reveals strengths and fractures within poetic representations. There is, particularly in stateside and early veteran poetry, an imaginative failure to grasp any real quality of the Vietnamese experience, so that the war becomes a site for exploring American pathologies and traumas. This failure reveals cultural assumptions deeply embedded in collective experience. In unravelling contradictions and mindsets, I wish to indicate a naïvety underlying some of the anti-war poetry, which is both a strength and a weakness of American writing. It is a strength because it allows for new and fresh perspectives; the writing is less constrained because it only understands from within its own self-confident bias. It is a weakness because, of course, this confidence is very frequently misplaced and imaginatively limited. Stateside poets interrogate the basic justifications for American involvement and some, like Robert Bly and Adrienne Rich, place Vietnam within a wider historical framework going back to the founding of the nation and the near extermination of the Native Americans. These poets help

[3] Robert Pinsky, 'Freneau, Whitman, Williams', *Poetry and the World* (New York: The Ecco Press, 1988), 137.
[4] Edward W. Said, *Culture & Imperialism* (London: Vintage, 1994), 385.

to create a climate of conscience that refuses to condone the immorality of the war or to see it as a fundamentally unique event in the country's history. Within a dominant atmosphere of support for involvement in Vietnam and a post-war reconstruction of the conflict as an essentially laudable but failed crusade, the poetic statements are crucial representations of alternative perspectives and histories. There is, however, an element of solipsism and moral élitism that characterizes the notion of poet as prophet so evident in the utterances of Allen Ginsberg. One aspect of the poet-seer collocation is an excess of empathy that constructs absolute oppositions between an 'evil' America and a 'good' Vietnam. The simplification of political and human realities in order to project certain ideological positions detracts from the poems, making them prescriptive and didactic.

Some of this naïvety is available in veteran poetry as well, with its privileging of combat experience as if that were removed from the contingencies of politics and history, memory and individual bias. The stance of the poet as teacher and prophet, exhorting an apathetic nation to moral recollection, is available in the poems of John Balaban and W. D. Ehrhart. Early veteran poems are marked by a sense of alienation and exile, and the poetic project is almost exclusively rooted in individual trauma. In their more recent poetry, however, some veterans articulate a desire to reach out to the 'other', the Vietnamese, and attempt to comprehend different experiences. This empathy may originate in guilt and a desire for expiation, but it represents a vital expression of solidarity. The poetry neither demonizes nor valorizes the former enemy (as the political establishment and some stateside poets were wont to do), and breaks out of a solipsistic dichotomous perception in its awareness of alterities and contradictions.

I conclude with a chapter on translations from some Vietnamese poems to expand the realm of the 'other'. This chapter has its limitations since the poems are all translated and my interpretations cannot delve into the nuances embedded in language and tone. It seems fitting, however, to conclude with Vietnamese voices, for it was their country and its people that bore the brunt of a long and brutal war. A love of the land, exile, and the pain of separations dominate the poems I have chosen to discuss. While the translations originate in American academia, and I point to the politics of the process, I do not perceive the enterprise as being entirely cynical. The desire to hear and know the 'other', available in some poems by American veterans, is extended through these translations. The circle of solidarity is enlarged as poets express and share, and thereby hope to move beyond the bitterness and horror of Vietnam.

Poetry by Vietnamese is representative of marginal voices and their expression resists the denigration of the 'other'. During the war and after it, the Vietnamese were either reviled as 'gooks' or idealized as heroes and victims. A study of their poetry breaks stereotypes, and individual voices reveal worlds of pain, memory, trauma, and exile. They speak to the 'centre' as manifested in political language, as well as to stateside and veteran poetry, and extend and reconfigure conceptions and imaginings of the Vietnam War. There are no definitive conclusions here, only an opening out of possibilities, of multiple worlds, memories, and experiences.

Throughout this study I offer interpretations predicated on the possibility of solidarity and hope as manifested in poetry. Like Said's reader and writer, I am implicated in a political position arising partly out of my own historical consciousness of colonialism and the terrors wrought by war this century. Perhaps I place too great a burden on poetry to address the politics and the human predicament of the Vietnam War, but I believe that poetic representation redresses some of the cynicism and horror inherent in that conflict. The lack of poetry would be a silence that could be construed as complicity. The courage of the poets I will be discussing and the value of their poetry lie in their refusal to be silenced. Poetry creates the possibility and hope of alternative and humane perceptions during and after Vietnam. As Carol Cohn writes: 'Our reconstructive task is a task of creating compelling alternative visions of possible futures, a task of recognizing and developing alternative conceptions of rationality, a task of creating rich and imaginative alternative voices—diverse voices whose conversations with each other will invent those futures.'[5] Cohn is positing ways of counteracting the rational and seemingly neutral language used by the proponents of nuclear weapons, but her formulation is appropriate for my perception of the poetry dealing with Vietnam. In the course of this study I hope

[5] Carol Cohn, 'Sex and Death in the Rational World of Defense Intellectuals', *Signs: Journal of Women in Culture and Society*, 12: 4 (Summer 1987), 687–718.

to outline some of the varied voices that participate in, enrich, and 'invent' a world of myriad and hopeful 'conversations'.

This study would not have been possible without the guidance, patience, and generosity of my former supervisor, Professor Jon Stallworthy. Whether it was nuances of interpretation and language, obtaining copies of a Vietnam veteran poetry magazine from Colorado, or organizing funding and sorting visa problems for a research trip to the USA, Professor Stallworthy has provided invaluable advice and unstinting help. It was an absolute privilege working with him.

I am indebted to John Baky, Vietnam veteran and director at the Connelly Library, La Salle University, Philadelphia, who placed his archive on Imaginative Representations of the Vietnam War at my disposal in February–March 1997. The archive is the most comprehensive one in the field of Vietnam studies and was invaluable for my study. I would like to thank John Newman at the State University of Colorado, Fort Collins, for access to his collection and for sharing the landscape and food of the 'real' West.

To Bill (W. D.) Ehrhart, Vietnam veteran, poet, editor, and memoirist, I owe a debt of gratitude for insights into the war, post-Vietnam trauma, and the travails and delights of writing. He has helped me to perceive the poetry of Vietnam in not merely academic terms, but as encompassing human, moral, and political tragedies. Reading his poetry, along with that of other veterans, has confirmed my conviction that poetry is invaluable within the dominant rewriting of the history of the war in America.

Sophie Goldsworthy as editor supervised the transition from thesis to book with tact and patience. I am grateful to her and to Matthew Hollis, who helped with copyright permissions. I would like to thank Dr David Robertson at St Hugh's, Oxford, for offering essential criticism on Chapter 1. I would also like to thank Suman Gupta, Carol Acton, Jane Potter, Richard Caplan, Luisa Calè, Liz Ashford, Tom Healy for comments, insights, and fine dinners. And Reena Sastri for an ongoing literary exchange peppered with incisive criticism. Many thanks to Diana Lewis, without whose skill and knowledge of computers, I would have been lost in a word-processing maze. Grateful thanks to the Felix Foundation, who provided the funding for me to undertake this study at Oxford. Finally, thanks to Neena and Mini, without whose love and support I would not have completed this work.

Throughout the study I use British English spelling except when I cite American sources that employ US English.

S.C.

Acknowledgements

ROBERT BLY, 'Watching Television' and 'War and Silence', from *The Light Around the Body* (London: Harper & Row Publishers, 1967) reprinted by permission of the author. Du Tu Le, 'The Dawn of a New Humankind', Tran Mong Tu, 'A New Year's Wish for a Little Refugee', and Tran Da Tu, 'The New Lullaby', from Huynh Sanh Thong, *An Anthology of Vietnamese Poems from the Eleventh Through the Twentieth Centuries* (New Haven and London: Yale University Press, 1996), reprinted by permission of Yale University Press. Richard Baker, 'Hoedown', from *Shellburst Pond* (Tacoma, Wash.: Vardaman Press, 1982), reprinted by permission of the author. Bruce Weigl, 'Burning Shit at An Khe' and 'Dialectical Materialism', from *Song of Napalm* (New York: Atlantic Monthly Press, 1988), and 'Her Life Runs Like a Red Silk Flag', from *What Saves Us* (Evanston, Ill.: TriQuarterly Books, 1992), reprinted by permission of the author. Van Ky, 'My Birthplace, Nam Binh', from Thanh T. Nguyen and Bruce Weigl (sel. and trans.), *Poems From Captured Documents* (Amherst, Mass.: The University of Massachusetts Press, 1994), © University of Massachusetts Press. Reprinted by permission of University of Massachusetts Press and the translator. Howard Nemerov, 'Redeployment', from *The Collected Poems of Howard Nemerov* (Chicago and London: The University of Chicago Press, 1977), 'The Language of the Tribe', from *Sentences* (Chicago and London: The University of Chicago Press, 1980), 'Ultima Ratio Reagan', from *War Stories: Poems About Long Ago and Now* (Chicago and London: The University of Chicago Press, 1987), 'On Getting Out of Vietnam', 'On Being Asked for a Peace Poem', and 'The War in the Air', from *Trying Conclusions: New and Selected Poems, 1961–1991* (Chicago and London: The University of Chicago Press, 1991), reprinted by permission of Margaret Nemerov. Horace Coleman 'D-Day+50; Tet+25', from *In The Grass* (Woodbridge, Conn.: Viet Nam Generation Inc., & Burning Cities Press, 1995), reprinted by permission of the author. Morton Marcus, 'Confession', from Walter Lowenfels (ed.), *Where Is Vietnam? American Poets Respond* (Garden City, NY: Doubleday & Company, Inc., 1967), reprinted by permission of the author. Basil T. Paquet, 'Morning—A Death', reprinted from Larry Rottman, Jan Barry, and Basil T. Paquet (eds.), *Winning Hearts and Minds: War Poems by Vietnam Veterans* (Brooklyn: 1st Casualty Press, 1972), by permission of the author. David Connolly, 'After the Firefight' and 'Another Chance', from *Lost in America Grass* (Woodbridge, Conn.: Viet Nam Generation Inc., & Burning Cities Press, 1994), reprinted by permission of the author. 'What Were They Like?' by Denise Levertov, from *Poems 1960–1967*. Copyright © 1966 by Denise Levertov. Reprinted by permission of New Directions Publishing Corp. 'The Distance' and 'In Thai Binh (Peace) Province' by Denise Levertov, from *The Freeing of the Dust*. Copyright © 1975 by Denise Levertov. Reprinted by permission of New Directions Publishing Corp. 'An Interim', 'Overheard Over S.E. Asia', and 'Scenario' by Denise Levertov, from *Poems 1968–1972*. Copyright © 1968, 1972, 1972 by Denise Levertov. Reprinted by permission of New Directions Publishing Corp. Jim Nye, 'Chimaera', from *After Shock: Poems and Prose from the Vietnam War* (El Paso, Tex.: Cinco Puntos Press, 1991). Copyright © by Jim Nye. Used by permission of the author and Cinco Puntos Press. 'Face to Face' and 'North American Time', from *The Fact of a Doorframe: Poems Selected and New, 1950–1984* by Adrienne Rich. Copyright © 1984 by Adrienne Rich. Copyright © 1975, 1978 by W. W. Norton & Company, Inc. Copyright © 1981 by Adrienne Rich. Used by permission of the author and W. W. Norton & Company, Inc. Igor Bobrowsky 'I hate you . . .', from Larry Rottman, Jan Barry, and Basil T. Paquet (eds.), *Winning Hearts and Minds: War Poems by Vietnam Veterans* (Brooklyn: 1st Casualty Press, 1972) reprinted by permission of the author. 'Saying Goodbye to Mr. and Mrs. My', from John Balaban, *After Our War* (Pittsburgh: University of Pittsburgh Press, 1974), reprinted by author's permission. John Balaban, 'The Book and the Lacquered Box', 'After Our War', and 'In Celebration of Spring', from *Locusts at the Edge of Summer: New and Selected Poems*. Copyright © 1997 by John Balaban. Reprinted with the permission of Copper Canyon Press, P. O. Box 271, Port Townsend, WA 98368-0271, USA. Lee-lee Schlegel (ed.), *DEROS*, for 'Simple Truth' and 'Rule of Thumb'.

W. D. Ehrhart, 'Fragment: 5 September 1967', is reprinted from Larry Rottman, Jan Barry, and Basil T. Paquet (eds.), *Winning Hearts and Minds: War Poems by Vietnam Veterans* (Brooklyn, NY: 1st Casualty Press, 1972), by permission of the author. All other poems of W. D. Ehrhart are reprinted from *Beautiful Wreckage: New & Selected Poems* (Easthampton, Mass.: Adastra Press, 1999), by permission of the author. Kevin Bowen, 'Incoming' and 'A Conical Hat', from *Playing Basketball With the Vietcong* (Willimantic, Conn.: Curbstone Press, 1994), reprinted by permission of the author. Walter McDonald, 'Black Granite Burns Like Ice', from *Where Skies are Not Cloudy* (Denton, Tex.: University of North Texas Press, 1994), reprinted by permission of University of North Texas Press. 'The Food Pickers of Saigon', reprinted from *After the Noise of Saigon*, by Walter McDonald (Amherst, Mass.: University of Massachusetts Press, 1988), copyright © 1988 by Walter Macdonald. Walt McDonald, 'Caliban in Blue', from *Caliban in Blue* (Lubbock, Tex.: Texas Tech Press, 1976). © 1976 Texas Tech University Press. Reprinted by permission of the author and Texas Tech University Press. Yusef Komunyakaa, 'Starlight Scope Myopia' and 'A Greenness Taller Than Gods', from *Dien Cai Dau* (Middletown, Conn.: Wesleyan University Press, 1988), reprinted by permission of the author and Wesleyan University Press. Nguyen Ba Chung, 'Non-Attachment', from Kevin Bowen and Bruce Weigl (eds. and introd.), *Writing Between the Lines* (Amherst, Mass.: The University of Massachusetts Press, 1997), © William Joiner Center. Reprinted by permission of the author and The University of Massachusetts Press. Nguyen Duy, 'Red Earth, Blue Water', and Le Thi May, 'Wind and Widow', from *Manoa: A Pacific Journal of International Writing*, 7: 2 (Winter 1995), reprinted by permission of *Manoa*. PFC Pilarsky Harley, 'The Soldier's Call', and PFC Thomas W. Piper, 'Why Am I Here', from Forest L. Kimler (ed. and compiler), *Boondock Bards* (APO San Francisco 96503: Pacific Stars and Stripes, 1968) reprinted by permission of Pacific Editor, *Stars and Stripes*.

Contents

Foreword by Jon Stallworthy	vii
Preface	xi
Acknowledgements	xix
1. POLITICS AND POETRY: SOME CONTEXTS AND PROBLEMS FOR AMERICAN POETRY OF THE VIETNAM WAR	1
2. STATESIDE POETRY: PROTEST AND PROPHECY	26
3. VETERAN POETRY: PROTEST AND ANGUISH—BRINGING THE WAR HOME	98
4. VETERAN POETRY: COMBAT EXPERIENCE—THE ACTUALITY AND THE NEED TO BEAR WITNESS	119
5. VETERAN POETRY: THE AFTERMATH	141
6. THE 'OTHER': VIETNAMESE POETIC REPRESENTATIONS	201
Bibliography	227
Index	246

I
Politics and Poetry
Some Contexts and Problems for American Poetry of the Vietnam War

'THE IDEA of the nation is inseparable from its narration: that narration attempts, interminably, to constitute identity against difference, inside against outside, and in the assumed superiority of inside over outside, prepares against invasion and "enlightened" colonialism.'[1] Throughout its history America has narrated itself in terms of a paternalistic, messianic mission, the 'City upon a hill' that would be a beacon of hope for the world.[2] This teleological narration constitutes a complex reality and is the site of immense contradictions. The contradictions arise out of the disjunction between rhetorical constructions (such as the desire to civilize the 'savage' Indian) and the actual barbarity of that process. Dominant foundational and national myths were largely successful in sustaining the momentum and coherence of American ideals such as freedom and democracy and, although there were dissenting voices (such as William James's scathing comments on American imperialism in the Philippines) it was not until the Vietnam War that there was a serious attempt to question the elements comprising a seemingly coherent narrative.[3] The Vietnam War moulded the outlook as well as the imagination of an entire generation, confronting the arrogance of the American

[1] Geoffrey Bennington, 'Postal Politics and the Institution of the Nation', in Homi K. Bhaba (ed.), *Nation and Narration* (London: Routledge, 1990), 132.

[2] 'For we must consider that we shall be as a City upon a hill. The eyes of all people are upon us.' John Winthrop, 'A Modell of Christian Charity', in *Life and Letters of John Winthrop, 1630–1649*, ii, ed. Robert C. Winthrop (Boston: Ticknor and Fields, 1867), 19.

[3] On the US invasion of the Philippines, William James wrote in the *Boston Transcript*, 1 Mar. 1899: 'We are destroying down to the very root every germ of a healthy national life in these unfortunate people.... We must sow our ideals, plant our order, impose our God.' Cited by Frank Lentricchia, 'In Place of an Afterword—Someone Reading', in Frank Lentricchia and Thomas McLaughlin (eds.), *Critical Terms For Literary Study* (Chicago and London: The University of Chicago Press, 1990), 334.

enterprise with failure and disillusionment. Ironically, involvement in Vietnam seemed a natural sequel to an earlier war, interpreted as the apotheosis of American goals and ideals, the 'good war': the Second World War. While this chapter is primarily concerned with the political contexts of Vietnam, and does not imply a simplistic link between the two wars, it is interesting to note the ways in which the Second World War continued the narration of American values and concerns, and how that was reflected in the policy and language of commitment in Vietnam.

My purpose in outlining a dominant thread in American foreign policy is to highlight certain cultural imperatives that led America into Vietnam. Policy-making is a complex process often impelled by contradictory factors and diverse interests. My idea is not to unearth intentions or motivations of policy-makers but to indicate continuities and assumptions underlying American policy in Vietnam. The justifications for those policies, and the dissensions articulate 'a structure of attitude and reference' that circumscribes debates about the war.[4] Given certain cultural and political imperatives such as democracy and freedom, most policy debates on Vietnam do not question particular premises and problems inherent in the involvement. Robert Schulzinger comments on this consensus that underpins the larger framework of American foreign policy:

> no one should overlook the near unanimity of opinion among foreign policy advisers on certain fundamentals.... they felt that America was superior to other nations.... they feared that other countries presented dangers. And finally, they shared an optimistic faith that American military strength, wealth, and political values could be artfully applied to improve the lot of the world's peoples.[5]

In this chapter I will briefly sketch some modes of consensus-building and the role of language in the furtherance of particular assumptions about Vietnam. An outline of American political imperatives provides a framework within which the poetry of the war can be placed. The political context, however, is not a mere placid, historically removed 'background'. The poetry and the war are closely imbricated, and it is necessary to recognize the contingency, the historical specificity of certain poetic represen-

[4] Edward W. Said, *Culture & Imperialism* (London: Vintage, 1994), 73.
[5] Robert D. Schulzinger, *American Diplomacy in the Twentieth Century* (New York and Oxford: Oxford University Press, 1994), 10–11.

tations. The history of the war (the Second World War or Vietnam), to use Pierre Macherey's formulation, 'is not in a simple, external relation to the work, in so far as the emergence of the work required this history, which is its only principle of reality and also supplies its means of expression'.[6]

The American involvement in the Second World War follows several of the theoretical notions about national narration outlined by Geoffrey Bennington. The inside–outside oppositional framework available in America's opposition to Nazi Germany, fascist Italy, and militarist-imperial Japan, helped to consolidate the idea of a democratic power's crusade against evil enemies. The fact that the war was brought home to America, in Japan's audacious attack on Pearl Harbor, intensified the notion of national peril. Throughout the war, therefore, the sense of a noble cause, the need to save the world, dominates the language of war. At least the threat here was much more real and horrible than the threat to the world in Vietnam. The fact that the endeavour was successful created the 'good war', 'feel good factor', and firmly placed America at the centre of world politics and power equations. The end of the Second World War and the beginning of the Cold War furthered the need for continuous vigilance against a new enemy, communism. Following the US–USSR alliance against fascism during the war this construction, as Eric Hobsbawm points out, is one of the decisively paradoxical moments in twentieth-century history:

In many ways the period of capitalist–communist alliance against fascism—essentially in the 1930s and 1940s—forms the hinge of twentieth-century history and its decisive moment. In many ways it is a moment of historical paradox in the relations of capitalism and communism, placed, for most of the century—except for the brief period of anti-fascism—in a posture of irreconcilable antagonism.[7]

Post-war reconstruction presented boundless possibilities and the new frontiers telescoped directly into American foundational myths of the 'original' frontier. The occasional isolationism and reticence in American foreign policy (although this did not occlude the colonization of the Philippines or intervention in

[6] Pierre Macherey, *A Theory of Literary Production*, trans. Geoffrey Wall (London, Henley, and Boston: Routledge & Kegan Paul, 1978), 93–4.
[7] Eric Hobsbawm, *Age of Extremes: The Short Twentieth Century 1914–1991* (London: Michael Joseph Ltd., 1994), 7.

Cuba, Guatemala, and Nicaragua) was now replaced by a desire to contain the communist menace and make the world safe for democracy (a factor underlying the conflict in Korea). The seeds of American intervention in Vietnam lay in the rehabilitation of originary frontier myths, now translated on to a world scenario. The newly independent Vietnam represented no security threat *per se*, but successive US administrations worked to undermine the legitimacy of Ho Chi Minh by projecting Hanoi as a puppet government (either of China or the USSR, or both), and constructing the overarching domino theory to justify intervention. American involvement in Vietnam was justified and consolidated, made available to the individual 'conscience', partly on the basis of an assumption that the modern-day American pioneer would rescue a nation from the evils of communism. The paternalistic, white-man's-burden political attitude is evident in some of John F. Kennedy's speeches. He rationalized the necessity for intervention by characterizing the United States as the 'godparents' of 'little Vietnam'. He went on to say, 'We presided at its birth, we gave assistance to its life, we have helped to shape its future.'[8] The rhetoric emphasizes the disinterested generosity underlying US policy. President Johnson, responsible for major troop commitments and escalating the war, stated that 'the larger purpose of our involvement has always been to help the nations of South-east Asia become independent and stand alone, self-sustaining, as members of a great world community—at peace with themselves, and at peace with all others'.[9] Rhetorical justifications became more pronounced as US armed might seemed inadequate to the task of defeating the menacing minions of a dangerous ideology. For instance, President Nixon's Address to the Nation, of 3 November 1969, encapsulates the moralistic, self-defined American projection of peace and freedom:

Today we have become the strongest and the richest nation in the world. And the wheel of destiny has turned so that any hope the world has for the survival of peace and freedom will be determined by whether the

[8] Cited in Norman Podhoretz, *Why We Were In Vietnam* (New York: Simon and Schuster, 1982), 20. In Stanley Kubrick's *Full Metal Jacket*, a character echoes Kennedy's sentiments: 'I'm fighting this war because I believe that inside each gook is a freedom loving American waiting to get out.'
[9] Cited in Marvin E. Gettleman, Jane Franklin, Marilyn Young, and H. Bruce Franklin (eds.), *Vietnam and America: A Documented History* (New York: Grove Press Inc., 1985), 401.

American people have the moral stamina and the courage to meet the challenge of free world leadership.[10]

The term 'free world' is a legacy of the Second World War where the war, as Paul Addison noted, 'served a generation of Britons and Americans as a myth which enshrined their essential purity, a parable of good and evil'.[11] Similarly, Nixon presents constructed political realities as essentialist moral choices, and the morality is a manichaean one. The grim threat of communism must be challenged by 'the moral stamina and the courage' of the American people. The American intervention is predicated on the desire to validate national will, even if that validation involves impinging on the sovereignty and lives of another nation, and it is significant that neither president questioned America's right to be in Vietnam. It is taken as an a priori basis for fulfilling the larger political responsibility and destiny that has been bequeathed to America.

Nixon's apocalyptic vision of a just struggle against communism is one instance of a domestic consolidation based on a sense of threat. There was no ideological and intellectual refutation of communism within the American political establishment, merely the construction of an all-encompassing evil. The threat without was mirrored in the threat within. The idea of an internal insurrection created a climate of fear, insecurity, and absolute opposition. Its most comprehensive and bizarre manifestations were the House [of Representatives] Un-American Activities Committee, and, a few years later, the anti-communist crusade of Senator Joseph McCarthy. McCarthyism, as Douglas Tallack points out, 'might be regarded as the twisted image of hopes that were disappointed when the rest of the world, including European allies, proved recalcitrant in the face of American offers to redesign the world along the lines of freedom and democracy'.[12] The rhetoric of freedom and the need to repulse communism

---

[10] Ibid. 439.
[11] Paul Addison, 'East is East', *New Statesman* (24 Mar. 1978), 404–5. Addison also writes that, during and after the Second World War, 'The Americans believed all too naively in spreading the American way of life among benighted peoples, a motive which went hand in hand with an eager search for new export markets and investment opportunities, not to speak of the plans of the US Navy for annexing various Pacific islands which belonged to friendly nations' (404).
[12] Douglas Tallack, *Twentieth Century America: The Intellectual and Cultural Context* (London and New York: Longman, 1991), 192.

created an internal schism in America. The split within and the necessity for eternal vigilance was evident in the spy trials that followed, from Klaus Fuchs (an atomic scientist) and David Greenglass (a machinist) at the atomic energy centre at Los Alamos, to Ethel and Julius Rosenberg. The Rosenbergs were accused of selling atomic secrets to Russia, and their trial and execution were emblematic of the national desire for consolidation, security, and patriotism. The polarization of American society was predicated on the idea of a monolithic and fundamentally evil communist conspiracy. As Victor Navasky observes, this polarization pitted ' "patriots" (the hunters) against "subversives" (the hunted), right against left, the ins against the outs— even as the international cold war seemed to split the planet between those who sided with "the free world" and those who identified with "aesthetic communism"'. ' "There is no room in America today for the neutral patriot!" said Earl Cocke Jr., national commander of the American Legion in 1951. "You cannot be indifferent toward Communism any more than you can be indifferent toward cancer." '[13]

The perceived communist threat not only dominated American politics, but also sustained the post-war military–industrial complex. The war to defeat Nazism and fascism created a massive economic boom in the USA, and this was partly reflected in new economic (as well as political) investments in post-Second World War Europe.[14] The Marshall Plan, for instance, was a means of containing communism and expanding political spheres of influence through economic aid. Since the threat of communism was omnipresent, the American State had to be geared to combat this constant menace. This implied a state of war-preparedness, an idea that could be 'sold' to the American public. As Samuel F. Downer, financial Vice-President of LTV Aerospace Corporation, said in an interview to the *Washington Post*, on 8 December 1963:

[13] Victor S. Navasky, *Naming Names* (New York: The Viking Press, 1980), 20.

[14] Eric Hobsbawm, in *Age of Extremes*, writes that 'wars were clearly good to the US economy. Its rate of growth in both wars was quite extraordinary, especially in the Second World War when it grew at the rate of roughly 10 per cent per annum, faster than ever before or since. In both the wars the USA benefited from being both remote from the fighting, and the main arsenal of its allies, and from the capacity of its economy to organize the expansion of production more effectively than any other. Probably the most lasting effect of both world wars was to give the US economy a global preponderance' (48).

If you're President and you need a control factor in the economy, and you need to sell this factor, you can't sell Harlem and Watts but you can sell self-preservation, a new environment. We're going to increase defense budgets as long as those bastards in Russia are ahead of us. The American people understand this.[15]

The cost was irrelevant since this was a noble cause (and the military-industrial complex benefited economically). The bogey of an internal and external communist threat found an ideal battleground in Vietnam.

Graham Greene's *The Quiet American* accurately portrays America's obsession with making the world safe for democracy, the 'quasi religious fervour' with which the quiet American, Alden Pyle, determines that south Vietnam shall be the 'proving ground for democracy'. The white-man's burden sits heavily on his shoulders:

Perhaps only ten days ago he had been walking across the Common in Boston, his arms full of the books he'd been reading in advance on the Far East and the problems of China . . . he was absorbed already in the dilemmas of Democracy and the responsibilities of the West; he was determined . . . to do good, not to any individual person but to a country, a continent, a world. Well, he was in his element now with the whole universe to improve.[16]

Pyle's sense of mission and manifest destiny, the absolutizing of the 'other' as the site for the fulfilment of this mission, formed the crux of a complex political myth that led America to Vietnam. The justification involved the diabolization of the enemy and the necessity for American intervention in terms of Cold War rhetoric. Justifying the escalation of war under the guise of 'Vietnamization', Nixon declared on 30 April 1970: 'If, when the chips are down, the world's most powerful nation, the United States of America, acts like a pitiful, helpless giant, the forces of totalitarianism and anarchy will threaten free nations and free institutions throughout the world.'[17] This speech repeats the commitment to peace and freedom (manifested, ironically, in the bombing of north Vietnam and Cambodia), in the face of anarchy

---

[15] Cited in Noam Chomsky, *At War With Asia* (London: William Collins Sons & Co. Ltd., 1971), 23.
[16] Graham Greene, *The Quiet American* (Harmondsworth: Penguin Books Ltd., 1955), 18.
[17] Cited in Gettleman *et al.*, *Vietnam and America*, 451.

and threat. The imperial sweep of the assertion is matched by an equally simplistic definition of collective interests that must be defended at all costs. Nixon's language is emblematic of 'the paranoid style' that Richard Hofstadter perceives in US foreign policy statements:

> The distinguishing thing about the paranoid style is not that its exponents see conspiracies or plots here and there in history, but that they regard a 'vast' or 'gigantic' conspiracy as *the motive force* in historical events. History is a conspiracy, set in motion by demonic forces of almost transcendent power, and what is felt to be needed to defeat it is not the usual methods of political give-and-take, but an all-out crusade.[18]

The image of the USA as 'a pitiful, helpless giant' is a curious juxtapositioning of force (shackled perhaps by American lack of will manifested in aberrations like the anti-war movement) and insecurity, of gung-ho macho malespeak ('the world's most powerful nation') and vulnerability (a vulnerability reluctantly and painfully acknowledged only after the loss in Vietnam). The political-pioneer agenda was stated in absolute terms and, once Vietnam was locked into a grid of geopolitical strategic interests (defined in terms of American self-interest), successive administrations in America chose to construct reality around these preconceived interests. The war, as John Carlos Rowe points out, 'had been a collective fantasy . . . waged by a Pentagon and Congress blind to their own ethnocentricism and narrow nationalism, and doomed by stubborn commitments to outdated foreign policies and simple-minded myths about Reds and Dominoes'.[19] Rowe's critique is accurate in so far as he points to the misrepresentation of Vietnamese politics for the sake of justifying America's involvement. However, his absolutizing of foreign policy frameworks ignores more complex factors within that paradigm. Insecurity, the fear of failure, and a concomitant obsession with the 'credibility' of US power, the USA as reluctant reformer, and the need to avoid the taint of colonialism are important elements of the larger pattern of 'narrow nationalism' and 'outdated foreign policies'.

US involvement in Vietnam began not in the 1960s when

---

[18] Richard Hofstadter, *The Paranoid Style in American Politics and Other Essays* (London: Jonathan Cape, 1966), 29.

[19] John Carlos Rowe, 'From Documentary to Docudrama: Vietnam on Television in the 1980s', *Genre*, 21: 4 (Winter 1988), 451–77.

Kennedy decided to send 'advisers', but with its support of French recolonization after the Second World War, and its role in sabotaging the Geneva Agreement of 1954. As Stanley Karnow writes: 'By 1954, seeing the Indochina War as a struggle against global Communism, the United States had spent $2.5 billion to finance the futile French military effort—more assistance than France received in the Marshall Plan aid from America to rebuild its shattered postwar economy.'[20] Ngo Dinh Diem, a north Vietnamese Catholic who represented a client government of dubious value, was projected as a bulwark against communism, and backed by influential sections of the American polity.[21] He was welcomed by the Mayor of New York, who described him as a man 'to whom freedom is the very breath of life itself', 'a man history may yet adjudge as one of the great figures of the Twentieth Century', and defined the government he headed as a 'political miracle'.[22] In a joint declaration with Diem, Vice-President Johnson stated that Diem was 'in the vanguard of those leaders who stand for freedom on the periphery of the Communist empire in Asia'.[23] Diem's government, supported by US aid, killed thousands of so-called communist sympathizers, allowed little or no freedom of the press, and alienated the south Vietnamese through his patronage of north Vietnamese Catholics. Diem's dependence was evident when the USA backed a coup against him for apparently sending out peace feelers to Hanoi. Yet even while virtually controlling the Diem administration, and in its collaboration with French colonialism, the USA was acutely sensitive to charges of American colonialism. A high-ranking American diplomat said in 1966:

First of all, we ardently desire to avoid anything that smacks of colonialism. If our leverage were to be used brutally, it might achieve more in a given situation, but it will also really make us look like colonialists and

---

[20] Stanley Karnow, *Vietnam: A History* (London: Pimlico, 1994), 148. One of the ironies of the war is the pre-1945 American support for Ho Chi Minh. This was short-lived and supplanted by the post-war need to combat communism.

[21] I do not capitalize north and south Vietnam as they were not separate countries. The final declaration of the Geneva Conference stated: 'The Conference recognizes that the essential purpose of the agreement relating to Vietnam is to settle military questions with a view to ending hostilities and that the military demarcation line is provisional and should not in any way be interpreted as constituting a political or territorial boundary.' Cited in Gettleman et al., *Vietnam and America*, 79.

[22] Gettleman et al., *Vietnam and America*, 138.

[23] Ibid. 162.

would thus be the opposite of productive in the long run. . . . we prefer to reason, to use Anglo-Saxon logic, not to use our leverage too openly.[24]

The fear of being associated with colonial practices reveals some awareness of colonial underpinnings within the US enterprise (note that the diplomat does not deny the USA has leverage, since that would be to deny America's power), but policy-makers definitely disavow colonial desires.[25] It is interesting that this disavowal is bolstered by an appeal to 'Anglo-Saxon logic' and reason, presumably beyond the realm of the capable Diem.

The distancing from colonialism dovetailed nicely not only with the language of freedom outlined earlier, but also with the notion of disinterested intervention, a classic colonial strategy. The USA was the reluctant reformer forced into distant lands because of their need for protection and help. Kennedy's designation of America as the 'godparents' of 'little Vietnam' is typical of the paternal interest that the USA had in freedom and democracy. Kennedy's paternalism is reminiscent of earlier colonial enterprises, and Rudyard Kipling's 'The Head of the District' offers parallel insights in another age and country. When Yardley-Orde, the District Commissioner of Kot-Kumharsen district, dies, he is replaced by a Bengali, a Mr Grish Chunder Dé. The incompetent Mr Dé, despite being 'more English than the English', is despised by the fiercely independent and fanatical locals, who would rather be ruled by the English than a '*kala admi*', 'an eater of fish from the South'.[26] Apart from the manner in which racial stereotypes function amongst the natives (a similar division is apparent between north and south Vietnamese), Kipling's story presents a classic example of colonial paternalism. Yardley-Orde addresses his litter-bearers in their language and ends his admonitory speech thus: 'I speak now true talk, for I am as it were already dead, my children,—for though ye be strong

[24] Cited in Robert Shaplen, *The Road From War: Vietnam 1965–1970* (London: Andre Deutsch Limited, 1971), 65.
[25] The reality of US power was emphasized by Ambassador Henry Cabot Lodge, who said in an interview that 'the U.S. might be justified in staying in Viet-Nam even if a Saigon government asked us to leave'. Cited in Marcus G. Raskin and Bernard B. Fall (eds.), *The Viet-Nam Reader: Articles and Documents on American Foreign Policy and the Viet-Nam Crisis* (New York: Random House, 1967), 325.
[26] Rudyard Kipling, 'The Head of the District', in *Collected Stories*, selected and introduced Robert Gottlieb (London: David Campbell Publishers Ltd., 1994), 190, 193.

men, ye are children.'²⁷ The colonizer is not only the civilizing agent but also the father of his people, a myth that infantilizes the natives. Mr Dé can never succeed as district commissioner because he cannot hope to be an imposing father figure. The subtext of the tale is the necessity of English rule since the natives are incapable of leadership. The infantilizing process, however, is not one sided and this is evident in Khoda Dad Khan's reply: 'And thou art our father and our mother. . . . What shall we do, now there is no one to speak for us, or to teach us to go wisely!'²⁸ The colonizer gives voice to the colonized, speaks for him, and the process is effective and complete when the colonized speaks in his master's voice. A similar pattern is discernible in Vietnam where US political leaders repeated the voice of benign paternalism and this was assimilated by the south Vietnamese leadership. America projected itself as the guarantor of the rights of the free world and Kennedy concluded that if Vietnam were to fall 'victim to any of the perils that threaten its existence—Communism, political anarchy, poverty and the rest', the US would be held responsible and its prestige in Asia would 'sink to a new low'.²⁹

We find the familiar pattern of threat, protective response, and insecurity (under no circumstances must US prestige 'sink to a new low'). The USA is simultaneously a reluctant belligerent (because the ideals it values are threatened) and disinterested protector. As Douglas J. Macdonald puts it: 'The United States has consistently faced the same policy dilemma in a number of nations: it does not want to go in, but it cannot stay out—what could be termed, for the Cold War era, the dilemmas of commitment versus containment respectively.'³⁰ Macdonald attempts to explain and justify US support for French colonialism till 1954 using the paradigmatic 'dilemmas of commitment versus containment'. His analysis does not consider questions regarding the ethics of intervention; he begs the question by citing other countries' forays into third countries. The entire range of rhetorical

[27] Ibid. 188.
[28] Ibid.
[29] Cited in Podhoretz, *Why We Were In Vietnam*, 20.
[30] Douglas J. Macdonald, *Adventures in Chaos: American Intervention for Reform in the Third World* (Cambridge, Mass., and London: Harvard University Press, 1992), 49–50. A parallel is cited in Gettleman *et al.*, *Vietnam and America*, 28: 'Not since the Crusades has France undertaken such disinterested action. This war is the war of Vietnam for Vietnam.' General Jean de Tassigny explaining French reconquest of Vietnam after the Second World War.

arguments, from the threat posed by communism to the paternalistic defence launched by America, bolsters America's unique power and mission in the bipolar post-Second World War world. The compensatory 'positive' rhetoric is vital for justificatory purposes. As Ward Just points out: 'Since American wars are never undertaken for imperialistic gain (myth one), American soldiers always fight in a virtuous cause (myth two) for a just and goalless peace (myth three) . . . American wars are always defensive wars, undertaken slowly and reluctantly, the country a righteous giant finally goaded beyond endurance by foreign adventurers.'[31] Policy declarations, communiqués, rhetorical assertions with reference to Vietnam often serve as a linguistic mode of creating an atmosphere of consent. Language can be seen as instrumentalist, reiterating and reinforcing dominant national ideals and myths. It is a perpetuation of what Herbert Marcuse calls 'one-dimensional thought': 'One-dimensional thought is systematically promoted by the makers of politics and their purveyors of mass information. Their universe of discourse is populated by self-validating hypotheses which, incessantly and monopolistically repeated, become hypnotic definitions or dictations.'[32] The process of 'hypnotic definitions or dictations' reconstituting and re-presenting historical details and events which are difficult to assimilate into official mythology is evident in the post-Vietnam era. While it is not my intention in this chapter to provide a detailed analysis of the modes and implications of this process, I believe a brief outline will provide a further context within which American poetry about the war can be analysed.

Some dominant political terms employed by the US establishment to justify involvement in south Vietnam were: freedom, democracy, peace, help, defence (America did not attack and bomb south Vietnam, it was *defending* the territory against communist infiltrators), and the rights of the free world.[33] These terms functioned as metaphors that mediated the truth and reality of American involvement to its people. Since they were articulated by people in power, and it is the powerful who impose their

[31] Ward Just, *Military Men* (London: Michael Joseph, 1972), 7.
[32] Herbert Marcuse, *One-Dimensional Man: Studies in the Ideology of Advanced Industrial Society* (London: Routledge, 1964), 14.
[33] The emphasis on *defending* south Vietnam and north Vietnamese *aggression* implies that south Vietnam was a separate country. When the USA intervened in 1954 this was a fiction.

metaphors, they were taken to be the truth of the war. As George Lakoff and Mark Johnson point out: 'In a culture where the myth of objectivism is very much alive and truth is always absolute truth, the people who get to impose their metaphors on the culture get to define what we consider to be true—absolutely and objectively true.'[34] The particularity of certain repetitive rhetorical modes of distorting and thereby coping with reality prepares the way for a post-Vietnam rewriting of history. Except for the most diehard right-wing militarist, the US involvement in Vietnam was acknowledged as a mistake, an aberration, by policy makers and academics. John King Fairbank was critical of the war, stating that this is 'an age when we get our power politics overextended into foreign disasters like Vietnam mainly through an excess of righteousness and disinterested benevolence'.[35] Most academics agree that it was a 'failed crusade', 'noble' but 'illusory', and undertaken with the 'loftiest intentions', as Stanley Karnow puts it.[36] Robert McNamara acknowledges errors and his sense of unease at the way the war was conducted, but he concludes his memoir with a reiteration of basic goals:

> Let me be simple and direct—I want to be clearly understood: the United States of America fought in Vietnam for eight years for what it believed to be good and honest reasons. By such action, administrations of both parties sought to protect our security, prevent the spread of totalitarian Communism, and promote individual freedom and political democracy.[37]

The admission of defeat or error is counterbalanced by referring to the pristine motives and practice of US policy. The stringing together of 'righteousness', 'benevolence', 'crusade', 'noble', 'honest', and 'loftiest intentions' creates the idea of a power that laudably set out to combat evil forces, and was defeated not so much by them as by its own naïvety and simple-minded goodness. The language draws upon a collective memorialized notion of America's past and its pristine originary history. The new frontier (the free world threatened by communism) is a rhetorical and

---

[34] George Lakoff and Mark Johnson, *Metaphors We Live By* (Chicago and London: The University of Chicago Press, 1980), 160.
[35] Cited in James Peck (ed.), *The Chomsky Reader* (London: The Serpent's Tail, 1988), 131.
[36] Karnow, *Vietnam: A History*, 9.
[37] Robert S. McNamara, *In Retrospect: The Tragedy and Lessons of Vietnam*, with Brian Van De Mark (New York: Times Books, 1995), 333.

mythical extension of the old frontier (how the west was won, etc.), and erases uncomfortable political and moral questions. America's history of colonialism prior to Vietnam (of which I shall indicate a few instances) and in Vietnam is smothered in the self-validating rhetoric used to 'explain' the involvement in Vietnam.

There are instances of political and academic revisionism that are more partisan and seem to ignore basic events and realities. Nixon, in *No More Vietnams*, writes: 'We won the war in Vietnam, but we lost the peace. All that we had achieved in twelve years of fighting was thrown away in a spasm of congressional irresponsibility.'[38] This is a common refrain in post-Vietnam America: the idea that the USA won, and defeatism during and after the war (the 'Vietnam syndrome') was fostered by the media, the un-American anti-war protesters who were expressing their distaste for the violence unleashed in Vietnam, and Congress, 'which turned its back on a noble cause and a brave people'.[39] Another thread in revisionist history tends to reverse political realities and thereby their interpretation. Douglas Macdonald, who begs the question on the issue of the ethics of US intervention, is a moderate version of Guenter Lewy who writes: 'Shrill rhetoric created a world of unreality in which the North Vietnamese Communists were the defenders of self-determination, while US actions designed to prevent the forceful takeover of South Vietnam stood branded as imperialism and aggression.'[40] The situation designated by Lewy is, ironically, accurate, but he asserts it is a 'world of unreality'. To admit to the truth of the situation, namely that America had displayed colonial aggression, would be to see it as it really was, but that would destroy the entire edifice of benevolent intervention. General Bruce Palmer, deputy to Westmoreland, quarrels over details in his account of Vietnam. He blames political civilian interference for the defeat, and indulges in innocent special pleading: 'They [Hanoi] also painted the U.S. effort as an immoral, illegitimate, and unlawful war against a weak, small country (North Vietnam) seeking to

[38] Richard Nixon, *No More Vietnams* (London: W. H. Allen, 1986), 165. Nixon was convinced of the morality of US intervention: 'Our goals were noble in Vietnam. ... We were morally right in trying to help South Vietnam defend itself, but we made crucial errors in how we went about it' (47). [39] Ibid. 202.
[40] Guenter Lewy, *America in Vietnam* (New York: Oxford University Press, 1978), 435.

unify its people under one government.'[41] Like Lewy, Palmer describes a complex but 'unacceptable' version of the war. In this framework, the war itself is not immoral but Hanoi successfully portrayed it as such.

John Carlos Rowe's comment on American policy (cited earlier) is an accurate indictment of some of the motivations that led to and sustained the war. Implicit in his critique is the idea that, if the assumptions were suspect, there might have been a radical restructuring of policy and attitudes. There seems to be no such serious, sustained reconsideration of national goals and official policy attempts to rehabilitate the nationalist, imperial myths that led America to Vietnam.

Philip Melling quotes one of Jimmy Carter's lectures on human rights wherein Carter 'explained that America had no responsibility to give Vietnam any assistance because "the destruction was mutual". In other words, "we went to Vietnam without any desire to impose American will. . . . I don't feel that we ought to apologize or castigate ourselves. . . . I don't feel that we owe a debt".'[42] George P. Schultz, Secretary of State in the Reagan administration, was equally forthright. In an address at the Department of State, on 25 April 1985, he said: 'We carry the banner of liberty, democracy, the dignity of the individual, tolerance, the rule of law. Throughout our history, including the period of Vietnam, we have been the champion of freedom, a haven of opportunity, and a beacon of hope to oppressed peoples everywhere.'[43] In a post-Vietnam world these assertions are ironic, reflecting a lack of historical consciousness, and a reinstating of dominant 'establishment' positions. The statements are indicative of a polity cocooned in self-righteous rhetoric. Of course, there is no single, monolithic polity; but there is a continuity of rhetoric from Kennedy to Nixon to Carter to Reagan and, most recently,

---

[41] General Bruce Palmer, Jr., *The 25-Year War: America's Military Role in Vietnam* (New York: Simon & Schuster, Inc., 1984), 180.

[42] Philip Melling, *Vietnam in American Literature* (Boston: Twayne Publishers, 1990), 85–6. Carter's disavowal of debt may be contrasted with an item in Nixon's letter of 1 Feb. 1973 to the Prime Minister of the Democratic Republic of Vietnam, Pham Van Dong: 'The Government of the United States of America will contribute to postwar reconstruction in North Vietnam without political conditions.' Cited in Gettleman *et al.*, *Vietnam and America*, 488. In *No More Vietnams*, Nixon blames Congress for the lack of reconstruction aid to north Vietnam.

[43] Cited in Robert Emmet Long (ed.), *Vietnam Ten Years After* (New York: The H. W. Wilson Company, 1986), 155.

to Robert McNamara. Ronald Reagan merely ignored the unpleasant complexity of the war. On his way out of a memorial service for Vietnam veterans in 1986, he stated: 'We are beginning to appreciate that they were fighting for a just cause.'[44] The extended statements of earlier politicians are now distilled as simple fact, as earlier deviations (the lack of appreciation for the 'just cause') are weeded out.

Macdonald, McNamara, Nixon, Lewy, Palmer, Carter, and Schultz offer examples of what Edward Said calls the 'academic-research consensus or paradigm'.[45] Said is writing about the seemingly neutral, academic 'scholarship' on the Middle East that perpetuates orientalist myths about that area and its people, but the paradigm is equally applicable to Vietnam. This consensus is occasionally questioned, but it is a powerful and influential paradigm. It dominates the debate, occupies the centre of discussions on Vietnam, and feeds into various cultural productions such as television and film (the Rambo figure in *First Blood* is a good example of this sort of cultural rewriting).

Thus far I have outlined dominant narrative patterns during and after the war that justify and rewrite the reasons for involvement and subsequent loss. There are examples, however, of dissent within and outside the establishment. The latter manifested itself in the anti-war movement and in the poetry which is the subject of this study. The former is available in two memos George Ball, a senior State Department official in the Kennedy and Johnson administrations, wrote in June and July 1965 outlining his objections to US policy:

> The loss of South Vietnam does not mean the loss of all of Southeast Asia to the Communist power. . . . The Viet Cong—while supported and guided from the North—is largely an indigenous movement. Although we have emphasized its cold war aspects, the conflict in South Vietnam is essentially a civil war within that country. . . . Once we suffer large casualties, we will have started a well-nigh irreversible process. Our involvement will be so great that we cannot—without national humiliation—stop short of achieving our complete objectives. *Of the two possibilities I think humiliation would be more likely than the achievement of our objectives—even after we have paid terrible costs.*[46]

---

[44] Long (ed.), *Vietnam Ten Years After*, 63.
[45] Edward W. Said, *Orientalism* (Harmondsworth: Penguin Books Ltd., 1978), 275.
[46] Cited in Gettleman *et al.*, *Vietnam and America*, 278–9. Italics in original text.

Ball questions some fundamental assumptions guiding US policy in Vietnam: the domino theory, the external nature of the threat in south Vietnam, and the character of the conflict. He is also prescient in his estimation of the costs of escalation. Yet at that juncture his was a lone voice not heeded by McNamara, Dean Rusk, and President Johnson to whom he addressed these memos. Johnson had committed US Marines to Vietnam and McNamara was optimistic about the outcome of that intervention. Apart from policy wranglings that sideline Ball, it is significant that his opposition is premised on pragmatic questions of cost and credibility, not morality; he is immersed in the world of realpolitik. His concerns centre around the possible 'humiliation' of America, a trope that is repeated by Nixon in his 'pitiful, helpless giant' speech. Ball's critical observations paradoxically highlight the power of the dominant discourse and the manner in which debate is confined within narrow parameters. Another example of this type of exclusion is available in a speech in May 1966 by General David Shoup:

I believe that if we had and would keep our dirty, bloody, dollar-crooked fingers out of the business of these nations so full of depressed, exploited people, they will arrive at a solution of their own. That they design and want. That they fight and work for. [Not one] crammed down their throats by Americans.[47]

Shoup's is a more direct and moral indictment of American policy and remarkable in the general atmosphere of consent within the military establishment. Once again, however, it was overwhelmed by the prevailing political and ideological environment. The 'structure of attitude and reference' that defined policy was not shaken, and generals such as Westmoreland, Palmer, and Le May continued to wage a war of attrition in Vietnam.

The two instances are crucial indices of dissension within a largely monolithic projection of political rhetoric and reality. At the same time they highlight the ineffective nature of dissent within a wider consensus (a problem confronted by anti-war poetry as well). The rehabilitation of nationalist myths and the rewriting of Vietnam are indicative of the ways in which the 'academic-research consensus' supplements and supports the political consensus.

[47] Cited in Noam Chomsky, *Rethinking Camelot: JFK, the Vietnam War and U.S. Political Culture* (Boston: South End Press, 1993), 103.

Geoffrey Hartman in an article, 'Public Memory and its Discontents', defines 'contemporary *public* memory' in contradistinction to 'traditional *collective* memory'.[48] In the case of Vietnam, policy and rhetoric justifying that policy were defined in terms of the 'traditional *collective* memory' of manifest destiny, freedom, and democracy. However, the events in Vietnam and protest at home seemed to unravel the mythic consensus. The revisionist pronouncements of politicians and academics attempt to erase the unpalatable aspects of the 'contemporary *public* memory' vis-à-vis Vietnam. In a sense, the rewriting of the Vietnam period attempts to create a 'contemporary *public* memory' that is at one with the 'traditional *collective* memory', a return to the 'innocent' America of immense possibilities and good intentions. America's role in the Second World War constituted part of this 'traditional *collective* memory', and the 'just war' paradigm was imported to Vietnam as well. The paradigm does not, however, adequately reflect the problems in this war. As William O'Brien notes, 'in our time the substance of the just-cause condition of just war has been essentially the issue of being either Red or dead'.[49] Whereas the Second World War was started by Germany and Hitler was clearly identifiable as evil, the USA went halfway round the world to attack a country that had done it no harm. In the 'good war', it was the Japanese who attacked Pearl Harbor without provocation and provided a clear basis for US outrage and intervention. It is interesting that intervention in Vietnam was justified using the language of the Second World War. While Vietnam was seen as a good winnable war, the connections with the earlier war were highlighted. Vietnam veterans such as Philip Caputo testify to the influence of the 'good war' rhetoric, particularly as reflected in John Wayne films. However, the connections were severed when Vietnam turned out to be a war of loss and trauma, and revisionist history now projects it as a unique, aberrant war without any historical contexts. Some critics and poets of the Vietnam War question this new consensus and thereby disrupt the deliberate process of historical reconstruction.

[48] Geoffrey Hartman, 'Public Memory and Its Discontents', *Raritan*, 13 (Spring 1994), 24-40.
[49] William V. O'Brien, *The Conduct of Just and Limited War* (New York: Praeger Publishers, 1981), 21.

The process of reconstituting history does, occasionally, accept that America might have done wrong to commit itself in Vietnam. For instance, Robert McNamara confessed: 'We of the Kennedy and Johnson administrations who participated in the decisions on Vietnam acted according to what we thought were the principles and traditions of this nation. . . . Yet we were wrong, terribly wrong.'[50] I have outlined what these 'principles and traditions' were as construed by policy-makers. McNamara's confession of wrongdoing is part of the tradition which maintains that America failed in Vietnam because of its naïve desire to help other nations achieve enlightened democracy. Ironically, McNamara points to the crucial fissures in that tradition, and leads us to an examination of what precisely these 'principles and traditions' were. While the American nation narrates itself in terms of a new Eden, settled and developed by a new Adam, that narration contains a less savoury aspect: the American history of colonialism, both within the North American land mass and abroad. It is not my intention to enter into a detailed analysis of American colonialism, but a few examples will help to place Vietnam within this other, non-idealistic framework. This 'alternative' tradition and history problematizes the essentially triumphalist rewriting and representation of Vietnam in official and some cultural circles.

The history of American colonialism began with the massacre of the native inhabitants of the land: the American Indians.[51] Occasionally blood was shed, but it was for a noble set of ideals, and the annihilation of entire tribes and lifestyles was a small price to pay for the foundation of the 'City upon a hill'. The dichotomy between ideals and actuality, rhetoric and policy, so pronounced in the Vietnam era, has its roots in the foundation of the American State.

Once the scattered set of colonies, originating in Jamestown, Virginia, had spread and consolidated itself into the United States of America (a complex process beyond the scope and object of this study), the rhetoric of empire became more strident and

---

[50] McNamara, *In Retrospect*, p. xvi.
[51] T. D. Allman observes that for the colonists the Indians 'were not human beings; they were only obstacles to the inexorable triumph of American virtue, who must be swept away to make room for a new reality of American freedom'. Cited in Peck (ed.), *The Chomsky Reader*, 123.

confident. President McKinley asserted American superiority in justifying the occupation of the Philippines:

We could not turn the islands over to France and Germany, our commercial rivals—that would be bad business and discreditable. We could not give them back to Spain—that would be cowardly and dishonorable. We could not leave them to themselves—they were unfit for self-government. . . . There was nothing left for us to do but to take them all, and to educate the Filipinos, uplift them and Christianize them.[52]

And Woodrow Wilson, the champion of democracy and self-determination, wrote in 1902 that it is 'our peculiar duty' to teach colonial peoples 'order and self-control . . . [and] . . . the drill and habit of law and obedience'.[53] These two examples are emblematic of classic colonialist rhetoric and practice. Business interests, national honour, self-imposed duty towards less fortunate peoples are all combined to perpetuate colonial rule. They create the same rhetorical spaces found in the apologias for intervention in Vietnam.[54] In fact, the modes of distorting and coping with reality are extremely similar, so that while there is a steady emphasis on freedom and democracy, there is, equally, a plethora of colonialist statements and practices in Vietnam. The latter is the less pleasant side of the same coin. McNamara's contention that policy-makers had betrayed the great traditions of the country is not quite accurate when we consider some of the connections and continuities.

The 'new frontier' in Vietnam was expressed through US plans of building schools, hospitals, and digging wells. The 'pacification' and Strategic Hamlets Program were designed to fulfil these purposes, although they did degenerate into the creation of refugee camps (or concentration camps, depending on where one was situated). Occasionally, as Mary McCarthy points out, they provided unwitting comic relief: 'When I asked an OCO man in Saigon what his groups actually did in a Vietnamese village to prepare—his word—the people for elections, he answered curtly,

---

[52] Cited in Robert J. McKeever, 'American Myths and the Impact of the Vietnam War: Revisionism in Foreign Policy and Popular Cinema in the 1980s', in Jeffrey Walsh and James Aulich (eds.), *Vietnam Images: War and Representation* (Basingstoke and London: The Macmillan Press Ltd., 1989), 45.

[53] Cited in Peck (ed.), *The Chomsky Reader*, 63.

[54] Nixon wrote: 'We fought in Vietnam because there were important strategic interests involved. But we also fought because our idealism was at stake.' *No More Vietnams*, 210.

"We teach them Civics 101."⁵⁵ South Vietnamese police and administrators were trained at Michigan State University, and, like any effective imperial power, America succeeded in creating a class of bureaucrats that would collaborate with it. American colonial endeavours are a palimpsest of the earlier conquest of America, and similar enterprises all over the world.

If language is instrumental in creating the conditions and justifications for intervention, it is also a precursor to action. One of the shocking aspects of the Vietnam War was the level of destruction—of people, and of the country, particularly its forest cover. The level of atrocity was curiously at odds with the stated US policy of spreading democracy and defending south Vietnam. One possible explanation for the disjunction is racist and colonial attitudes expressed by people in charge of the war. Noam Chomsky quotes an army general, whose attitude explains the level of redundant violence in the American campaign: 'You've got to dry up the sea the guerrillas swim in—that's the peasants—and the best way to do that is to blast the hell out of their villages so they'll come into our refugee camps. No villages, no guerrillas: simple.'⁵⁶ The reworking of Mao's notion of guerrilla warfare strips away all rhetorical illusions and any pretence to a civilizing mission. In a sense, it is a more honest appraisal of motives and objectives, and exposes the violence underlying colonialism. Another example is a statement by General Westmoreland, Commander-in-Chief of the US army in Vietnam, 1965–68. He makes a distinction between the value of life in America and in Vietnam: 'Life is plentiful, life is cheap to those people. That is the philosophy of the Orient. You have to realize that an individual life there isn't as important as an individual life in America.'⁵⁷ Westmoreland enunciates a classic paradigm and paradox of colonial practice.

⁵⁵ Mary McCarthy, *Vietnam* (Harmondsworth: Penguin Books Ltd., 1967), 26.
⁵⁶ Noam Chomsky, *For Reasons of State* (New York: Pantheon Books, 1970), 224. General Curtis Le May expressed a similar sentiment: 'My solution? Tell the Vietnamese they've got to draw in their horns and stop aggression or we're going to bomb them back into the Stone Age.' Cited in Felix Greene, *Vietnam! Vietnam!* (London: Jonathan Cape, 1966), 154.
⁵⁷ Cited in Nigel Gray (ed.), *Phoenix Country* (London: The Journeyman Press, 1980), 99. General Palmer supports Westmoreland's assertion, albeit more subtly: 'Indeed, American military professionals who fought in the Pacific in World War II or in Korea became acutely aware of differing oriental values with respect to human life, and knew the pitfalls of putting too much store in the impact of heavy casualties on the morale of a determined foe or on the will of a ruthless totalitarian government' (*The 25-Year War*, 165).

Although the colonizing nation undertakes the onerous mission of civilizing the native (in this particular case 'saving' south Vietnam from communism), that task involves a rhetoric of contempt and difference, which prepares the way for violence. Atrocities in Vietnam during the American engagement are well documented, particularly the My Lai massacre, and they highlight an utter disregard for Vietnamese life. The objectification of a Vietnamese person in terms of a 'philosophy of the Orient' highlights what James C. Thompson defines as 'cryptoracism' amongst policymakers, bureaucrats, and the men in the field. Thompson wonders why the so-called 'backroom boys'—the bureaucrats and administrators—managed to remain so neutral and detached. He avers that

> bureaucratic detachment may well be compounded by a traditional Western sense that there are so many Asians, after all; that Asians have a fatalism about life and a disregard for its loss; . . . that they are very different from us (and all look alike?) . . . the upshot of such subliminal views is a subliminal question whether Asians, and particularly Asian peasants, and most particularly Asian Communists, are really people— like you and me.[58]

Thompson's observations are relevant to the sort of attitude expressed by Westmoreland. As US troops poured into Vietnam, the rhetoric of a civilizing mission and the reality of wanton destruction seemed totally incompatible. For instance, 35 per cent of south Vietnam's 14 million acres of dense forests were sprayed with defoliants one or more times, two-thirds of bomb tonnage— 6,300,000 tons—were deployed in south Vietnam. This, however, was the only way in which the guerrillas could be deprived of support and, besides, civilian casualties amongst Vietnamese did not really count (except when they were used to bolster the 'body count').

Frantz Fanon wrote that 'the colonial world is a Manichaean world', it constructs absolute categories of good and evil, the chosen and the damned.[59] This rhetoric of exclusion is particularly effective in blanking out the Vietnamese and their concerns. The dominant discourse speaks for the colonized; the subaltern does not utter a word, unless it is in praise of his colonial masters.

---

[58] Cited in Chomsky, *At War With Asia*, 233–4.
[59] Frantz Fanon, *The Wretched of the Earth*, trans. Constance Farrington (1967; Harmondsworth: Penguin Books Ltd., 1990), 31.

Throughout this chapter I have highlighted American voices, concerns, and criticisms. It seems necessary and appropriate now to focus on some Vietnamese voices. These indicate not only the extent to which the colonized internalized the language of the colonizer (the problem of internalizing dominant rhetoric is also manifest in American poetry on the war), but also the ways in which opposition perspectives differ. It is interesting that, both in the political realm (for the north Vietnamese, the war was a patriotic one to oust an imperial aggressor) and in the poetic, manichaean frameworks are maintained. It is almost as if the two sides were bound by the logic of colonialism and anti-colonialism. However, neither side is so constrained that it is totally unable to perceive nuances and problems in its respective stances. The poetic responses (which I discuss in subsequent chapters) are often problematic and simplistic, but they do provide insights into the horror and moral morass that was the Vietnam War.

For the purposes of this chapter, however, two statements will serve as representative. President Diem in a letter to President Kennedy, on 7 December 1961, wrote:

it is not only our freedom which is at stake today, it is our national identity. For, if we lose this war, our people will be swallowed by the Communist bloc, all our proud heritage will be blotted out by the 'Socialist society' and Vietnam will leave the pages of history. We will lose our national soul.[60]

The letter, which begins by stating that south Vietnam had honoured the 1954 Geneva Agreement (a dubious assertion given its sabotaging of the elections due in 1956 to unify the country), parrots the anxieties and ideas of national identity that American leaders had already spoken for Vietnam. This act of political ventriloquism is indicative of the extent to which the language justifying colonialism is embedded in the political psyche of the colonized. Language, particularly political slogans and rhetoric oft repeated, is the most effective agent of enslavement. The creation of a consensus in American policy and academic circles is followed up and strengthened by a type of consensus in south Vietnam. The latter, as the coup against Diem showed, was a precarious one, and it represented not so much a winning of hearts and minds (a much vaunted US programme to 'pacify'

[60] Cited in Gettleman *et al.*, *Vietnam and America*, 163–4.

south Vietnam), as a colonizing of hearts and minds. Of course, not all voices were silenced. A delegation of ninety-three Catholic priests said in a joint declaration on 15 October 1969: 'Those whom the USA accuses in its ignorance as Communist, are in reality our relatives, our brothers, our sisters, our friends dispersed in villages and hamlets. . . . They only ask one thing: to be masters of their own home and to gain a livelihood by the sweat of their brow.'[61]

The statement breaks the monolithic characterization of the 'other' as communist and therefore evil. There were nationalists in south Vietnam who opposed Diem and the US presence, but alternative human and political dimensions were repressed. While the USA could function as an external colonial power, Diem functioned as one who was oppressing his own people.[62] The significant aspect of the declaration is that it was made by Catholic priests because Catholics were the main source of political support for Diem. It was partly his Catholic partisanship (particularly with those from north Vietnam) that cemented opposition against him. Political agendas are stated in absolute, unidimensional terms, and admit little or no room for dissension. They articulate themselves as truth, and the declaration tears this façade, indicating fissures, contradictions, complexities.

I began by stating that the Second World War was constructed as a 'good war' and that the American success provided the impetus, ideological and military, for intervention in various parts of the world, Vietnam being the most prominent one. Vietnam was significant not only because America lost the war, but because there were unprecedented levels of dissent during the conflict. Stateside poets were part of this larger framework of protest. The purpose of tracing this genealogy of political and rhetorical modes is also to emphasize that Vietnam was not an aberration in American history. The most effective way in which American popular culture and the polity have rewritten and recuperated Vietnam is to 'admit' that it was a mistake, an error

---

[61] Cited in Chomsky, *At War With Asia*, 54.

[62] Truong Nhu Tang highlights this aspect of repression: 'It was part of the regime's ideology that anyone who opposed them must be a Communist. They could not accept the fact that there might be people who hated them for the travesty they had made of the country's life, for their intolerance and corruption and cold indifference to the lot of their countrymen.' Truong Nhu Tang, *Journal of a Vietcong* (London: Jonathan Cape, 1986), 113.

made in good faith. As Noam Chomsky and other critics have pointed out, this stance is a misrepresentation of the planning and violence evident in a dispassionate analysis of the war. The rhetorical aspect of the war is crucial because it played a substantial role in obscuring the extent of American involvement and atrocity in Vietnam. The 'honest error' position is subtly transformative in that the loss and trauma in Vietnam then becomes emblematic of a loss of innocence, a betrayal of pristine originary impulses. The idea is a seductively important one and recurs as a trope in some of the poetry. Vietnam, however, does not exist in a political vacuum. As Evelyn Cobley points out, 'Vietnam was not so much an aberration of American values as it was their most striking expression.'[63]

It would not be entirely accurate, however, to project the post-Second World War American consensus as being seamlessly woven into aggressive anti-communism, and culminating in Vietnam, without dissenting voices. As a prologue to the following chapter I consider responses by two American poets to the Second World War to highlight this aspect of dissent. Poetic representations of the 'good war' provide a valuable critical context for the poetry of Vietnam and, although this is not a comparative study, it is important to note that American poetry on Vietnam does not exist in a critical, literary vacuum.

[63] Evelyn Cobley, *Representing War: Form and Ideology in First World War Narratives* (Toronto, Buffalo, and London: University of Toronto Press, 1993), 218–19.

2

Stateside Poetry

Protest and Prophecy

PROLOGUE: THE SECOND WORLD WAR: POETRY OF THE 'GOOD WAR'

The Second World War in its global reach, its effect on vast civilian populations, the extermination of 6 million Jews, and the use of atomic bombs in Hiroshima and Nagasaki, was an exercise in mass destruction. That the allies, and particularly America, won the war and constructed a post-war mythology of a righteous triumph over evil, cannot mitigate the actual evil: the war itself. Numbers give us an idea of the extent of the carnage, but as Paul Fussell points out,

> the sheer numbers defeat attempts to flesh them out with actual, unique human beings. Killed and wounded were over 78 million people, more of them civilians than soldiers. Close to 6 million Jews were beaten, shot, or gassed to death by the Germans. One million people died of starvation and despair in the siege of Leningrad.... If the battle of the Somme constitutes a scandal because 20,000 British soldiers were killed in one day, twice the number of civilians were asphyxiated and burned to death in the bombing of Hamburg. Seventy thousand died at Hiroshima, 35,000 at Nagasaki, and the same at Dresden.[1]

Collateral damage, particularly the deaths of civilians, seemed an inevitable aspect of the war. While the scale was unprecedented in the Second World War, it was not a unique feature of the war. Billy Prior, a character in Pat Barker's *The Ghost Road* (part of her trilogy on the First World War), writes that civilian deaths are part of the package of all war: 'Five civilians killed. When did we stop thinking of civilians as human? Quite a long time ago, I think.'[2] Although civilian deaths might have been taken for granted, retrospective horror at the scale of death is not pre-

---

[1] Paul Fussell (ed.), *The Bloody Game* (London: Abacus, 1991), 307.
[2] Pat Barker, *The Ghost Road* (London: Viking, 1995), 244.

cluded. Faced with such mind-numbing statistics and destruction on a worldwide scale (America was the only major power whose land mass was unscathed by the war), the victors had to set about reconstructing a 'new' world. This is where America, with its booming post-war economy, stepped in to provide economic aid predicated on ideological solidarity. After the defeat of Nazism and fascism, the battle was now joined with a new enemy: communism. American poets, however, were not as triumphalist as the rest of their society and many of their poems attempt to deal with the horrors and ambiguities of the war.

Paul Fussell laments the fact that America has learned nothing from the war:

in unbombed America especially, the meaning of the war seemed inaccessible. As experience, thus, the suffering was wasted. The same tricks of publicity and advertising might have succeeded in sweetening the actualities of Vietnam if television and a vigorous uncensored moral journalism hadn't been brought to bear. America has not yet understood what the Second World War was like and thus been unable to use such understanding to re-interpret and re-define the national reality and to arrive at something like public maturity.[3]

The media coverage of Vietnam was not as 'uncensored' or as 'moral' as Fussell suggests, and his unqualified endorsement of its role is open to debate.[4] However, his characterization of post-Second World War and post-Vietnam America is insightful and accurate. In fact, it was precisely the lack of understanding, the inability to 're-interpret and re-define national reality' that led the USA into Vietnam. In the realm of public historical memory and insight Fussell's sense of despair is comprehensible and justified. However, there is another form of critical enquiry into the war that attempts to redress some of the problems he pointed out. The dynamics of public debate and discourse on the Second World War were not radically altered by poets writing on the war, but they do attempt to re-describe and probe the dominant myths that the war generated.

In an essay, 'Thirteen Ways of Looking at a Skylark', Howard

---

[3] Paul Fussell, *Wartime: Understanding and Behavior in the Second World War* (New York and Oxford: Oxford University Press, 1989), 268.
[4] For a critical analysis of American media coverage of Vietnam, see Edward S. Herman and Noam Chomsky, *Manufacturing Consent: The Political Economy of the Mass Media* (London: Vintage, 1994), ch. 5.

Nemerov muses on the role of poetry, and provides an insight into his poetry dealing with the Second World War:

> One way regarded, it is the traditional business of poetry to inspire, even to invent, human purpose. But simultaneously the opposite is true: poetry is the traditional means of confronting the hopelessness of human purpose.[5]

In two poems, 'Redeployment' and 'The War in the Air', Nemerov provides stark counterpoints to the national sense of triumph, purpose, and fulfilment. 'Redeployment' is a post-war meditation on irredeemable horror:

> They say the war is over. But water still
> Comes bloody from the taps, and my pet cat
> In his disorder vomits worms which crawl
> Swiftly away. Maybe they leave the house.
> These worms are white, and flecked with cat's blood.
>
> The war may be over. I know a man
> Who keeps a pleasant souvenir, he keeps
> A soldier's dead blue eyeballs that he found
> Somewhere—hard as chalk, and blue as slate.
> He clicks them in his pocket while he talks.
>
> And now there are cockroaches in the house,
> They get slightly drunk on DDT,
> Are fast, hardy, shifty—can be drowned but not
> Without you hold them under quite some time.
> People say the Mexican kind can fly.
>
> The end of the war. I took it quietly
> Enough. I tried to wash the dirt out of
> My hair and from under my fingernails,
> I dressed in clean white clothes and went to bed.
> I heard the dust falling between the walls.[6]

The poem begins on a note of unconvinced neutrality: 'They say the war is over.' The speaker of the poem is sceptical and the opinion of the disembodied 'They' is contrasted with signs of decay and degeneracy. The bloody water from the taps and

---

[5] Howard Nemerov, 'Thirteen Ways of Looking at a Skylark', *Figures of Thought: Speculations on the Meaning of Poetry and Other Essays* (Boston: David R. Godine, Publisher, 1978), 12.

[6] Howard Nemerov, 'Redeployment', *The Collected Poems of Howard Nemerov* (Chicago and London: The University of Chicago Press, 1977), 61. Subsequent references are indicated after the quotation.

the pet cat vomiting worms are indicative of a monumental disorder in the world and in nature. The images of urban decay—bloody tap water, cats vomiting worms, cockroaches drunk on DDT, 'the dust falling between the walls'—are reminiscent of T. S. Eliot's descriptions of chaos and disorder. The Chorus in *Murder in the Cathedral* picture a world of horror as the Knights prepare to kill Thomas Becket:

> I have
> tasted
> The savour of putrid flesh in the spoon. I have felt
> The heaving of earth at nightfall, restless, absurd.
> . . . .
> I have tasted
> The living lobster, the crab, the oyster, the whelk and
> the prawn; and they live and spawn in my bowels,
> and my bowels dissolve in the light of dawn. I
> have smelt
> Death in the rose, death in the hollyhock, sweet pea,
> hyacinth, primrose and cowslip.[7]

Death and corruption haunt all that is normally associated with nature, beauty, and regeneration. All norms have been inverted and the purposelessness (or malevolent purpose) of existence, the existential void in which the speaker finds himself, unravels the sense of definitive purpose that the rhetoric of war, and post-war triumph created. His is a totally private, enclosed world of horror and encroaching dirt. His only interaction is with the cat, cockroaches, and a soldier with a grisly fetish. The souvenir, 'a soldier's dead blue eyeballs', is an uncanny presentiment of Vietnam, where soldiers collected 'gooks' ears as trophies. This strange mode of self-validation with strong sexual overtones ('He clicks them in his pocket while he talks') is a counterpart to the disorder in the natural world described in the first stanza. The psychic dislocation highlights further the hopelessness of investing a brutal enterprise with lofty purpose. The Second World War was a long and terrible war, but it has been reconstructed as a 'good' one. To quote Fussell again:

Now fifty years later, there has been so much talk about 'The Good

---

[7] T. S. Eliot, *Murder in the Cathedral* (London: Faber and Faber Limited, 1938), part II, 66–7.

War', the Justified War, the Necessary War, and the like, that the young and the innocent could get the impression that it was not such a bad thing after all. It's thus necessary to observe that it was a war and nothing else, and thus stupid and sadistic, a war, as Cyril Connolly said, 'of which we are all ashamed . . . a war which lowers the standard of thinking and feeling . . . which is as obsolete as drawing and quartering . . .'[8]

The 'dead blue eyeballs' could also be a grim echo of the concentration camps where seemingly every bit of the human body was converted into useable commodities, a total dislocation of purpose and use.

Concurrent with images of dirt and horror, are images of a desire to sanitize the world after the war. The DDT to counter cockroaches and the clean white clothes the speaker wears to bed cannot overcome an overwhelming tide of literal, moral, psychic dirt. The Holocaust looms large in the background, but it is the individual sense of contamination that dominates the last stanza:

> . . . I tried to wash the dirt out of
> My hair and from under my fingernails,
> I dressed in clean white clothes and went to bed.
> I heard the dust falling between the walls.

The personal situation is a metaphor for horror that cannot be washed away, analogous to the tribulations of Lady Macbeth. While she was personally responsible for murder, the speaker in the poem is responsible by virtue of participating in the war, and he bears a civilizational burden. There is another striking parallel in Eliot's *Murder in the Cathedral*. While the Knights kill Thomas, the Chorus describe a world eternally defiled:

> We are soiled by a filth we cannot clean, united to
>   supernatural vermin,
> It is not we alone, it is not the house, it is not the city
>   that is defiled,
> But the world that is wholly foul.
> Clear the air! clean the sky! wash the wind! take the
>   stone from the stone, take the skin from the arm,
>   take the muscle from the bone, and wash them.
> Wash the stone, wash the bone, wash the brain,
> Wash the soul, wash them wash them![9]

---

[8] Fussell, *Wartime*, 142.
[9] Eliot, *Murder in the Cathedral*, part II, 77.

Is it possible to exorcise the concentration camps and other horrors, particularly since there is no redemptive framework as in the case of Becket's murder? Nemerov seems to say that not all the perfumes of Arabia can cleanse the stench emanating from Auschwitz and Belsen, Hiroshima and Dresden.

Scepticism regarding the end of the war and its significance is indicated throughout the poem, and specially the first line of stanzas one, two, and four. The fourth stanza offers a telling contrast to the actual scenes of jubilation that occurred once the war was over: 'The end of the war. I took it quietly | Enough.' The deliberate incongruity and scepticism are inherent in the poem's title. 'Redeployment' is a military term applied to a post-war, angst-ridden private world. Is the speaker going to be redeployed for another war? Or is there a necessity for a redeployment of forces, of energies to fight the war within the psyche, and the nation? The psychic struggle, an attempt to maintain order and cleanliness, is evident in the poem. Perhaps 'Redeployment' also hints at the ways in which the state would redeploy the same myths and similar language to lead soldiers into further wars such as Vietnam. The connections are interesting and evident, particularly the ways in which Nemerov highlights the instrumentalist nature of state language in his poems on Vietnam, which I discuss later.

'Redeployment' is a personal, inward-looking subversion of post-war myths. 'The War in the Air' is a more direct interrogation of the 'good war' myth:

> For a saving grace, we didn't see our dead,
> Who rarely bothered coming home to die
> But simply stayed away out there
> In the clean war, the war in the air.
>
> Seldom the ghosts came back bearing their tales
> Of hitting the earth, the incomprehensible sea,
> But stayed up there in the relative wind,
> Shades fading in the mind,
>
> Who had no graves but only epitaphs
> Where never so many spoke for never so few:
> Per ardua, said the partisans of Mars,
> Per aspera, to the stars.
>
> That was the good war, the war we won
> As if there were no death, for goodness' sake,

> With the help of the losers we left out there
> In the air, the empty air.[10]

The clinical distancing of the war is its 'saving grace', with the dead as mere counters in a war game. The dichotomy between the action (firing) and its effect (death) probably leads to the psychic disorders outlined in 'Redeployment'. The obsession with order and cleanliness crops up again, and the horror of war is heightened by the detachment from the blood-and-guts aspect of ground warfare. The Second World War saw the largest deployment of air power in the history of warfare, rivalled in its destructive quality only by the pulverizing of Vietnam, Laos, and Cambodia. The air force of Allied powers (particularly the RAF in Britain) became a new, heroic élite. Their defence of Britain against unrelenting German attacks was heroic. This heroism, however, is qualified retrospectively by mass destruction unleashed on civilian populations, particularly in carpet bombing raids on cities like Dresden. There was, perhaps, no direct intent to kill civilians (the Blitz launched by the Germans was an exception), but they did die and their 'ghosts' do 'c[o]me back bearing' testimony to the horrible price of war. The poem maintains a quiet balance within the good–evil dichotomy that the war created, and highlights a conscious awareness of contradictions. Nemerov's ironic twist to the Churchillian 'so much owed by so many to so few' places this notion of heroism in a different context: 'Where never so many spoke for never so few.'[11] In reaching for the stars, aspiring to fulfil codes of heroism propagated by the war machine, the pilots (of whom Nemerov had been one) destroyed the earth, its people, and themselves. And that, as the last stanza forcefully states,

> was the good war, the war we won
> As if there was no death, for goodness' sake,
> With the help of the losers we left out there
> In the air, the empty air.

---

[10] Howard Nemerov, 'The War in the Air', *Trying Conclusions: New and Selected Poems, 1961–1991* (Chicago and London: The University of Chicago Press, 1991), 129–30.
[11] Paul Fussell highlights the series of blunders in Allied operations that led to Allied and civilian deaths: 'The confusions and delays prompted this graffito scrawled in the troop space of one of the transports: "Never in the history of human endeavour have so few been buggered about by so many."' *Wartime*, 28.

The use of the colloquial 'for goodness' sake' emphasizes Nemerov's anger and impatience at the formulation and efficacy of the 'good war' myth. How could one possibly believe this after the war? As Dellie Hahn points out:

The good war? That infuriates me. Yeah, the idea of World War Two being called a good war is a horrible thing. I think of all the atrocities. . . . I think of the destruction of the Jews, the misery, the horrendous suffering in the concentration camps.[12]

Hahn refers to the most notable atrocity, and Nemerov's questioning is more generalized in its indictment of the entire heroic, triumphalist culture spawned by the war. He inverts the winner–loser paradigm by collating meaningless deaths (which led to 'victory') with 'the losers we left out there | In the air, the empty air'. In a sense, the pilots are representative of a culture and civilization in the grip of a Freudian 'death wish', mindlessly destroying itself in pursuit of a 'better' world. The vehemence with which Nemerov wishes to deconstruct the 'good war' myth is attributable not only to anger or impatience, but fear, the fear that this myth will sustain future wars. In this he was prescient, as the myths of the Second World War fuelled American involvement in Vietnam, in its continuing crusade against evil in the world. Nemerov's poetry, 'confront[s] the hopelessness of human purpose' underlying seemingly purposive projects. This confrontation is not an invitation to despair but a composite and more enlightened perception, a retrospective musing on war and history.

Randall Jarrell's 'The Death of the Ball Turret Gunner', written in 1945, is a minimalist poem encapsulating the absurd brevity of such a gunner's existence:

> From my mother's sleep I fell into the State,
> And I hunched in its belly till my wet fur froze.
> Six miles from earth, loosed from its dream of life,
> I woke to black flak and the nightmare fighters.
> When I died they washed me out of the turret with a hose.[13]

In a note to the poem Jarrell described the actuality of the gunner's situation:

A ball turret was a plexiglass sphere set into the belly of a B-17 or B-24,

[12] Cited in Fussell, *The Bloody Game*, 595.
[13] Randall Jarrell, 'The Death of the Ball Turret Gunner', *Selected Poems* (New York: Alfred A. Knopf, 1955), 137.

and inhabited by two .50 caliber machine-guns and one man, a short small man. When this gunner tracked with his machine-guns a fighter attacking his bomber from below, he revolved with the turret; hunched upside-down in his little sphere, he looked like the foetus in the womb. The fighters which attacked him were armed with cannon firing explosive shells. The hose was a steam hose.[14]

The paring down of language is appropriate and effective within a context where the war and its heroes were described in glowing, euphemistic terms. The cynical manipulation of language and information by the government bred a profound distrust of language. The womb-to-death narration is punctuated by an awareness only of 'the State', 'black flak', 'nightmare fighters', 'the belly' of the aircraft where the ball turret gunner would be positioned, and death. The first line delineates a transition from innocence to horror, a falling 'into the State' of post-lapsarian nightmares. At another level 'the State' could be the aircraft (with, perhaps, an echo of the political state, into which one is acculturated), a monstrous Leviathan within which the ball turret gunner is scarcely human with his frozen 'wet fur'. The short flash of recognition before death encompasses the basic facts of his life: 'black flak and the nightmare fighters'. That stark recognition is too much to bear, and his life is 'mercifully' snuffed out. The Beckettian brevity of the poem heightens the existential pointlessness of life during the war. The anonymity and lack of individuation is typical of a situation where individuals were merely cogs in the war machine. E. B. Sledge, a participant in, and memoirist of, the war, wrote about this obliteration of all value and identity normally attributed to individuals: 'We were expendable. It was difficult to accept. We come from a nation and culture that values life and the individual. To find oneself in a situation where your life seems of little value is the ultimate in loneliness. It is a humbling experience.'[15] 'The Death of the Ball Turret Gunner' is dominated by silence and loneliness. The gunner can neither understand nor interpret his experience, he merely catalogues it. There is no possibility of heroism given that there is scarcely a history that heroic paradigms would recognize.

---

[14] Randall Jarrell, 'Introduction', *Selected Poems*, p. xiii. Joseph Heller's *Catch-22* deals wonderfully with the frightening and absurd aspects of a gunner's life, particularly in the figure of Yossarian.
[15] Fussell, *Wartime*, 293.

Yet, paradoxically, the poem is a succinct summation of the kernel of life and death in a war that is then reconstructed to mythify and justify war. It also conveys with devastating accuracy the dehumanizing violence of the war; violence visited not only on enemy personnel, but home participants who outlive their usefulness. The 'I' in the poem is a passive being, and the sense of a person acted upon is forcefully reiterated in the image of the dead gunner hosed out of the turret. An image that affirms and dignifies life (the washing of a dead body) contrasts with the force of the hose. The latter creates an impression of violent wrenching akin to an abortion (the 'foetus' image in Jarrell's note heightens the impression of deadly severance). The gunner's life is abruptly terminated, he has no voice and agency, and no dignity in death.[16]

The poem restores ambiguities absent in official representations of the war and attempts to point to alternative truths. Jarrell was constantly aware of, and expressed ideas at variance with, the dominant ones of his time. In a letter to Margaret Marshall, Literary Editor of the *Nation*, in September 1945, he wrote about his dismay at the reaction to the nuclear bombing of two Japanese cities:

I feel so rotten about the country's response to the bombings at Hiroshima and Nagasaki that I wish I could become a naturalized dog or cat. I believe our culture's chief characteristic, to a being from outside it, would be that we are *liars*. That all except a few never tell or feel anything near the truth about anything we do.[17]

There is an element of excessive bitterness and disillusionment in the statement, but the power of post-war reconstructive myths in glorifying the war justifies some of the outrage. Jarrell's poems on the war are animated by a desire to 'tell or feel anything near the truth', to restore a sense of integrity and value in a world of myth and prejudice. He is largely convincing in this enterprise and

---

[16] Yossarian, musing on Snowden's death, realizes the fragility of human existence: 'Man was matter, that was Snowden's secret. Drop him out of a window and he'll fall. Set fire to him and he'll burn. Bury him and he'll rot, like other kinds of garbage. The spirit gone, man is garbage. That was Snowden's secret. Ripeness was all.' Joseph Heller, *Catch-22* (London: Jonathan Cape, 1962), 429–30.

[17] Mary Jarrell (ed.), *Randall Jarrell's Letters* (London: Faber and Faber, 1985), 130. An alternative point of view is provided by Admiral Halsey, who said in a victory message to his fleet when the Japanese surrendered, 'The forces of righteousness and decency have triumphed.' Cited in Fussell, *Wartime*, 129.

James Dickey's comments on Jarrell's poetry in a lecture on 'Some Guesses at the Future of American Poetry', accurately sum up the qualities of integrity and communication: 'One believes it, and therefore the poem can act either as human communication or poetry or both, without the reader's having to kill off one side of his receptiveness so that the other can operate.'[18] In its refusal to construct or accept justificatory myths, 'The Death of the Ball Turret Gunner' is a telling riposte to the 'good war' myth.

Theodor Adorno, in his essay on 'Commitment' in literature and particularly poetry, reiterated his famous statement about lyric poetry after Auschwitz: 'I have no wish to soften the saying that to write lyric poetry after Auschwitz is barbaric; it expresses in negative form the impulse which inspires committed literature.'[19] However, a little later in the same essay, he went on to write that 'it is now virtually in art alone that suffering can still find its own voice, consolation, without immediately being betrayed'.[20] While lyric poetry might domesticate horror and seem inadequate to the task of representing the Holocaust, it is significant that Adorno emphasizes the importance of art in a world of unimaginable suffering. He is not advocating silence and sees in art the only possibility of committed utterance and redemption. The poems of the Second World War discussed here, and the poetry on the Vietnam War, give voice to the suffering of a violent century. These poetic utterances are not necessarily consolatory, and, perhaps, they are not meant to ameliorate (cannot ameliorate?) the complex fate humankind has created for itself. The importance of the poetry, however, lies in the responsibility that poets bear by continuing to write, to witness and record the politics, wars, and travails of their lives and lives around them. In this, the poetry is deeply committed and political. As Robert Pinsky writes: '"All poetry is political." The act of judgement prior to the vision of any poem is a social judgement. It always embodies, I believe, a resistance or transformation of communal values.'[21] The process and modes of 'resistance

---

[18] James Dickey, 'Spinning the Crystal Ball: Some Guesses at the Future of American Poetry', a lecture delivered at the Library of Congress, 24 Apr. 1967 (Washington: The Library of Congress, 1967), 11.
[19] Theodor Adorno, 'Commitment', in Fredric Jameson (ed.), *Aesthetics and Politics* (London and New York: Verso, 1980), 188.
[20] Ibid. 189.

Stateside Poetry 37

or transformation of communal values' is crucial in evaluating the poetry inspired by major political upheavals such as the Second World War and Vietnam. Quite often, as we shall see in American poetry on Vietnam, the language of the poem is complicit in dominant political utterances and strategies. In some ways the task of the Second World War poets was even more daunting since they returned to a jubilant nation, unwilling to consider critically the contradictions in the 'good war'. Part of the value of their poetry lies in their sense of personal and historical responsibility, their refusal to evade the unpleasant aspects of the war and their country which triumphed in that war. These political concerns are mediated by personal experiences of the war. While the political establishment projected the Second World War as the 'good war', the poets ask for an honest reappraisal of the major military conflict of their times. They accept the sort of responsibility that Friedrich Dürrenmatt believes politicians shun:

In the Punch-and-Judy show of our century ... there are no more guilty and also, no responsible men. It is always, 'We couldn't help it' and 'We didn't really want that to happen.' And indeed, things happen without anyone in particular being responsible for them.[22]

This attitude is terribly convenient, and some poets do succumb to the temptation of non-responsibility. The poetic response is often complex and contradictory, and the poet's protest may be implicated with dominant ideological utterances. It may essentialize personal experience, or it may move beyond complicity to Herbert Marcuse's notion of 'the Refusal'.[23] Writing about moral dilemmas after the Vietnam War, Peter Marin wondered whether a deeply righteous country could actually come to terms with the consequences: 'How does a country like ours, with its mythical sense of itself as a force for good in the world, deal with a moral defeat, a moral tragedy?'[24] This mythical construction of moral

---

[21] Robert Pinsky, 'Responsibilities of the Poet', *Poetry and the World* (New York: The Ecco Press, 1988), 97–8.
[22] Cited in Paul Fussell, *The Great War and Modern Memory* (New York and London: Oxford University Press, 1975), 204.
[23] Herbert Marcuse, *An Essay on Liberation* (London: Allen Lane The Penguin Press, 1969), 8.
[24] Cited in Robert Emmet Long (ed.), *Vietnam Ten Years After* (New York: The H. W. Wilson Company, 1986), 131.

nationhood was consolidated by the US success in the Second World War and the poetry, in its myriad responses to both the wars, attempts to answer the question raised by Marin. In the answers and the questions to the question, lies the beginning of political, moral, intellectual, and poetic responsibility.

STATESIDE POETRY AND THE VIETNAM WAR

'From 1964 to 1972, the wealthiest and most powerful nation in the history of the world made a maximum military effort, with everything short of atomic bombs to defeat a nationalist revolutionary movement in a tiny peasant country—and failed.'[25] Howard Zinn's stark binary characterization of the American foray into Vietnam is indicative of the visceral importance of that involvement in a particular period of American social, political, and cultural history. For the first time in its collective history the USA had to cope with military defeat and with an anti-war movement of unprecedented vehemence. America, which had always emphasized the moral and millennial basis of its founding and continued existence, now saw itself on the brink of an apocalyptic precipice. Of course, both the perceived polarities were exaggerations. Nevertheless, the polarities were the parameters within which much of the political and cultural debates and productions took place. While this chapter is primarily concerned with stateside poetry protesting against the Vietnam War, a brief outline of some of the concerns of the movements of the 1960s provides not only a valuable context for the poetry, but highlights some of the debates and contradictions that permeate it.

Within the context of the anti-war movement of the 1960s, Vietnam was imaged in apocalyptic terms. There was a collective sense of a civilizational burden that the protestors not only had to bear but to exorcise as well. Whatever values prosperous middle America represented and was proud of—from the media to the consumer culture and militarism—were the most visible aspects of a corrupt society. Todd Gitlin comments on this sense of corruption:

---

[25] Howard Zinn, *A People's History of the United States* (New York: Harper Collins Publishers, 1980), 460.

Stateside Poetry 39

Look at TV, *Newsweek* or *Time:* Interspersed between the ads for the American way of life, here was *this* child seared by napalm, *this* suspect tortured by our freedom-loving allies, *this* village torched by Marines with cigarette lighters, *this* forest burned to the ground . . . a seemingly endless procession of pain and destruction. So much punishment inflicted by one nation against another: the sheer volume of it seemed out of line with any official, self-contradictory, incomprehensible reasons of state. There had to be something radically, unredeemably wrong at the dark heart of America. By the late Sixties many of us had concluded that the problem simply wasn't bad policy but a wrongheaded social system, even a civilization. The weight of decades, or centuries, even millennia had to be thrown off overnight—because it was necessary.[26]

The protest movement exploded the complacency of what Robert Lowell called the 'tranquilized *Fifties*', relentlessly exposing the hypocrisy and venality of those in charge of the political and cultural system.[27] The 1950s, however, were not entirely 'tranquilized' and it is important to bear in mind the influence of the counter-culture and the Beats, both of which originated in the 1950s, on the protest movement in the next decade. There is a tendency amongst 1960s historians and memoirists to privilege that period as a unique one with no background whatsoever. The Vietnam War was perceived as the most grotesque symptom of this system and the protest against the war centred on the desire for social and political change. The need, expressed primarily by non-combatant poets, was radically to transform social and political vocabulary as a first step towards social change. As Herbert Marcuse put it, 'the sociological and political vocabulary must be radically reshaped: it must be stripped of its false neutrality; it must be methodically and provocatively "moralized" in terms of the Refusal'.[28] Marcuse's theory of 'the Refusal' involves the ability to perceive the manipulations of contemporary politics and provide coherent alternatives to them. While his insights into the functioning of modern democracies are pertinent, his 'solutions' are sometimes difficult to put into practice. However, his idea of 'the Refusal' is a useful context for several poets who attempt to deconstruct the language of state. Chapter

[26] Todd Gitlin, *The Sixties: Years of Hope, Days of Rage* (New York and London: Bantam Books, 1987), 255–6.
[27] Robert Lowell, 'Memories of West Street and Lepke', *Life Studies* (London: Faber and Faber, 1959), 57.
[28] Marcuse, *An Essay on Liberation*, 8.

I dealt with some aspects and implications of this seemingly neutral political vocabulary employed *vis-à-vis* Vietnam. In the course of analysing individual poems I will attempt to highlight the ways in which poets both question and are complicit in (even if unintentionally) certain dominant modes of representing the worlds of conflict.

The anti-war movement was truly revolutionary in its denunciations of the war, although quite often the criticism of contemporary politics verged on the creation of exaggerated contrasts. Tom Hayden, a leading figure of the movement, believed that absolute polarization was the best way to stop the war:

> Since the country, provably, has no soul that is operational, no conscience that works, only a kind of tattered remnant of a democratic tradition that doesn't prevail when the chips are down—given that, then you have to make a cold calculation . . . to raise the internal cost to such a high level that those decision-makers who only deal in cost-effectiveness terms will have to get out of Vietnam.[29]

While it highlighted a set of problems, this strategy was destined to fail for the simple reason that the state had at its disposal greater resources of violence and coercion than the protest movement. Moreover, this stance did not involve any radical difference or great 'Refusal', merely an attempt to stalemate the state at its own game. The logical extension of this argument was the degeneration of the movement into the bizarre and pointless violence of the Weathermen.

It is necessary to emphasize this atmosphere of conflict and the need to create either-or oppositions, because non-combatant poetry was written within this context. Non-combatants wrote anti-war poetry and expressed anti-war sentiments for reasons which vary from poet to poet. Individual concerns, however, can be seen to be mediated by three major factors: the role and influence of the media, the need to express personal and national guilt, and the influence of the counter-culture. The outpouring of anti-war stateside poetry is significant not only in its content, but in its volume. At no other comparable period in American history, not even during the Civil War (commemorated most notably by Walt Whitman and Herman Melville), was poetry such a major mode of protest. Unlike any previous war in their

---

[29] Cited in Gitlin, *The Sixties*, 289.

history, Vietnam was brought home to Americans by the media. Vietnam was America's first TV war, and although the media did not question the fundamental premises of US involvement, it did make the war and its attendant atrocity difficult to ignore. Similarly *Time*, *Life*, and *Newsweek* helped to disseminate the often unpleasant aspects of the war. The media constituted one mode of representing the war (and still does through Hollywood projections of Vietnam 'reality' such as *Platoon* and *Apocalypse Now*), a powerful and intrusive language occasionally questioned by poets such as Allen Ginsberg and Howard Nemerov.

Non-combatant poetry may be seen as an expression of the collective guilt that this war, in sharp contrast to the Second World War, provoked in the aggressor. The term 'collective guilt' is a misnomer in that there was no nationwide consensus that the war was an immoral and brutal undertaking. As Todd Gitlin and Charles de Benedetti among other analysts of this period point out, one of the many contradictions of the war lay in the domestic response to war protestors. As an increasing majority believed that the war was a mistake and a bad investment, that majority equally asserted its absolute contempt and hatred for the anti-war movement.[30] Protest poets attempt to represent the landscape of America during a time of domestic and international crisis. They question the dominant vocabulary presented by the state, and this interrogation further highlights a divide in national opinion. Protestors and anti-war poets were seen as fifth columnists, an enemy within. Spiro Agnew designated the anti-war movement as consisting of 'Malcontents, radicals, incendiaries, civil and uncivil disobedients, yippies, hippies, yahoos, Black Panthers, lions and tigers—I would swap the whole damn zoo for a single platoon of the kind of young Americans I saw in Vietnam.'[31] Agnew's vituperation is just one example of the sort of hate speech that was also used to

---

[30] See ibid. 414. Also Charles de Benedetti, *An American Ordeal: The Antiwar Movement of the Vietnam Era* (Syracuse, NY: New York University Press, 1990), 137–8: Harris reported in mid-December [1966?] that 'popular hostility toward antiwar critics was so deep that one-third of Americans believed that citizens did not have the right to demonstrate against the war ... The great majority of people ... believed instead that antiwar demonstrators were either motivated by personal exhibitionism, communist manipulation, or a desire to avoid the draft.'

[31] Cited in W. D. Ehrhart, 'The United States Screw & Bolt Company', *In The Shadow of Vietnam: Essays, 1977–1991* (Jefferson, NC, and London: McFarland & Company, Inc., Publishers, 1991), 42.

demonize the Vietcong, the enemy without. To protest against indiscriminate murder and destruction in Vietnam in the name of democracy was to be branded an anti-American, a communist sympathizer. The stateside poets reflect upon, and are emblematic of, a deeply divided nation. They wish to bear witness to the immorality of the war, and the lies and manipulations of the state that sustain the war. Their witnessing is implicated in certain problems, but it is interesting to contrast it with another kind of witnessing that was sanctioned in the USA in the 1950s, and equally indicative of a divided society. The House Un-American Activities Committee (HUAC) was based on a different sort of witness: the professional informer, who helped to create 'the cartoon history of the cold war', the good guys versus the bad, the us–them syndrome. Within the HUAC context, to be anti-war was to be pro-communist. As Victor Navasky notes: 'It was a function of the professional witnesses to distort a political environment by defining the Communist conspiracy as not merely alien but also immoral.'[32] Thus the non-combatant poets' wish to emphasize the necessity of acknowledging collective responsibility in a society that readily blamed the conspiratorial 'other', both within and without, to explain problems at home.

Apart from the media's bringing the war home and the need to express personal and national guilt, stateside poetry was mediated by its position within the counter-culture. The Beat generation, hippies, flower power, the civil rights movement, and the women's movement were the most prominent within a myriad movements of varying seriousness and import. Since the system was seen to be corrupt, opting out was one mode of protest. It was also a mode that gained notoriety because of its association with drugs and irresponsibility, an invitation to chaos. However, as Morris Dickstein points out, 'Their [the Beats'] attitude was not based on an indifference to morality but was an attempt to freshen the petrified sources of moral behavior.'[33] More than the Beats, however, the civil rights and women's movements were instrumental in opening up American society by exposing inequalities and injustices within the country. The specific and complex contributions of these movements is

[32] Victor Navasky, *Naming Names* (New York: The Viking Press, 1980), 3, 44.
[33] Morris Dickstein, *Gates of Eden: American Culture in the Sixties* (New York: Basic Books, Inc., Publishers, 1977), 20.

beyond the scope of this study, but one of the profound ironies inherent in the rhetoric of the fight for democracy and equality in Vietnam was the problematic nature of these within America. The lynchings and brutality which the southern black American had to contend with for his basic rights, the influence and example of Martin Luther King Jr. and Malcolm X, the break from the New Left by women who were oppressed by familiar patriarchal patterns, are significant contexts for the Vietnam War, and the protest poetry originating therein. These movements highlighted the schisms within America as much as the war, which helped to exacerbate them.

Allen Ginsberg personified in significant ways the atmosphere of protest, division, complicity, and contradiction. He was, as *The Times* obituary stated, a great survivor:

Whether as a prophetic bard or pretentious beatnik, Allen Ginsberg has survived for four decades as an icon of the American counterculture. He was one of the last survivors of the Beats, a cool cabal of mid-Fifties writers who, centring on Jack Kerouac, sought to rebel against staid, middle-class convention.[34]

More than any other protest poet of the era, he cultivated a public persona of protestor-poet-prophet, he revelled in the role of iconoclast and Beat generation guru. As Morris Dickstein observes:

It was not as a poet, it seemed, that he lent his magnetic spiritual presence to so many of the most obscene and solemn moments of the 1960s, from New York to Berkeley and London to Prague; rather, he was the elder statesman, the wise and worldly Lord of the Revels, a live link with the germinal protest culture of the fifties.[35]

The public persona, while being important in highlighting the poet as activist role, tends to obscure the poetry, reducing it, occasionally, to the level of 'sustained shrieks of frantic defiance'.[36] 'Howl', which is the subject of that comment by M. L. Rosenthal, embodies a more complex reflection on, and interrogation of, America in the 1950s than Rosenthal implies.

---

[34] 'Allen Ginsberg', Obituary in *The Times*, Monday, 7 Apr. 1997, 23.
[35] Dickstein, *Gates of Eden*, 6.
[36] M. L. Rosenthal, ' "Poet of the New Violence": "Howl" and Other Poems by Allen Ginsberg', *Our Life in Poetry: Selected Essays and Reviews* (New York: Persea Books, 1991), 73.

However, his emphasis on the public aspect, the hysterical denunciation of American values does form a part of Ginsberg's poetics. In an essay titled 'Pound's Influence', Ginsberg advocated a more public and oral poetics: 'The seventh heritage we have is Pound's renewal of the public function of poetry. Prophetic, critical, educational, the poet intruding on society again. . . . The intrusion of the person, Whitman's Person, back into politics or social activity and social judgement.'[37] The invocation of 'Whitman's Person', the larger-than-life persona striding across and celebrating American democratic vistas, is important in ascertaining the political and aesthetic ambition and desire in Ginsberg's poetry. At a time of political complacency, Ginsberg asserted a language of feeling to counter the atrophied language propagated by the state: 'Poetry is a rhythmic vocal articulation of feeling and the content of poetry is feeling as well as whatever else you would call it if it were removed from feeling—I suppose conditioned reflex language chain associations.'[38] In the 'rhythmic vocal articulation of feeling' lay the justification for public poetry reading sessions, an empathic reaching out to kindred souls. The individual poetic voice was perceived as a more genuine representation than inauthentic mass culture. War, Ginsberg believed, was as much a part of this mass culture as TV, and these were as corrupting as political language, which used the media as one of its vehicles. In opposition to order imposed by the state, Ginsberg posited personal and poetic vitality and authenticity. Some of these concerns are evident in his poetry, but so are the contradictions which complicate his position and utterances as poet and self-designated prophet.

'Howl', published in 1956, is not only a paean to an age, but amazingly prescient in its critique of American society and some of its characteristics which were manifested in the Vietnam War. The poem constitutes a significant break in a largely conservative and self-satisfied society, and prepares the ground in some ways for the protest culture of the 1960s. In his characterization of the Beat generation, Ginsberg conveys the manic energy and simultaneous death drive and confusion of the counter-culture:

[37] Allen Ginsberg, 'Pound's Influence', *The American Poetry Review*, 15: 4 (July/Aug. 1986), 7–8.
[38] Allen Ginsberg, *Allen Verbatim: Lectures on Poetry, Politics, Consciousness*, ed. Gordon Ball (New York and London: McGraw-Hill Book Company, 1974), 28.

I saw the best minds of my generation destroyed by madness, starving
  hysterical naked,
dragging themselves through the negro streets at dawn looking for an
  angry fix,
angelheaded hipsters burning for the ancient heavenly connection to the
  starry dynamo in the machinery of night[39]

The energy described is reminiscent of Jack Kerouac's evocation of the same period in *On the Road*. As personal and political protest, the counter-culture seemed to advocate an opting out of the mainstream of respectable society. While this was an alternative, it was often a destructive and despairing one, and 'Howl' conveys some of this anguish and loneliness. The violence that was to take place in Vietnam (this is the period when American advisers and aid were propping up the south Vietnamese government of Diem) seems to be prefigured in the figure of Moloch:

What sphinx of cement and aluminum bashed open their skulls and ate
  up their brains and imagination?
Moloch! Solitude! Filth! Ugliness! Ashcans and unobtainable dollars!
  Children screaming under the stairways! Boys in sobbing armies! Old
  men weeping in the parks!
.   .   .   .
Moloch whose mind is pure machinery! Moloch whose blood is running
  money! Moloch whose fingers are ten armies! Moloch whose breast
  is a cannibal dynamo!

('Howl', 131)

Moloch is emblematic of a capitalist consumption-obsessed society that would look upon Vietnam as an economic opportunity, an enclave of US economic and political interests. The language is declarative and asserts ideas rather than mediating them for the reader/listener to dwell on. Ginsberg projects himself as visionary poet and shaman, exorcizing the evil influence of Moloch. However, the curse on Moloch, the archetypal false god in Milton's *Paradise Lost*, while indicating American degeneration, seems to imply the possibility of redemption. Behind the illusion that Moloch perpetrates there is, perhaps, a 'real' god, a better sense of mission that the US can and ought to discover. This implication is surprisingly conservative in the context of

---

[39] Allen Ginsberg, 'Howl', *Collected Poems 1947–1980* (New York: Viking, 1984), 126. Subsequent references are indicated after the quotation.

Ginsberg's self-professed iconoclasm, and does fit in conveniently with national regenerative myths. It could be seen as a contradictory, idealistic strain in his poetics.

'A Supermarket in California' evokes the poetry and myth of Walt Whitman to emphasize this sense of loss:

> Where are we going, Walt Whitman?
> . . . .
> Will we stroll dreaming of the lost America of love past blue automobiles in driveways, home to our silent cottage?
> Ah, dear father, graybeard, lonely old courage-teacher, what America did you have when Charon quit poling his ferry and you got out on a smoking bank and stood watching the boat disappear on the black waters of Lethe?
>
> ('A Supermarket in California', 136)

There is a poignancy in the evocation of the democratic myth celebrated by Whitman, a myth which culminated in the America of supermarkets, driveways, and death. 'Lonely old courage-teacher' posits affinity and difference: like Whitman, Ginsberg positions himself as a lonely prophet-poet crying in the wilderness, but unlike him, Ginsberg sees himself in a world less amenable to the word of the poet. Whitman's was a more robust, optimistic vision, and Ginsberg wonders if that vision can ever be recovered. Despite his rants, he hopes to identify himself with a nation he can value and cherish, and opposition does not imply a total rejection of possibilities within America.

'America', written on 17 January 1956, is the best example of a complex protest that also encodes a desire to belong. The poetry is political in its awareness of the intertwining of personal lives and testimony with political and historical forces. It is also against all war, imperialism, corruption in government, and the media:

> America when will we end the human war?
> . . . .
> I'm addressing you.
> Are you going to let your emotional life be run by *Time* Magazine?
> I'm obsessed by *Time* Magazine.
> I read it every week.
>
> ('America', 146–7)

The influence of the Cold War and mass media productions are so pervasive that even the protest poet is 'obsessed' by them. The dominant culture saps one's imagination and leaves one incapable of independent judgement: 'America I've given you all and now I'm nothing' ('America', 146). The nihilism is a precursor of the feelings of betrayal and helplessness expressed by anti-war protestors in the 1960s, for whom protest was an expression of responsibility, a valuable and ethical type of patriotism. For the vast majority of the population, however, protest was an unrepresentative and unpopular activity that was construed as betrayal. Seymour Hersh, whose *My Lai 4* documented the atrocity, received a spate of hate mail. One correspondent wrote:

You are a lousy stinking anti-American and should be kicked out of the U.S. You went on an ego trip on the My Lai affair just to get your name in the papers. All lousy jews are alike. Give them protection and let them come into the Country, and immediately they start an underground revolution. Heads of every country know this and Hitler was wise to the Jews. Too bad he didn't get rid of them all—what a lovely planet this would be without them.[40]

It was against this sort of xenophobia that poets like Ginsberg were to protest as well, wishing to live in a more humane society. In 'America' there is an underlying hope that the nation will shed its paranoia and inhibitions and fulfil its possibilities:

> America when will you be angelic?
> When will you take off your clothes?
> When will you look at yourself through the grave?
> When will you be worthy of your million Trotskyites?
> America why are your libraries full of tears?
>
> ('America', 146)

The poem ends with the desire to contribute to this new, 'angelic' nation:

> It's true I don't want to join the Army or turn lathes in precision parts factories, I'm nearsighted and psychopathic anyway.
> America I'm putting my queer shoulder to the wheel.
>
> ('America', 148)

The collaboration will be on the poet's terms, and the desire

---

[40] Cited in Fussell (ed.), *The Bloody Game*, 715.

expressed is a combination of protest, self-deprecation, and commitment. The commitment coexists with the protest—'America I'm putting my queer shoulder to the wheel'—and believes in a better world. In an interview in March 1973, Ginsberg expressed awareness of a type of complicity: 'Except that the time has in a sense perhaps inured me to the social lie and made me part of the large social lie of hope. Kerouac was essentially hopeless, finally saw no hope. . . . And I keep thinking that I'm too comfortable in this chamber of horrors.'[41] This is an awareness achieved in hindsight, for in earlier poetry dealing with the problems he perceived in American society, even when he delineated the 'chamber of horrors', he implicitly accepted certain oppositional paradigms.

In 'Wichita Vortex Sutra' and 'Iron Horse', he projects Vietnam as a ubiquitous presence in America. The earlier critique of US political and cultural modes is now sharpened by a particular example, the involvement in Vietnam. The site of his poetry, however, is constituted of American society, culture, values, and politics, so much so that Vietnam is merely imaged as the absent presence that is yet another symbol of the sickness within America. Ginsberg seems rhetorically aware that this incapacity to conceptualize the 'other' is a factor that contributed to the ferocity of US violence in Vietnam:

> Who's the enemy, year after year?
> . . . .
> Television shows blood,
>   print broken arms burning skin photographs,
>   wounded bodies revealed on the screen
> Cut Sound out of television you won't tell who's Victim
> Cut Language off the Visual you'll never know
>   Who's Aggressor—
> cut commentary from Newscast
> you'll see a mass of madmen at murder.
>
> ('Iron Horse', 454)

Ginsberg is acutely conscious of the manner in which language is manipulated to create political consensus and construct the enemy. He is also aware of the need to negotiate the labyrinth of media created images. The deliberate lack of form, the rambling lines, the often casual syntax are devices to undermine what

---

[41] Ginsberg, *Allen Verbatim*, 235.

Thomas Merton defines as the 'unconscious aspiration to *definitive* utterance, to which there can be no rejoinder'.[42] In significant ways,

> The war is language,
>   language abused
>   for Advertisement,
>   language used
> like magic for power on the planet
>
> ('Wichita Vortex Sutra', 401)

Ginsberg's harangues in poetic format create space for the rejoinder, for a re-description of American ideals, goals, and policies. He is the most polemical and didactic of the stateside poets I discuss, convinced that the power of poetic language would or could negate the influence of war language. The problem with this conviction is that it converts Vietnam into a linguistic and media hyper-reality. Rhetorical awareness does not translate into actual conception of the reality of war and the 'other'. While there was an element of the hyper-real in political projections of Vietnam, to see the war as language *per se*, is to ignore and misrepresent its terrible actuality.

An aspect of this minimizing is evident in 'Iron Horse', where Ginsberg allegorically re-enacts the expansion of America through a train journey. The journey is interspersed with descriptions of, and reflections on, ninety-nine soldiers off to Vietnam:

> A consensus around card table beer
>   'It's my country,
>   better fight 'em over there than here,'
>   afraid to say 'No it's crazy
>   everybody's insane—
>   This country's Wrong,
>   the Universe, Illusion.'
>
> ('Iron Horse', 441)

The critique of American imperialism and nationalistic paranoia and fervour is unexceptionable. America being in the wrong does not, however, easily translate into the universe being an illusion, particularly from the Vietnamese point of view, or that of US

---

[42] Thomas Merton, 'War and the Crisis of Language', in Robert Ginsberg (ed.), *The Critique of War* (Chicago: Henry Regnery Company, 1969), 103.

soldiers fighting the war. Although Cold War paradigms of reds and dominoes were ghastly illusions, they constituted notions of reality that led to inconceivable misery, and this is something that the poem ignores.

When Ginsberg stresses the umbilical connection between violence perpetrated in Vietnam and resounding in the States, he makes a more valuable comment which moves beyond rhetorical assertiveness. It is analogous to Frantz Fanon's notion of 'involution' as a result of imperialism.[43] Additionally it is the violence within America that vents itself in Vietnam:

where bodies twitch arm from leg torn heart beat spasmed brainless in
    dynamite Napalm rubble Song-My to West 11th Street Manhattan
as war bomb-blast burns along the neckbone-fused nations Hanoi to
    Chicago Tu-Do to Wall Street

('Friday the Thirteenth', 538)

It is interesting that the poem makes a connection between two seemingly disparate and desperate events, the massacre of civilians in My Lai and the blast in a house in Manhattan that killed several Weathermen who were convinced that violence was the most effective way to oppose the war. James Merrill, who lived in that house till he was 5, writes about the blast in his poem '18 West 11th Street'. The first two stanzas cited here convey the confused desperation of these anti-war activists:

> In what at least
> Seemed anger the Aquarians in the basement
> Had been perfecting a device
>
> For making sense to us
> If only briefly and on pain
> Of incommunication ever after.[44]

Merrill's is a quieter and more insightful meditation on the betrayal of ideals, on the inability of the Weathermen to conceive

---

[43] Frantz Fanon, *The Wretched of the Earth*, trans. Constance Farrington (1967; Harmondsworth: Penguin Books Ltd, 1990), 23. Fanon writes: 'today violence, blocked everywhere, comes back to us through our soldiers, comes inside and takes possession of us. Involution starts; the native recreates himself, and we, settlers . . . ultras and liberals, we break up.'
[44] James Merrill, '18 West 11th Street', *From the First Nine: Poems 1946–1976* (New York: Atheneum, 1982), 253. Subsequent references are indicated after the quotation.

of non-violent, regenerative protest, and the failure of communication not only within the peace movement, but within American society at large. What was the point of protest that killed people, what were the values the Weathermen hoped to spread? As Merrill writes a little later in the poem:

> The point
> Was anger, brother? Love? Dear premises
> Vainly exploded, vainly dwelt upon.
>
> ('18 West 11th Street', 253)

The Weathermen agenda was a self-destructive one and Merrill highlights the element of hysterical protest that acquired many of the characteristics of the war against which they were protesting. This was most evident in the designation of the federal government as the 'enemy' by elements in the peace movement. Merrill's poetic voice intertwines the personal and the political; the destruction of an abode of childhood is analogous to the blasting of American myths and ideals that occurred during the 1960s. Ginsberg's voice is characteristically more assertive, but he does point to the tragic yoking of the two nations by violence. To explain the proliferation of violence, he provides an aesthetic of 'lack-love': 'the *awareness* that we all carry is too often painful, because the experience of rejection and lack-love and cold war— I mean the whole cold war is the imposition of a vast mental barrier on everybody, a vast antinatural psyche.'[45] The inability to see the 'other' and the creation of absolute oppositions was an important factor in sustaining the Cold War and Vietnam. However, Ginsberg often displayed an equal inadequacy in imagining the 'other', retreating into a private alternative world of language and drugs, or taking on the prophetic mantle. This does not invalidate his poetry, but it does circumscribe it. He is an important voice and witness to the 1950s, the 1960s, and Vietnam precisely in his contradictory impulses towards rant, commitment, a sense of belonging, and an equally strong sense of alienation. As Robert Pinsky observes, the 'double view' is an inherent aspect of American poetry: 'That double view—the poet celebrating the idea of democracy and liberty, the poet angry and despairing at the place,

---

[45] Allen Ginsberg, 'A Blake Experience', interview with Thomas Clark, *Paris Review* (Spring 1966), in Lewis Hyde (ed.), *On the Poetry of Allen Ginsberg* (Ann Arbor: The University of Michigan Press, 1984), 128.

in the actual United States, of democracy, liberty and poetry—has been historically a kind of basic motive force.'⁴⁶ During a period of acute conflict, such as the Vietnam War, the distinctions seem sharper, and each poet discussed in this chapter had to contend with, and position him/herself *vis-à-vis* the crisis. As is evident in some cases, within a polarized society, poets do tend to create and occupy positions of absolute opposition.

Robert Bly shares with Ginsberg the tendency towards prophecy, the idea that poetry can be revelatory. In 'As the Asian War Begins', he avers that political poetry can 'Give us a glimpse of what we cannot see, | Our enemies, the soldiers and the poor.'⁴⁷ With this idea in mind, Bly does 'give us a glimpse' of what America did not want to see and, unlike Ginsberg, formulates a more coherent aesthetics of the politics–poetry conjunction. 'A true political poem', Bly writes, 'is a quarrel with ourselves, and the rhetoric is as harmful in that sort of poem as in the personal poem. The true political poem does not order us either to take any specific acts: like the personal poem, it moves to deepen awareness.'⁴⁸ Bly's statement echoes Yeats, who wrote in 'Anima Hominis': 'We make out of the quarrel with others, rhetoric, but of the quarrel with ourselves, poetry. Unlike the rhetoricians, who get a confident voice from remembering the crowd they have won or may win, we sing amid our uncertainty.'⁴⁹ In an interview in 1970, Bly reiterated the difference between opinion and thought, propaganda and poetry: 'A poem should be a matter of thought, not of opinion. It is possible to think about the war.'⁵⁰ He sees no contradiction between the personal and the public manifesting themselves in political poetry. As Edward Lense comments: 'The rhetoric of prophecy subsumes any distinction between "public" and "private". Like the Old Testament prophets, Bly speaks as a public and private man simultaneously; in his public role he criticizes the State and

---

⁴⁶ Pinsky, 'Freneau, Whitman, Williams', *Poetry and the World*, 102.
⁴⁷ Robert Bly, 'As the Asian War Begins', *The Light Around the Body* (New York, Evanston, and London: Harper & Row, Publishers, 1967), 33. Subsequent references are indicated as *The Light* after the quotation.
⁴⁸ Robert Bly, 'Leaping Up Into Political Poetry', *Talking All Morning* (Ann Arbor: The University of Michigan Press, 1980), 101.
⁴⁹ W. B. Yeats, *Essays* (London: Macmillan and Co. Limited, 1924), 492.
⁵⁰ Robert Bly, interview with Gregory Fitzgerald and William Heyen, *Talking All Morning*, 81.

its actions, in his private role he upholds a moral code that the State has broken.'[51] The prophetic mode, the desire 'to deepen awareness', the simultaneity of public and private voices, is articulated in some parts of *The Teeth Mother Naked at Last*. At an obvious but important level Bly, like Howard Nemerov, deals with the issue of disinformation—and its conceptual matrix, rationalizing, justifying—in an idiom (unlike Nemerov's) of force and insistence. The agenda is not one of unearthing 'true' or 'authentic' information, it is one of highlighting the proliferation of the war, and the polyphony of that spread. The poem counterpoints brutal destruction with clinical military jargon:

> This is what it's like for a rich country to make war
> this is what it's like to bomb huts (afterwards described as 'structures')
> this is what it's like to kill marginal farmers (afterwards described as 'Communists').[52]

The appropriation of language and its manipulation for projecting doctored versions of reality is obvious and sinister. 'Huts' become 'structures', and 'farmers' are demonized into 'Communists'. It is a process of naming that the political establishment was very adept at, and Chapter 1 dealt with some examples. The fact that some 'farmers' may have been 'Communists' as well is not as important as all farmers being classified as such. From the perspective of the National Liberation Front (NLF) often referred to as the Vietcong, or the north Vietnamese, with a long anti-imperialist history, the farmers can never actually have been 'marginal'.[53] 'Marginal' is itself a naïve epithet employed from a metropolitan, abstract standpoint, and this is Bly's position as well, especially in his more didactic outbursts. The naïve generalizations are indicative of a lack of comprehension of the 'other', who is objectified and dehumanized by the politicians and the military. The military establishment in Vietnam generated its

---

[51] Edward Lense, 'The Assyrian Lion Above the Soybean Fields: Bly's *The Light Around the Body* as Prophecy Against the Vietnam War', *Journal of American Culture*, 16: 3 (Fall 1993), 89–95.
[52] Robert Bly, *The Teeth Mother Naked at Last* (San Francisco: City Lights Books, 1970), 13. Subsequent references are indicated as *Teeth Mother* after the quotation.
[53] The term 'marginal' could also refer to the status of the farmers who were largely subsistence farmers.

own argot (just as the soldier developed a very different slang to describe the war): MACV, I Corps, II Corps, DMZ, 'body count', pacification, Strategic Hamlet Program. These helped to create an easily definable and therefore containable reality, and served to depersonalize and dehumanize the enemy. Bly highlights 'the horrors of abstraction—... the cartographic work of reinscribing Vietnam as a military arena'.[54] Once the process of reinscription, reinforced by the politicians, was entrenched, the war could safely be consigned to an event happening in a distant part of the world. While the distance was a literal fact, the war had everything to do with the way America perceived itself and its role in the world. The basic myths justifying US involvement were accepted by a large majority, and the images of horror beamed daily coexisted placidly with the American way of life. Bly does not wish this placid response to continue, and collapses the distance between the war 'out there' and the war 'within' America— its collective psyche and national ethos as manifested in Vietnam, the civil rights movement, and the general atmosphere of strife. Some of these connections are drawn out in poems such as 'Watching Television', 'War and Silence', and 'Driving Through Minnesota'. Bly refuses to distance the war:

> If one of those children came toward me with both hands
> in the air, fire rising along both elbows,
> I would suddenly go back to my animal brain,
> I would drop on all fours screaming,
> my vocal chords would turn blue, so would yours,
> It would be two days before I could play with my
> own children again.
>
> (*Teeth Mother*, 19)

Regressing to the 'animal brain' is essential in Bly's opinion to comprehend the problems represented by Vietnam. The poem is a psychic analysis of American history based on the myth of the Teeth Mother, which posits an opposition between the Good Mother and the Death (or Teeth) Mother. This may be compared to Ezra Pound's 'Hugh Selwyn Mauberly', where the poet characterizes his own generation as being tainted by war and its lies:

[54] Frank Lentricchia, 'In Place of an Afterword—Someone Reading', in Frank Lentricchia and Thomas McLaughlin (eds.), *Critical Terms for Literary Study* (Chicago and London: The University of Chicago Press, 1990), 336.

> Died some, pro patria,
>   non 'dulce' non 'et decor'
> . . . .
> walked eye-deep in hell
> believing in old men's lies, then unbelieving
> came home, home to a lie,
> home to many deceits,
> home to old lies and new infamy;
> usury age-old and age-thick
> and liars in public places.[55]

The most direct echo occurs a little later in the poem:

> There died a myriad,
> And of the best, among them,
> For an old bitch gone in the teeth,
> For a botched civilization
>
>   ('Hugh Selwyn Mauberly', 191)

Pound's evocation of a rottenness at the heart of civilization reinforces the idea of a terrible cyclicity, almost the inevitability of war fought in every generation for spurious ideals. In Bly's vision of America, the Teeth Mother 'suggest[s] the end of psychic life, the dismembering of the psyche'.[56] It is this dismembering of a personal and collective psyche that he presents. Normal, personal relationships seem like a weird aberration, and the prospect of playing with one's children is as incongruous as the nonchalance with which the two pilots seek to 'take out as many structures as possible'.

The Teeth Mother motif, in so far as Bly uses it to analyse American society, leads to further aesthetic insights regarding political poetry. He posits a core of impulses and ideas that must be tapped to rejuvenate the polity and poetry:

It's clear that many of the events that create our foreign relations and our domestic relations come from more or less hidden impulses in the

---

[55] Ezra Pound, 'Hugh Selwyn Mauberly', *Personae: The Collected Poems of Ezra Pound* (New York: Liveright Publishing Corporation, 1926), 190. Subsequent references are indicated after the quotation.

[56] Robert Bly, *Sleepers Joining Hands* (New York, London, Evanston, and San Francisco: Harper & Row Publishers, 1973), 42. Bly writes about the revelation that the war has brought about: 'the Vietnam war has helped everyone to see how much of the Teeth Mother there is in the United States. The culture of affluence opens the psyche to the Teeth Mother and the Death Mother in ways that no one understands' (43).

American psyche. It's also clear I think that some sort of husk has grown around that psyche, so that in the fifties we could not look into it or did not. The Negroes and the Vietnam War have worn the husk thin in a couple of places now. But if that is so, then the poet's main job is to penetrate the husk around the American psyche, and since that psyche is inside *him* too, the writing of political poetry is like the writing of personal poetry, a sudden drive by the poet inward.[57]

The darkness-at-the-heart-of-America kind of psycho-poetic analysis is valuable in its awareness of historical and collective memory, in its perceptions of the connections between the war and the civil rights movement, and the need for the poet to introspect and internalize the collective, psychic tremors surrounding him. The acknowledgement of the poet's complicity—'since that psyche is inside *him* too'—is essential and ironic, particularly for poets such as Bly and Ginsberg, who often forget this and take on the stance of the neutral prophet. The formulation is suspect in its attempt to search for the essential causes or flaws that have led to Vietnam. Implicit in this statement is the idea that the poet has the answer/s to the dilemmas facing the country. Such an analysis is couched in absolute and prophetic terms, and substitutes one set of certainties (the rhetoric surrounding the war) with another (the evil at the heart of America), obliterating the complex histories of the past in the very process of recovery.

In Bly's poetics and representation of Vietnam there is a calculated attempt to establish the extent to which brutalization within American society is responsible for its actions in that country. He does not see the war as an aberration in America's pristine history, but rather as an extension of earlier histories of conquest, and these histories constitute a collective repressed memory, the psyche that must be probed by the poet:

I think the Vietnam war has something to do with the fact that we murdered the Indians. We're the only modern nation that ever stole its land from another people. . . . What you do first when you commit a crime is you forget it and then you repeat it. So therefore in my opinion what we're doing is repeating the crime with the Indians. The Vietnamese are our Indians.[58]

[57] Bly, 'Leaping Up Into Political Poetry', 98.
[58] Robert Bly, quoted in James F. Mersmann, *Out of the Vietnam Vortex: A Study of Poets and Poetry Against the War* (Lawrence, Manhattan, and Wichita, Kan.: The University Press of Kansas, 1974), 123.

Stateside Poetry

The comfortable lobotomy of Vietnam from US historical memory, traditions, and values, practised not only by ordinary Americans and politicians, but by academics and Hollywood over the past twenty years, is something that Bly will not perform. Passages in *Teeth Mother* refer to the connections between seemingly disparate imperial encounters:

> The ministers lie, the professors lie, the television lies,
>   the priests lie
> . . . .
>
> These lies mean that the country wants to die.
> Lie after lie starts out into the prairie grass,
> like enormous trains of Conestoga wagons.
>
> (*Teeth Mother*, 10)

There is a rhetorical assertiveness and shrillness in these lines that project the poet as truthteller. Concurrently, however, the awareness of a historical legacy and climate of 'lies' enables Bly to interpret various connections in US history that are often suppressed.

'Watching Television' is a vision of America as a society convulsed by violence:

> Sounds are heard too high for ears,
> From the body cells there is an answering bay;
> Soon the inner streets fill with a chorus of barks.
>
> We see the landing craft coming in,
> The black car sliding to a stop,
> The Puritan killer loosening his guns.
>
> Wild dogs tear off noses and eyes
> And run off with them down the street—
> The body tears off its own arms and throws them into the air.
> . . . .
>
> The filaments of the soul slowly separate:
> The spirit breaks, a puff of dust floats up,
> Like a house in Nebraska that suddenly explodes.
>
> (*The Light*, 6)

As a phantasmagoric representation of, and meditation on, historic, psychic, and societal violence, this poem is unexceptionable. Themes adumbrated in *The Teeth Mother* recur here: the violence within the heart and mind of America, the combination of the crusader-killer ('The Puritan killer loosening his guns') and guilt-ridden reformer individual ('The filaments of the soul slowly separate'). The fundamental contradiction between the millennial hopes and brutal actualities to fulfil that vision comes to a head in a society at war with itself. The individual seems to have lost control and violence takes on a life of its own: 'The body tears off its own arms and throws them into the air.' This dislocated violence mirrors the act of watching the Vietnam War on television. Television allowed the viewer to spectate without responsibility, to maintain a comfortable distance from the war. No responsible citizen, however, could totally dissociate her/himself from the war. The fact that a majority of citizens treated it as being 'outside' their domain and their lives was indicative of dislocated violence; treating the violence committed by their compatriots as if it was being done by anonymous 'others'. These 'others' could be the politicians or the soldiers, but the fact that they constituted an integral part of the nation was often overlooked. While particular groups were held responsible for the war, national myths and ideologies were seldom questioned. The passivity that the great majority displayed during the war is the object of Bly's criticism. Vietnam, as pointed out earlier, was the first war brought directly into the homes of every television owner in the USA. Individual citizens watched American power destroy another nation and this is Bly's central point: that by not protesting the war, they silently participated in the dismemberment of the nation's spirit: 'The spirit breaks, a puff of dust floats up.' There is a disturbing involution that occurs in the act of watching this war on television: a society watching itself destroy itself in its desire to fulfil noble ideals. It is a society inured to violence, unable or unwilling to acknowledge the depth of violence within the country that manifests itself in Vietnam.

In 'War and Silence', Bly makes a direct connection between the war and the civil rights movement:

> The bombers spread out, temperature steady
> A Negro's ear sleeping in an automobile tire
> Pieces of timber float by saying nothing
>
> Bishops rush about crying, There is no war,
> And bombs fall,
> Leaving a dust on the beech trees

> One leg walks down the road and leaves
> The other behind, the eyes part
> And fly off in opposite directions
> Filaments of death grow out
> The sheriff cuts off his black legs
> And nails them to a tree
>
> (*The Light*, 31)

The obsessive death impulse (the Teeth Mother element) within America, the fact that the two countries are sites of great violence, and that this violence emanates from within, are themes repeated in Bly's poems. While he does delve into originary history to explain contemporary violence, he also contemplates and excoriates the bitter irony and complicity of contemporary history. The obsession with violence is not surprising in the context of political assassinations (the Kennedys, Martin Luther King Jr., and Malcolm X), lynchings and brutalities against blacks, violence against war protestors (at the Democratic Convention in Chicago for instance), and Vietnam. The extremely violent resistance to the civil rights movement (manifested in police action and groups like the Ku Klux Klan) gave the lie to, and provided a vicious ironic context for America's crusade in favour of democracy and freedom in Vietnam. President Johnson's 'Great Society' seemed to have no moral authority and Martin Luther King was aware of this irony when he wrote in *Ramparts* in April 1967: 'We were taking the young black men who had been crippled by our society and sending them 8000 miles away to guarantee liberties in Southeast Asia which they had not found in Southwest Georgia and East Harlem.'[59]

The erosion of all moral authority is indicated in Bly's bishops' lies: 'Bishops run about crying, There is no war.' This is a theme common in war poetry, particularly that of the First World War, where it was the old men—the generals and the bishops—who were despised for sacrificing innocent youth in meaningless battle. Siegfried Sassoon's 'They' exposes the hypocrisy of people in positions of authority. The two stanzas delineate a contrast between the rhetoric of the clergy and the stark reality of war. The poem tellingly reiterates the rhetoric of 'just war', which was

---

[59] Martin Luther King Jr., 'Declaration of Independence From the War in Vietnam', cited in Marvin E. Gettleman *et al.*, *Vietnam and America: A Documented History* (New York: Grove Press Inc., 1985), 307.

modified for circulation in Vietnam as well. '"The ways of God are strange!"' precisely because they are interpreted by men who have their own agendas to fulfil.[60] Similarly, the title of Bly's poem not only indicts authority figures such as the bishops, but an entire society that permits the wars to continue. Silence for Bly implies consent, a refusal to take a stand; silence leads to death and petrifaction of the spirit. The juxtapositioning of the civil rights movement, Vietnam (as subtext and ever-present context), the death of each individual black American, and the death of American ideals, is poignantly contained in the trope of silence: 'A Negro's ear sleeping in an automobile tire | Pieces of timber float by saying nothing.' The conflict created a situation described by Tim O'Brien as one of 'moral schizophrenia', a paralysis of moral will, a hideous continuation of, and participation in, violence.[61] Bly presents a graphic and anthropomorphic aspect of this schizophrenic state:

> One leg walks down the road and leaves
> The other behind, the eyes part
> And fly off in opposite directions

It is a state of perpetual motion and violence, and it is a horror Bly wants America to recognize and rectify.

The desire for peace in a time of turmoil is detailed in 'Turning Away From Lies':

> If we are truly free, and live in a free country,
> When shall I be without this heaviness of mind?
> When shall I have peace? Peace this way and peace that way?
> I have already looked beneath the street
> And there I saw the bitter waters going down,
> The ancient worms eating up the sky.

(*The Light*, 43)

Although Bly writes poems of political protest, he does want to believe that the American ideals of peace and liberty were articulated in good faith and can be achieved. While peace and freedom are universal ideals, the pursuit of happiness and the ideals of equality have a particular political and moral resonance

---

[60] Siegfried Sassoon, 'They', *Collected Poems 1908–1956* (London: Faber and Faber, 1961), 23–4.
[61] Tim O'Brien, interviewed by Sheila Rogers on 'Arts Week', Canadian Broadcasting Corporation, 20 Jan. 1991.

in America. The betrayal of these founding ideals creates an acute sense of loss and anger. 'When shall I have peace?' is similar to Ginsberg's appeal: 'America when will you be angelic?' The intrusion of the singular 'I' indicates a greater sense of a personal burden than in Ginsberg and, unlike him, Bly has a deep sense of despair. As poet and seer, delving into personal and political consciousness, he can only see decay. The democratic vistas are clogged by 'ancient worms', the lies, evasions, and repression of historical memory that Bly sees at the heart of the American darkness. The personal, historical, and political visions coalesce in the image of 'ancient worms eating up the sky'.[62] As James F. Mersmann observes: 'Not only has he [Bly] succeeded in giving us the psyche of the nation, but he has articulated what our individual psyches feel—our oppression, hysteria, and deep sadness have found a tongue.'[63] Mersmann's observation is largely true, but needs to be qualified. Bly, like Ginsberg, is acutely aware of the power of language (and the way it was wielded in the course of the war), the problem of truth (the emphasis on lies and lying in the poems discussed is evident), and the importance of poetic dissent. Within the poetics, however, Bly, like his more controversial fellow poet, is immersed in the role of prophet and truthteller. This self-designated role exposes a particular problem in the poetry: the inability to be truly ironic. This lack leads to the hysterical, stilted tone and quality of some of the poems and arises out of a desire to emphasize the cultural centrality of the poet. In the process, both poets overstate the problems in terms of simplistic binary oppositions. They forget that they are 'marginal' and that their influence lies paradoxically in that very marginality. Ideally, this position would allow them the freedom to question the 'centre' without being contained by it. In campaigning for a more visible, public poetics they lose the voice of authentic private protest. The absence of irony creates a poetry that is often self-obsessive, flat, and stilted. The result of the prophetic mode, occasionally, is poetry which consists of banal diatribe and has limited poetic value. For instance, Bly's 'Asian Peace Offers Rejected Without Publication' resembles a

[62] Bly's image recalls the amphisbaena, 'a fabulous venomous serpent with a head at each end and able to move in either direction'. Betty Kirkpatrick (ed.), *Brewer's Concise Dictionary of Phrase & Fable* (Oxford: Helicon Publishing Ltd., 1995), 29.
[63] Mersmann, *Out of the Vietnam Vortex*, 152.

government handout: 'Men like Rusk are not men: | They are bombs waiting to be loaded in a darkened hangar' (*The Light*, 30). These lines betray Bly's formulation of political poetry mentioned earlier. They express a particular opinion (with which one may or may not agree), but they do not involve 'the sudden drive by the poet inward'. They are totally bound by immediate political context, and there is no objective correlative in the poem that would explain why 'Men like Rusk are not men'. Both Ginsberg and Bly recognize the contingency of final vocabularies deployed by the state to justify America's involvement in Vietnam. Both of them relate that discourse to America's history of colonization and repression. However, while criticizing that vocabulary they tend to substitute vocabularies for it which desire to be interpreted as *the* voice of dissent. They find it difficult to debunk authority without claiming it for themselves, and are trapped in a self-proclaimed prophetic mode.[64] When they take on the role of moral arbiter, they articulate anti-war representations which are as absolute and fundamental in their assertions as government-speak.

In some of his interviews Bly seems aware of the problem, particularly the need to re-energize the language, but this is not always translated into his poetry. Responding to a question about *The Teeth Mother*, he said:

In one passage of 'The Teeth Mother' I mentioned that the pilots bomb 'huts', afterwards described as 'structures.' So in that line you can see that the technocrats have withdrawn energy from the word 'structures' in order to tell lies about what they're doing.... Since so many words have had their energy corrupted, it's very difficult to write poetry, and I'm not surprised that people work for five to six months on a single short poem, I do myself.[65]

In an article titled 'Whitman's Line As a Public Form', Bly aligns himself with the declarative Whitmanesque syntax and indicates the limitations of such a form: 'The Smart-Blake-Whitman line

---

[64] See Richard Rorty, *Contingency, irony, and solidarity* (Cambridge and New York: Cambridge University Press, 1989): 'For us ironists, nothing can serve as a criticism of a final vocabulary save another such vocabulary; there is no answer to a redescription save a re-re-redescription.... It is the problem of how to overcome authority without claiming authority' (80, 105). For a poetic insight into the self-proclaimed prophetic mode adopted by some stateside poets, see Jon Stallworthy, 'A poem about Poems About Vietnam', *Critical Quarterly*, 10 (1968), 57.

[65] Robert Bly, interview with Kevin Powers, *Talking All Morning*, 229–30.

belongs in general to declaration rather than inquiry, to prophecy rather than meditation, to public speech rather than the exchange of feelings, and in this last quality we see its major flaw.'[66] This later critical, theoretical position, juxtaposed with the earlier formulation that the 'true political poem is a quarrel with ourselves, and the rhetoric is as harmful in that sort of poem as the personal poem', is a largely consistent development. In passing, we may note that Bly does simplify Whitman's syntactical strategies, and that Ginsberg is more finely attuned to the resonances and cadences of Whitman's poetry and vision. The problem lies in the inadequacy of some of the political poetry which fails to transcend the purely rhetorical mode, and in its assumption of absolute stances. In contrast, Howard Nemerov adopts a less strident mode and achieves a more acutely critical poetic discourse.

Nemerov's poetry on the Vietnam War is informed by a personal sense of context and continuity arising out of his combat experience in the Second World War. He questions the national mythology of the 'good war' and the heroic paradigms available in that war. His Vietnam poems are reflections on historical and cultural amnesia which creates the cynical cyclicity of the war. 'Ultima Ratio Reagan' encapsulates the idea that Vietnam is another example of this terrible continuity:

> The reason we do not learn from history is
> Because we are not the people who learned last time.
>
> Because we are not the same people as them
> That fed our sons and honor to Vietnam
> And dropped the burning money on their trees,
>
> We know that we know better than they knew,
> And history will not blame us if once again
> The light at the end of the tunnel is the train.[67]

There is an understated awareness of the ignorance and arrogance of each generation that believes in its ideals as absolute entities: 'We know that we know better than they knew.' This

---

[66] Robert Bly, 'Whitman's Line As a Public Form', *The American Poetry Review*, 15: 2 (Mar./Apr. 1986), 5

[67] Howard Nemerov, 'Ultima Ratio Reagan', *War Stories: Poems About Long Ago and Now* (Chicago and London: The University of Chicago Press, 1987), 6. The title is a subtle variation on Stephen Spender's poem 'Ultima Ratio Regum'. It is likely that both poets were looking back to its origin, the inscription on Louis XIV's canon.

arrogance is a contributory factor in the destruction of Vietnam which, paradoxically, America was trying to 'save'. The underlying economic agenda reflects ironically on the rhetoric of the democratic vision, and is coupled with wanton destruction: 'And dropped the burning money on their trees.' The consumer culture, symptomatic of the American way of life, is dovetailed with the violence visited on Vietnam. 'The light at the end of the tunnel' is the phrase that General Westmoreland uttered a few weeks before the Tet Offensive in 1968, and it is emblematic of the refusal on the part of authority figures to come to terms with reality in Vietnam. The credibility gap and the problem of linguistic manipulation is a theme that Nemerov is obsessed with, and General Westmoreland's optimistic assertions fit into the larger generational and collective lying that allowed the war to proceed. It is significant that Ronald Reagan should figure in the title since he played a major role in rehabilitating the image of the Vietnam veteran and recuperating the war for American consumption. In a dominant culture unable to cope with defeat, Reagan redefined the war as a 'just cause'. In that sense, 'The light at the end of the tunnel is [inevitably] the train', since as a collective entity the nation refuses to learn the lessons of Vietnam.

'On Getting Out of Vietnam' presents an allegory of some of the themes of lying and cyclicity evident in 'Ultima Ratio Reagan':

> Theseus, if he did destroy the Minotaur
> (it's hard to say, that may have been a myth),
> Was careful not to close the Labyrinth.
> So After kept on looking like Before:
> Back home in Athens still the elders sent
> Their quota of kids to Knossos, confident
> They would find something to die of, and for.
>
> (*Trying Conclusions*, 47)

Vietnam had turned into a kind of Borgesian labyrinth: a strange combination of fact and fiction where the justifications for involvement were tenuous at best and charged with dubious rhetoric. It was a moral maze created by policy-makers and politicians. Once they designated something as 'real' ('The light at the end of the tunnel' or the Strategic Hamlet Program) they stuck to that notion of 'reality', even when events contradicted it.

The desperation of that situation is heightened by the *need* for war, the necessity for 'something to die of, and for'. By providing Theseus and Knossos as historical, mythical referents, Nemerov heightens the futile, relentless continuity of war. The mythological allusions add a perspective, a grounding in history and myth, that Ginsberg and Bly seldom possess. It is an awareness of similarity and difference, not mere continuity, that gives Nemerov's poetry an ironic, resonant quality. The myths of nationalism, valour, honour, and war as a means of fulfilling these are extremely powerful. Vietnam did provide a generation with 'something to die of, and for', at least until the disillusionment set in, and this in itself, as Adrienne Rich points out, represents a problem: 'War comes at the end of the twentieth century as absolute failure of imagination, scientific and political. That a war can be represented as helping people to "feel good" about themselves, their country, is a measure of that failure.'[68]

Nemerov's war poetry is marked by wit, humour, the logical progression of an argument, and a minimalist economy of expression. His style is often elliptical and the references to Vietnam almost casual or seemingly non-existent. This elliptical and sharply ironical mode is basic to his poetics. In an essay, 'The Careful Poets and the Reckless Ones', he makes a comment about James Merrill's poetry which is equally applicable to his own: 'It is a part of my pleasure in some of this poet's works that he [Merrill] does not appear to regard it as a duty to spend all or most of his time being angry at something; the indignant scream has so nearly become the poet's stipulated tone that this is quite a relief.'[69] The absence of 'the indignant scream' is apparent in all of Nemerov's war poems, even the ones that deal more directly and angrily with the war.

In 'The Language of the Tribe', he reproduces the discourse of official doublespeak to indicate the inadequacy of a representational mode that presumes a monopoly on 'truth':

> The Secretary spoke of the 'facilities.'
> Under his bald dome the mouth opened and spoke.

---

[68] Adrienne Rich, 'What Would We Create?', *What Is Found There: Notebooks on Poetry and Politics* (London: Virago Press Limited, 1995), 16.
[69] Howard Nemerov, 'The Careful Poets and the Reckless Ones', *Poetry and Fiction: Essays* (New Jersey: Rutgers University Press, 1963), 196.

> The raids, he said, were protection reaction responses
> Against the enemy's anti-aircraft facilities.
>
> That were harassing our unarmed reconnaissance
> Surveillance over their facilities.
>
> But might the bombs have damaged other targets?
> Under his bald dome the mouth opened and spoke.
>
> Possibly, he said, the bombs might have
> Deprived the enemy's facilities
>
> Of access to logistic and supply
> Facilities in close proximity
>
> To primary targets; by which he meant, I think:
> 'The bastards kept the bullets near the guns.'[70]

The poem is a striking example of what Hugh Kenner defines as the 'phosphorescent quotation': 'It was long supposed that a politician was best mocked by parody; by isolating traits and exaggerating them. But in the mid 1950s satirists discovered that to mock Dwight Eisenhower it was sufficient to quote him verbatim.'[71] The formal tone of the poem is deliberately foregrounded so that it can be undercut by the intervention of an alternative 'personal' voice and idiom. There is no single referent for Vietnam, no precise definition that can locate, isolate, and categorize the war, and this poem highlights the hierarchy of discourse operative in representations of the war. The 'centre', the 'truth', is constituted and articulated by particular administrations, and policy and military planners. At a press conference, which is an arena for the dissemination of this 'truth', the poet is 'marginal' by virtue of expressing an alternative and less acceptable 'truth'. However, the poetic statement is 'central' to any representation of the war (and this is even more apparent in poetry by veterans) since it locates Vietnam in a non-absolutist matrix. The centre-margin paradigm requires the poet to negotiate constantly the problematic and often invisible boundaries

---

[70] Howard Nemerov, 'The Language of the Tribe', *Sentences* (Chicago and London: The University of Chicago Press, 1980), 8. Subsequent references are indicated after the quotation.

[71] Hugh Kenner, *The Counterfeiters* (Bloomington, Ind.: Indiana University Press, 1968), p. ix. Michael Herr, in an interview with Salman Rushdie recalls 'a US military spokesman describing a bombing raid "north of the Dee Em Zee as having obtained 100% mortality response"'. Salman Rushdie, *Imaginary Homelands: Essays and Criticism 1981–1991* (Harmondsworth: Penguin Books Ltd., 1991), 333.

between authority and dissent, the absolute and the relativistic. In assuming absolute oppositional stances, Ginsberg and Bly tend to forget this and take on the language and tone of their 'opponents'.

The question of location (the poet and politician *vis-à-vis* the war) and proliferation of the war is a central concern in 'Continuous Performances': 'The war went on till everything was it' (*Sentences*, 19). The protean nature of Vietnam complicates the position of the anti-war protestor and poet. The anti-war poet can easily be assimilated into the larger framework of democratic pluralism (for instance, the way in which Ginsberg was perceived 'as a figure of patience, charm, and conciliation' even in the 1960s, and is now included in university syllabi in the USA), and a polity that can absorb and tolerate protest can parade its democratic credentials.[72] Of course, plurality does not necessarily imply actual debate, it involves the manufacture of consensus through the media and films, among other means:

> the growing war
> Already sponsoring movies about itself
> To let the children know what it was like.
> (*Sentences*, 19)

The influence of films harks back to the Second World War because it was the exploits of John Wayne and Audie Murphy that inspired many Americans to go to Vietnam.[73] The process of selective remembrance and re-presentation is evident in films about the Vietnam War, and Nemerov is anxious about its effects on collective national memory. Hollywood is not the only agent participating in the rewriting of the war. The documentary

---

[72] Dickstein, *Gates of Eden*, 261.

[73] There is now a resurgence of Hollywood films about the Second World War. Commenting on the influence and ideological orientation of the first crop of Second World War films, Stephen Amidon writes: 'In the first wave of second world war films to hit the beach, Hollywood served as a sort of adjunct to the allied imagination, churning out stories that cemented the public's moral certitude about the justice of the conflict, while paying homage to those who served. These ranged from overtly propagandist vehicles cranked out in the heady final days of the war to the more artistically accomplished efforts appearing somewhat later, such as Clark Gable's *Command Decision* (1948), Gregory Peck's *Twelve o' Clock High* (1949) and John Wayne's prototypical *Sands of Iwo Jima* (1949). In nearly all of these films, unflinching patriotism, selfless camaraderie and stoic bravery (even among those who stayed at home) were posited as the absolute values whose possible existence in the enemy was never really entertained.' Stephen Amidon, 'Back to the Front', *The Sunday Times*, sect. 11, 18 May 1997, 2–3.

Hearts and Minds analyses the immense power and resilience of mainstream nationalism. In the film, Lt. George Coker, a POW, lectures on patriotism and the American way of principled survival to schoolchildren and mothers. He is welcomed back as a national hero. The film analyses how the POW myth helped to create an acceptable heroism, in a war devoid of heroes, within the military-nationalist framework. While *Hearts and Minds* critically analyses some issues, another documentary titled *Vietnam Memorial* is essentially a healing, reconciliatory film. While there can be no objection to the desire for healing the wounds of the war, it becomes problematic when that healing is at the expense of historical accuracy and memory. In this film, Vietnam is included in the pantheon of glorious sacrifices and history is revised: 'We didn't lose the war. The politicians did' says a veteran in the film. The veteran is rehabilitated as a hero and absolved of all responsibility for trying to understand the war and its causes; so is the nation. The statement quoted is part of the extremely select remembrance to which the Vietnam Memorial as monument and document contributes, and that Hollywood films advance. A continual reappraisal and redescription of given realities is necessary if the poet is to resist the sort of convenient simplifications available in the culture.

In three lectures titled 'What Was Modern Poetry?' Nemerov, referring to Yeats's 'Nineteen Hundred and Nineteen', spoke about the necessity of coming to terms with contingency: 'The loss of innocence becomes a kind of brutal blessing, the stringent and salutary awakening from an illusion, as the poet savages himself and his contemporaries for their naïvety in never having realized how precarious, contingent, and uncertain were the certainties in which they lived.'[74] Vietnam represented a similar awakening, and 'the loss of innocence' trope recurs in much of the poetry. The poet's recognition of this collective naïvety is indicative of a commitment to the representation of contingent, disparate realities. The poet's negotiation of the quicksands of the centre–margin paradigm mentioned earlier indicates the precarious and, paradoxically, important position of the poet *vis-à-vis* society, politics, and the war. This seems to be the form and substance of Nemerov's political poetics. Yet in 'On Being Asked

---

[74] Howard Nemerov, 'What Was Modern Poetry? Three Lectures', *Figures of Thought*, 176.

For A Peace Poem', he gives voice to the 'anxiety of authenticity [that] surrounds the written response to all the major conflicts of the twentieth century'.[75] He wonders about the efficacy and value of poetry on the Vietnam War:

> Here is Joe Blow the poet
> Sitting before the console of the giant instrument
> That mediates his spirit to the world.
> He flexes his fingers nervously,
> He ripples off a few scaled passages
> (Shall I compare thee to a summers day?)
> And resolutely readies himself to begin
> His poem about the War in Vietnam.
> This poem, he figures, is
> A sacred obligation: all by himself,
> Applying the immense leverage of art,
> His is about to stop this senseless war.
> So Homer stopped that dreadful thing at Troy
> By giving the troops the *Iliad* to read instead;
> So Wordsworth stopped the Revolution when
> He felt that Robespierre had gone too far;
> So Yevtushenko was invited in the *Times*
> To keep the Arabs out of Israel
> By smiting once again his mighty lyre.
> Joe smiles. He sees the Nobel Prize
> Already, and the reading of his poem
> Before the General Assembly, followed by
> His lecture to the Security Council
> About the Creative Process; probably
> Some bright producer would put it on TV.
> Poetry might suddenly be the in thing.
>
> (*Trying Conclusions*, 50–1)

This is, at the simplest level, a parody of the instrumentalist agenda, the idea that Homer or Wordsworth or Nemerov could bring conflicts to an end. That poetry is fairly impotent in the face of the barbarity of the war is obvious, and Nemerov might have his more activist poet colleagues in mind when he parodies their desire for power and agency through poetry. W. B. Yeats's 'On Being Asked For A War Poem' expresses a similar sentiment in its disavowal of the instrumentalist agenda. While Yeats's antipathy

---

[75] Gill Plain, '"Great Expectations": Rehabilitating the Recalcitrant War Poets', *Feminist Review*, 51 (Autumn 1995), 41–65.

to one kind of war poetry was fairly clear (in his refusal to include Wilfred Owen in his *Oxford Book of Modern Verse*, for instance), Nemerov presents a less terse, more complex and humorous insight into the relationship between a poet and war. The poem is a tongue-in-cheek comment on 'the immense leverage of art'. Simultaneously the poet muses on the inconsequential position of the poet in American society as democratic plurality seems to pull the rug from under the poet's protesting feet. The poem is a combination of self-reflexive insight (the poet ought to eschew the prophetic mode à la Ginsberg), humour, doubt, and self-flagellation. The 'anxiety of authenticity' is reflected in the excessive, almost self-pitying language of sarcasm and parody. Nemerov's poetic and critical insights into the problems of memorializing and representation, give the lie to the caricature he presents here. Yet the anxiety he expresses is an important one, for it mediates the prophet-seer stance of Ginsberg and Bly on the one hand, and the activist commitment of Denise Levertov and Adrienne Rich on the other. Nemerov is aware of the dangers of trying to be a political spokesman and poet at the same time. He is a median figure in the opposites I have cast: calm, detached, almost Augustan in his poetic utterances, ironic, and superbly sensitive to the barbarities of actions and language perpetrated during the Vietnam War. In the aspirations of Joe Blow, he presents the ludicrous aspects of public poetry and its expectations as practised by poets such as Ginsberg. Yet he is divided and disturbed and the poem is an articulation of doubt. The poet in the General Assembly and on TV represents publicity and acceptance by mainstream society, and yet it compromises the protest in the very act of acceptance. The poet's effectiveness in re-describing and re-presenting the world lies in his resistance to the dominant vocabulary, his ability to stand back and see the humour and vanity of the idea of the poet as legislator. The ironic stance seems to be the most effective mode of criticizing the war and its banalities. Even irony, however, does not preclude the anxiety that is expressed in the poem, and the process of re-description without assimilation is a complex task with which all the poets discussed in the chapter are confronted.

Denise Levertov's war poetry is as acutely sensitive to the problems of history and language as Nemerov's is, but unlike him, she works on the basis of a more passionate political sense of commitment. In the essay 'Poetry, Prophecy, Survival', she articulates the idea that political poetry can be good poetry as well:

> A poetry of anguish, a poetry of anger, of rage, a poetry that, from literal or deeply imagined experience, depicts and denounces perennial injustice and cruelty in their current forms, and in our peculiar time warns of the unprecedented perils that confront us, can be truly a high poetry, as well wrought as any other.[76]

She perceives Vietnam as another part of this world of 'perennial injustice and cruelty', and believes that poetry in particular is 'a way *into* history': 'Intellect informs, but emotion—feeling—will not respond (especially to facts about events too distant or too vast to be experienced directly through the senses) unless imagination gives us the vision of them, presents (makes present) the unwitnessed, gives flesh to the abstract.'[77] Levertov is arguing for a non-combatant witnessing of the war, the idea that the poet will mediate the conflict in more authentic ways than the media or politicians. Poetry is a prophetic mode of witnessing (the desire for prophecy and witness in Ginsberg and Bly is comparable), and she is aware of the problems caused by distance and abstraction. The mediation of the war through television and *Time* and *Life* magazines muddies the presentation as does the reduction and dehumanization of Vietnam and its people by means of acronyms and abstractions. In such a political, ethical climate, the idea of witness was a powerful trope. It was not only a means of protest, but a way of maintaining one's integrity. As Morris Dickstein writes:

> At times we felt that because of our numbers and the justice of our cause the nation couldn't fail to take notice: policy would change, the voice of the people would have spoken. At other times, especially after years of similar manifestations, we recognized the practical futility of what we were doing. Yet somehow this feeling redoubled the need to do it. The prevailing mood on these occasions demanded a gesture of conscience; it arose from a compulsion to bear personal witness. . . . By marching we tried to purge ourselves of the least trace of inner complicity with the war; we stepped outside the national consensus and reached out for solidarity with others who shared an alternative idea of America.[78]

---

[76] Denise Levertov, 'Poetry, Prophecy, Survival', *New & Collected Essays* (New York: New Directions Publishing Corporation, 1992), 143–4.
[77] Ibid. 147.   [78] Dickstein, *Gates of Eden*, 261.

The solidarity and the community desired by the protest movement is an important context for Levertov's poetry, because it is informed by similar desires and limitations. Her poetry is vital in that it gives witness to the inhumanity of war, it desires a better world, and it expresses solidarity with the sufferers. As she states in 'Poetry, Prophecy, Survival', poetry makes 'empathy and compassion more *possible*, at least' (149). However, the solidarity defined by Dickstein is idealized and limited to America, the site of rage and involvement. The Vietnam War triggered the protest, but America remained the centre of concern. This solipsistic attitude is part of Levertov's poetics, and her reaching out to the 'other' is often inadequate and precious.

In 'Overheard Over S.E. Asia', Levertov personifies the horror of napalm in an imagined conversational mode that distances the horror and, through displacement, projects the sinister quality of American involvement. The poem is a magical, daemoniacal transformation of the 'Mirror, mirror on the wall' paradigm:

> 'White phosphorus, white phosphorus,
> mechanical snow,
> Where are you falling?'
> 'I am falling impartially on roads and roofs,
> on bamboo thickets, on people.
> My name recalls rich seas on rainy nights,
> each drop that hits the surface eliciting
> luminous response from a million algae.
> My name is a whisper of sequins. Ha!
> Each of them is a disk of fire,
> I am the snow that burns.
>   I fall
> wherever men send me to fall—
> but I prefer flesh, so smooth, so dense
> I decorate it in black, and seek
> the bone.'[79]

Images from the natural world—'rich seas on rainy nights', 'luminous response from a million algae'—create a distinction between the imagistic associations of beauty and regeneration, and the destruction of those associations in the process of death

---

[79] Denise Levertov, 'Overheard Over S.E. Asia', *Footprints* (New York: New Directions Publishing Corporation, 1972), 8. Subsequent references are indicated after the quotation.

by napalm. The characterization of napalm highlights the disjunction: on the one hand, it is an 'impartial' agent (mirroring the 'impartial' American agenda of promoting democracy, as well as the impassive 'backroom boys'—the scientists who produced the napalm with no moral qualms), and on the other hand, it is a morbid force with a 'mind' of its own (exposing the contradictions in that agenda). The obsession with napalm, evident here and in 'Scenario', relates directly to the depredations wrought by indiscriminate use of the substance to 'pacify' the Vietnamese. A study sponsored by the Pentagon stated that '388,091 tons of napalm bombs were dropped by the United States and its allies between 1963 and 1973. . . . In total, greater quantities of incendiary weapons were used than in any other countries in any other wars.'[80] Napalm was the archetypal image of horror in Vietnam and white phosphorus recalls the life of the sea as well as the death wrought by bombs: the words themselves embrace their own contradictions. The projection of a hitherto inconceivable reality exposes the luminous insanity of the war, but it also rationalizes and aesthetically sanitizes that insanity: making it material for ordered, well-chosen, moving language. This is perhaps the only mode in which a non-combatant can present the war poetically, since a disordered, random language would only convey a jumble. War is a jumble of disparate and confusing events, and absolute fidelity to that (a kind of reportage) may not constitute a viable poetic form. Even the poems of reportage (and there are quite a few by veterans) involve a linguistic reordering, a transmutation of reality, and the problem of poetic sensemaking of an event as horrific as war is something that veteran poets grapple with as well.

A similar aesthetic distancing operates in 'Scenario':

> The theater of war. Offstage
> A cast of thousands weeping.
>
> Left center, well-lit, a mound
> of unburied bodies,
>
> or parts of bodies. Right,
> near some dead bamboo that serves as wings,

---

[80] Cited in Nigel Gray (ed.), *Phoenix Country* (London: The Journeyman Press, 1980), 104.

> a whole body, on which
> a splash of napalm is working.
> Enter the Bride.
> half of her scalp is bald.
> She hobbles towards center front.
> Enter the bridegroom,
> young, thin, but without
> visible wounds. He sees her.
> he begins to shudder, to shudder,
> to ripple with shudders. Curtain.
>
> (*Footprints*, 9)

Levertov images the naïvety of American policy planners who hoped to 'contain' Vietnam by reducing it to a war-game scenario. The 'theater of war' metaphor allowed for the petrifaction of Vietnam, a reduction to abstraction that was necessary for the continuance of the war.[81] The bride and bridegroom re-enact a grotesque tableau. The poem, however, seems to contain the horror of the war in a manner similar to that of military strategists. 'Scenario' is dominated by the silence of its victims and forced participants: the 'other' is imaged, but has no voice. The Vietnamese are mute witnesses and sufferers with no agency to influence their lives. This is precisely the position of malleability desired by the Americans who wished to mould the Vietnamese in the likeness of Western models of democracy and capitalism. The poetry is directly implicated in the dominant political and cultural debates of the time. In a Rortyan sense it attempts to re-describe and reconstitute the 'final vocabulary' purveyed by the state to describe Vietnam.[82] Within this process of re-description Levertov hopes to collapse the aesthetic dichotomy between the lyrical and the didactic. In her essay 'The Nature of Poetry', she writes about this relationship: 'The didactic has a place in poetry, but only when it is inseparable from the intuitive—e.g. opinion is not a source of poetry, but the poetry of political anguish is at its best both didactic and lyrical.'[83] 'Scenario' is a poem of 'political

---

[81] Fussell, *The Great War and Modern Memory*, 192. Fussell observes that 'seeing warfare as theater provides a psychic escape for the participant: with a sufficient sense of theater, he can perform his duties without implicating his real self'.

[82] Rorty, *Contingency, irony, and solidarity*, 73.

[83] Denise Levertov, 'The Nature of Poetry', *Light Up the Cave* (1946; New York: New Directions Publishing Corporation, 1981), 60.

anguish' in that it highlights the terrible human dimension of the war, and thereby indicts the politics of the conflict. The expression of anguish and solidarity is, however, implicated in a poetics that descriptively contains the horror and the intuitive fails to transcend or transgress the boundaries of perception and opinion. The containment is not entirely successful since the ghastly silence of the poem does convey the quiet (because distant?) trauma of war. The shudders ripple outwards despite being muffled by the limitations pointed out.

The denial of voice and agency problematizes Levertov's stated notion of 'authentic' utterance. In 'Some Notes on Organic Form', she writes that 'A religious devotion to the truth, to the splendor of the authentic, involves the writer in a process rewarding in itself.'[84] One aspect of the 1960s movement was an emphasis on the idea of authentic existence, an existence that was best validated through the cultivation of personal beliefs and utterances. At its extreme it led to a cult of the personal as well as a belief 'that personal articulation cleanses language'.[85] The best and most notorious example of this was Ginsberg's poetry reading sessions. The authenticity and impact of poetry in Levertov's formulation would seem to depend on the ability to resist and interrogate dominant ideological positions. While the poetry by refusing the refuge of silence might sensitize a wilfully ignorant polity, it occasionally reinforces cultural, racial, and political strategies that sustain American involvement. 'What Were They Like?' presents a poeticized pastoral that ignores political and revolutionary contexts, and lyrically silences the 'other':

> Remember,
> most were peasants; their life
> was in rice and bamboo.
> When peaceful clouds were reflected in the paddies
> and the water buffalo stepped surely along terraces,
> maybe fathers told their sons old tales.

---

[84] Cited in Stephen Berg and Robert Mezey (eds.), *Naked Poetry* (New York and Indianapolis: The Bobbs-Merrill Co. Inc., 1969), 145.

[85] Cary Nelson, 'Whitman in Vietnam: Poetry and History in Contemporary America', *The Massachusetts Review*, 16: 1 (Winter 1975), 55–71. The Students for a Democratic Society Port Huron Statement emphasized similar notions of authentic existence: 'The goal of man and society should be human independence: a concern not with image [or] popularity but with finding a meaning in life that is personally authentic.' Cited in Gitlin, *The Sixties*, 108.

> When bombs smashed those mirrors
> there was only time to scream.
> There is an echo yet
> of their speech which was like a song.
> It was reported their singing resembled
> the flight of moths in moonlight.
> Who can say? It is silent now.[86]

The images conjure up a gentle, fragile world of Arcadian peasants: 'peaceful clouds', 'speech which was like a song', 'singing resembled | the flight of moths in moonlight'. The poem does convey the sense of a beautiful and timeless world destroyed by the war. This beautiful picture, it is implied, is torn apart by American bombs. The NLF and the North Vietnamese Army (NVA) do not figure in this equation. While American violence was horrendous, the poem ignores the violence visited on the Vietnamese peasantry by its own people from both parts of Vietnam. The legitimate outrage at US atrocity leads to an eliding of political complexity. A deeply felt personal sense of shame and guilt at the fact that she belongs to a polity and civilization that is destroying another country, manifests itself in the idealized 'other'. This desire for an ideal 'other' is available in representations of an earlier war at the turn of the century. M. Wyk Smith points to the biblical pastoralism and rural utopias in poems written on the Boer War: 'The Transvaal and the Orange Free State offered the rural myth as a reality and in a state of timeless preservation. Oversimplified as this view was, it became for many a subliminal vision of a lost European golden age.'[87] For some American protest poets, Vietnam was a site of all the 'good' betrayed within America. This transference did not always provide valuable insights into 'other' lives and their conflicts. 'Who can say?' is a rhetorical flourish that indicates the war machine's lack of interest and the poet's inability to articulate that voice. The silence marks a boundary of comprehension, engagement, and 'authentic' utterance.

The excess of empathy (which creates the idealized Vietnam), the desire to reach out to the 'other', often leads to a tortured

---

[86] Denise Levertov, 'What Were They Like?', *Poems 1960–1967* (New York: New Directions Publishing Corporation, 1975), 234.

[87] M. Van Wyk Smith, *Drummer Hodge: The Poetry of the Anglo-Boer War (1899–1902)* (Oxford: Clarendon Press, 1978), 262.

sense of inadequacy. In 'The Distance', Levertov compares two types of commitment, that of the anti-war protestor and the Vietnamese soldier:

> While we lie in the road to block traffic from the air-force base,
> over there the dead are strewn in the roads.
>
> While we are carried to the bus and off to jail to be 'processed,'
> over there the torn-off legs and arms of the living
> hang in burnt trees and on broken walls.
>   . . . .
> While we refuse the standard prison liverwurst sandwiches,
> knowing we'll get decent food in a matter of hours,
> over there free fighters, young and old, guns never laid aside,
> eat a few grains of rice and remember
> Uncle Ho, and the long years he ate no better, and smile.
>   . . . .
> They have seen and seen and heard and heard
> all that we will ourselves with such effort to imagine,
> to summon into the understanding . . .
>   . . . .
> I see their spirits
> visible, crowns of fire-thorn
> flicker over their heads.
>
> Our steps toward struggle
> are like the first tottering of infant feet.
> Could we,
>   if life lasts
>   find in ourselves
> that steady courage, win
> such flame-crowns?[88]

The effort of imagination, to 'summon into the understanding' the life of the 'other' is laudable in so far as the 'other' is seen to have a valuable existence. This is in obvious contrast to the military establishment, for instance, which preferred to see all Vietnamese as 'gooks'. The poem also effectively contrasts the luxury of protest in the USA and the very different and difficult resistance of the Vietnamese. The imaginative leap, however, fails to provide more than a stilted, valorized, stereotypical picture of the revolutionary fighter. Uncle Ho remains a smiling inspiration,

---

[88] Denise Levertov, 'The Distance', *The Freeing of the Dust* (New York: New Directions Publishing Corporation, 1975), 27–8. Subsequent references are indicated after the quotation.

the revolutionary fighters are crowned with 'fire-thorn', Christ-like in symbolic import. This idealized portrait can be effectively compared with the reflections of a north Vietnamese combatant in the novel *The Sorrow of War*, written by a Vietnamese veteran:

> But we also shared a common sorrow, the immense sorrow of war. It was a sublime sorrow, more sublime than happiness, and beyond suffering. It was thanks to our sorrow that we were able to escape the war, escape the continual killing and fighting, the terrible conditions of battle and the unhappiness of men in fierce and violent theatres of war.[89]

The smiling, ever-benevolent, and avuncular Ho is absent from this recollection. I will refer to Bao Ninh's novel in Chapter 6, but the point of the comparison here is to emphasize the stilted solipsism of even the best-intentioned American poetic representations. It is noteworthy that Levertov does not include the US combat figure in her poem. This is probably wise, given her lack of personal experience of combat, but it does point to a desire to blank out that aspect of the war. Part of the problem can be traced to a deep sense of betrayal and, following from that, the need to locate an alternative, ideal world. As Todd Gitlin notes in his study of the 1960s: 'The movement had to find the right relation to the American nation; having taken America's dream of itself seriously, it was quick to feel betrayed when the dream turned into nightmare, quick to relocate the promised land on some revolutionary soil elsewhere.'[90] In the mythology of anti-war protest, the north Vietnamese became representatives of that 'promised land', the revolutionary colossus guiding the infantile protestor in the oppressor country. The desire for a utopian community has been a guiding force in American history, from the early Puritan colonies, to Hawthorne's Brook Farm (although *The Blithedale Romance* is not an unqualified endorsement of the utopian fantasy), to People's Park in northern California in the 1960s. In a society riven with conflict, it was not surprising that

---

[89] Bao Ninh, *The Sorrow of War*, English version by Frank Palmos, based on the translation by Vo Bang Thanh and Phan Thanh Hao, with Katerina Pierce (London: Secker & Warburg, 1993), 217.

[90] Gitlin, *The Sixties*, 6. James Fenton indicates divergences and similarities in British and French responses to Vietnam: 'The broadest support for the antiwar movement came from disgust at what the Americans were doing.... Very few [in Britain] idolized the Vietcong, or the North Vietnamese, or Uncle Ho in quite the same way, for instance, the French Left did.' *All the Wrong Places: Adrift in the Politics of Asia* (London: Penguin Books, 1988), 4.

communitarian ideals were desired and, in the absence of ideal conditions at home, projected on to a distant, oriental, revolutionary 'other'. 'The Distance' is a more accurate title than it seems at first: it encompasses both the falling away from American ideals (the loss of innocence trope recurs) and the need to keep the ideal 'other' at a distance, lest unpleasant realities obtrude. When the unpleasant does interfere, the poet can still turn to her ideal construction of that world.

The poetic strategy in 'In Thai Binh (Peace) Province' is to project an idyllic image on to the horror that she had witnessed during her trip to Hanoi in 1972:

> I've used up all my film on bombed hospitals,
> bombed village schools, the scattered
> lemon-yellow cocoons at the bombed silk-factory,
> and for the moment all my tears too
> are used up, having seen today
> yet another child with its feet blown off
>   a girl, this one, eleven years old,
> patient and bewildered in her home, a fragile
> small house of mud bricks among rice fields.
>
> So I'll use my dry burning eyes
> to photograph within me
> dark sails of the river boats,
> warm slant of afternoon light
> apricot on the brown, swift, wide river,
> village towers—church and pagodas—on the far shore,
> and a boy and small bird both
> perched, relaxed, on a quietly grazing
>   buffalo.   Peace within the
>   long war.
>
> It is that life, unhurried, sure, persistent,
> I must bring home when I try to bring
> the war home.
>   Child, river, light.
>
> Here the future, fabled bird
> that has migrated away from America,
> nests, and breeds, and sings,
> common as any sparrow.
>
>   (*The Freeing of the Dust*, 35)

The particularization of the horror of war, specifically the wanton destruction caused by Nixon's 1972 bombing of north Vietnam, is vital for humanizing the 'other'. War photographers conveyed some of this violence in graphic terms, and photography is a means in the poem of accurate memorializing. The particularity, however, seems too great a burden to bear, and the poet decides to 'photograph within' her a constant and idyllic 'other'. The images probably do have an objective correlative in the real world, but they fulfil an internal need, the need to find 'Peace within the | long war.' This desire is not only a poetic one, but was a political one as well. In their various ways, political opinions and ideas ranging from Johnson's 'Great Society' to the 1960s movements to Martin Luther's campaign for civil rights and Nixon's cynical 'Vietnamization' policy, were proposing modes of finding peace in a troubled country. The pastoralizing of life in Vietnam (as in classic pastoral, it is nature and rural life that is the locale) was a means of countering the mechanized, bureaucratic nightmare that America was perceived to have turned into. The opposition was too neat and binary, and while this poem describes a Vietnamese landscape, the actual contested site is America and its values.

'An Interim' cites one of the most infamous examples of doublespeak during the Tet offensive to meditate poetically on the problems of language:

> And
> 'It became necessary
> to destroy the town to save it,'
> a United States major said today.
> He was talking about the decision
> by allied commanders to bomb and shell the town
> regardless of civilian casualties,
> to rout the Vietcong.
>
> O language, mother of thought,
> are you rejecting us as we reject you?
>
> Language, coral island
> accrued from human comprehensions,
> human dreams,
>
> you are eroded as the war erodes us.[91]

---

[91] Denise Levertov, 'An Interim', *Poems 1968–1972* (New York: New Directions Publishing Corporation, 1987), 20–1.

Despite its stilted and apostrophic style—'O language, mother of thought'—this poem expresses an important and familiar concern about language used and abused during the war. All the poets mentioned in this chapter are 'sensitive to the sickness of language—a sickness that, infecting all literature with nausea, prompts us not so much to declare war on conventional language as simply to pick up and examine intently a few chosen pieces of linguistic garbage'.[92] Language and poetic vision are blurred by Vietnam. If language is the 'weapon' the poet wields against the war and the state, Levertov expresses a deep anxiety at its erosion and complicity. Language cannot be corralled into convenient categories, in that poetic diction can be equally corrupted by the 'sickness of language' purveyed by the state. This awareness and anxiety varies and might explain the extreme oppositional stances adopted by poets, ranging from Ginsberg's harangues to Nemerov's doubtful tone in 'On Being Asked For A Peace Poem'. The 'anxiety of authenticity' and the problem of complicity coexist with a deeply felt commitment to clarity and 'authentic' utterance, as far as that is possible. It is almost the only option the poet has, for, without engagement, Levertov declares that the poet 'will negate whatever his words may say, and will soon have no world to say them in'.[93]

This position of apocalyptic opposition led to the publication of numerous anthologies of anti-war poetry in the 1960s and 1970s. Some of the more prominent ones were Walter Lowenfels's *Where Is Vietnam?*, Denise Levertov's *1968 Peace Calendar & Appointment Book: Out of the War Shadow*, Diane di Prima's *War Poems*, Robert Bly's *Forty Poems Touching On Recent American History*, Scott Bates's *Poems of War Resistance*, and Jack Sonenberg's *Artists and Writers Protest Against the War in Vietnam*. These anthologies represented a mode of activist protest that hoped to provide a counter-language to that of the media and the government. Poets anthologized in these collections were not always well known (nor were they always good poets!), but they represented voices who were willing to express outrage at the war. The war helped to create a kind of poetic community opposed to the dominant political community

---

[92] Merton, 'War and the Crisis of Language', 99–100.
[93] Denise Levertov, 'Great Possessions', *The Poet In the World* (New York: New Directions Publishing Corporation, 1973), 106.

and its ideology. The War Resisters League was one organization that hoped to create a climate of opinion against the war. Denise Levertov, who edited the 1968 *Peace Calendar* for the League, cited Albert Einstein's speech at Princeton in 1953 on the need for moral opposition:

> The War Resisters League is important because, by union, it relieves our courageous and resolute individuals of the paralyzing feeling of isolation and loneliness, and in this way gives them moral support in the fulfillment of what they consider their duty. The existence of such a moral élite is indispensable for the preparation of a fundamental change in public opinion, a change that, under present day circumstances, is absolutely necessary if humanity is to survive.[94]

Einstein's point of reference was a nuclear holocaust, and he occupied an interesting position of participation in, and opposition to, the bomb. His fears and sense of duty, however, were easily assimilated by an élite that perceived America's involvement in Vietnam in similar apocalyptic terms. Einstein's notion of 'a moral élite' is vital in this context, because that is exactly how most anti-war poets positioned themselves. Much of the moral rant in poets such as Ginsberg and Bly arose out of a sense of isolation and superiority in isolation. It was, paradoxically, the basis of some of the best poetry as well. Collectively, the anti-war poets saw themselves as exiles in the USA (this sense of alienation recurs in veteran poetry, and for more justifiable reasons), as intellectuals who, to use Edward Said's phrase, were 'author of a language that tries to speak the truth to power'.[95] The articulation of 'truth to power' was problematic and led to a kind of intellectual arrogance in some poets who did not recognize the pitfalls of the prophetic mode. The effort, however, was an important contribution to creating alternative points of view during the war. A brief discussion of some widely anthologized poems will highlight differences and continuities in the opposition, interrogative agenda.

Joel Oppenheimer's '17–18 April, 1961' is a direct, lengthy diatribe against American imperialism at a time when the Vietnam War was in its infancy:

---

[94] Denise Levertov (ed.), *1968 Peace Calendar & Appointment Book: Out of the War Shadow* (New York: War Resisters League, 1967), no pagination.
[95] Edward Said, cited in Jennifer Wallace, 'Exiled by foes, silenced by friends', *Times Higher Education Supplement*, 17 Jan. 1997, 17.

> the problem in your soul is that 63 years
> after mr mckinley we are still fucking
> around with dreams of empire, we still
> cannot bear to let people work out their
> own destiny, we still cannot believe in
> keeping our hands off, we have forgotten
> we once carried a flag into battle that
> read don't tread on me, we think we have
> the right to step anywhere, we are free,
> and therefor every other man is beneath
> us to be trod upon, i will not do it.[96]

If the title is any indication of the date of composition, Oppenheimer is prescient in presenting US involvement in Vietnam as an imperial one. The year of publication, 1968, was the year of the Tet offensive, the most significant jolt to the optimistic projections of the war by US officials. As protestor-poet he refuses to participate in the expansionist ambitions and politics of his country. Part of the context for protest is America's revolutionary past, its own fight against colonialism, and this seems to further the sense of anger and betrayal:

> america
> forget aguinaldo, forget the indians, forget
> the slaves, forget all that, just, for
> once america, admit it, stand up and admit
> you have killed everybody who stood in
> your way, quickly, to the wall, rarely,
> more often america, the slow stewing in
> the prisons and the reservations. and
> you keep on telling them you love them.
>
> when you have admitted it, america, then
> you can give it up. america you're no
> better than any of the rest of them,
> and i'm sorry for it.
>
> (*War Poems*, 72)

In the tradition of Bly, Oppenheimer catalogues the history of domination and colonization in America. The repetition of 'forget' highlights aspects of history that have been collectively

---

[96] Joel Oppenheimer, '17–18 April, 1961', in Diane di Prima (ed.), *War Poems* (New York: The Poets Press, Inc., 1968), 68. Subsequent references are indicated after the quotation.

repressed, that the nation wishes to forget, but the poet will not allow it to forget. It is only a national remembrance that will allow the country to forsake the trajectory of violence, both within and without. The poem articulates a fundamental fault line in US history, a divide between myth and actuality. As Adrienne Rich points out:

> Cruelty, greed, assassination of cultures are part of all history. But we, here, have been staggering under the weight of a national fantasy that the history of the conquest of the Americas, the 'westward movement,' was different—was a history of bravery, enlightenment, righteous claiming, service to religious values and civilizing spirit.[97]

It is this 'national fantasy' of righteousness and democracy that led the USA into Vietnam, and it is the intertwining of the possibilities and betrayal that the poet bemoans. 'i'm sorry for it' is a personal statement of contempt for America's collective lack of moral courage and for its present state. The line also encompasses a sense of loss at the possibilities corrupted (another form of the loss of innocence trope). Within a larger context of amnesia and historical duplicity, political poetry and personal testimony become vital. To quote Adrienne Rich again: 'in a history of spiritual rupture, a social compact built on fantasy and collective secrets, poetry becomes more necessary than ever: it keeps the underground aquifers flowing; it is the liquid voice that can wear through stone.'[98]

Walter Lowenfels's *Where Is Vietnam?* is a diverse anthology, containing well-known poets such as Ginsberg and Ferlinghetti, and not so familiar names such as Morton Marcus. The poetic purpose is similar to other anthologies published around the same time on the same theme. The question asked in the title is one with which all stateside poets were grappling. It is both a literal and metaphoric question: literal, because a majority of Americans did not know where Vietnam was, and figurative in that most poets seemed to locate Vietnam (the causes of American involvement and the war as symptoms of American pathologies) within the USA and its history. Vietnam exposed the rupture within America that Rich writes about.

---

[97] Adrienne Rich, 'What is an American Life?', *What Is Found There*, 122.
[98] Ibid. 122.

The expiation of national, civilizational guilt becomes an intense, internalized trauma in Morton Marcus's 'Confession':

> How do I say
> that I'm a murderer?
>
> I drag my shadow
> as if it were a sack
> full of discarded bodies.
>
> My count is indefinite
> but probably includes
> the 8 mothers
> who run through the caves
> of my colon
> with burning hair;
>
> the baby
> shaped like a scream;
> the two girls
> with hands and wombs
> of flaming water;
> and, on my spinal road,
> the boy who crawls
> farther and farther
> from his legs.[99]

Vietnam is imaged not only as an external atrocity but as physical and psychic laceration. Although most of the protest poets collapse the distance between the two countries, refusing to see it as a war 'out there', Marcus obliterates the inside–outside distinction altogether, so that the speaker's mind and body become a phantasmagoric palimpsest of the war. The disintegration of the physical self mirrors and re-enacts the physical violence wrought in Vietnam. Napalm and the 'body count' figure prominently as horror proliferates: 'My count is indefinite.' The internalization of horror here is in sharp contrast to Oppenheimer's expression of moral outrage in declarative poetry. In its tone and technique, 'Confession' is similar to Nemerov's 'Redeployment' and, like Nemerov's poem, it shatters any notion of glory in war. It also questions the typically American myth of expansionism, of moving west, of motion as being positive and redemptive. Jack

---

[99] Morton Marcus, 'Confession', in Walter Lowenfels (ed.), *Where Is Vietnam? American Poets Respond* (Garden City, NY: Doubleday and Company Inc., 1967), 85.

Kerouac's *On the Road* is a complex, celebratory meditation on this theme, and could be construed as a rather placid context for Marcus's variation on the theme:

> and, on my spinal road,
> the boy who crawls
> farther and farther
> from his legs.

It is a chilling image of dismemberment, of the literal highway metamorphosed into the 'spinal road' that registers the never ending insanity of the war. In its quietness and intensity, in its refusal to propagandize, 'Confession' is the more effective kind of political poetry that 'moves to deepen awareness'.

This brief survey of stateside poetry on Vietnam traverses a period beginning with Ginsberg's public declarations of anger and despair, and ending with Marcus's more private musing on trauma and guilt. These are, of course, arbitrary cut-off points, and the 'ending' may be extended a little by looking at the poetics of Adrienne Rich. As radical feminist and poet, her formulations of the necessity of political poetry are polemical. She sees poetry not only as a means of acknowledging the past (a vital need in a context of cultural amnesia), but as a means of working out a better future. As she wrote in the 'Preface' to *What Is Found There: Notebooks on Poetry and Politics*:

> This book is about desire and daily life. I began it because I needed a way of thinking about poetry outside of writing poems; and about the society I was living and writing in, which smelled to me of timidity, docility, demoralization, acceptance of the unacceptable. In the general public disarray of thinking, of feeling, I saw an atrophy of our power to imagine other ways of navigating into our collective future.[100]

She saw a society not only perpetrating violence in Vietnam, but convulsed with internal conflict. Within this context poetry could be a rejuvenating force, infuse politics with imagination and integrity. In keeping with the communitarian political desire of the 1960s, Rich aestheticizes politics: 'Politics *is* imagination or it is a treadmill—disintegrative, stifling, finally brutalizing—or ineffectual.'[101] She perceives poetry as activist, interventionist,

---

[100] Adrienne Rich, 'Preface', *What Is Found There*, p. xiii.
[101] Adrienne Rich, 'The Muralist', *What Is Found There*, 49.

and totally imbricated in historical and political contexts. The disintegration and repression of the American imagination and conscience is a theme in most protest poetry, particularly evident in Bly's poetics. In 'Face to Face', Rich dwells on the Puritan past that helped to fashion the present:

> Never to be lonely like that—
> the Early American figure on the beach
> in black coat and knee-breeches
> scanning the didactic storm in privacy,
>
> never to hear the prairie wolves
> in their lunar hilarity
> circling one's little all, one's claim
> to be Law and Prophets
> . . . .
> How people used to meet!
> starved, intense, the old
> Christmas gifts saved up till spring,
> and the old plain words,
>
> and each with his God-given secret,
> spelled out through months of snow and silence,
> burning under the bleached scalp; behind dry lips
> a loaded gun.[102]

Law and didacticism lie at the heart of the new civilization, and cut it off from all natural life. This process of denaturalizing is associated with patriarchy which expresses its urge to dominance and destruction. She returns to the foundational myth to indicate the wellsprings of violence in contemporary America. At the heart of the American notion of manifest destiny lies a type of prophetic zeal backed up by violence: 'behind dry lips | a loaded gun'. Violence arises out of repression and the inability 'to hear the prairie wolves | in their lunar hilarity'. Like the Beats, she emphasizes the need to break out of dominant social and ideological structures. Unlike the Beats, she sees poetry as an articulation of responsibility, as well as a privilege. It is not enough merely to fulminate against particular systems; the written word

---

[102] Adrienne Rich, 'Face to Face', *The Fact of a Doorframe: Poems Selected and New, 1950–1984* (New York and London: W.W. Norton & Company, 1984), 76. Subsequent references are indicated as *Doorframe* after the quotation.

stands as personal testimony. 'North American Time' dwells on privilege and responsibility in public, political poetry:

> II
> Everything we write
> will be used against us
> or against those we love.
> These are the terms,
> take them or leave them.
> Poetry never stood a chance
> of standing outside history.
> III
>
> .   .   .   .
>
> try telling yourself
> you are not accountable
> to the life of your tribe
> the breath of your planet
> IV
> It doesn't matter what you think.
> Words are found responsible
> all you can do is choose them
> or choose
> to remain silent. Or, you never had a choice,
> which is why the words that do stand
> are responsible
>
> and this is verbal privilege
>
> (*Doorframe*, 324–6)

The poem is polemical and there is a sense of oppositional paranoia in section II, but it is within this framework that Rich sees poetry, protest, and responsibility functioning. 'Verbal privilege' does not imply any kind of opting out. The poet must be responsible to the life of her tribe, the breath of her planet. Rich's notion of the poet as a central figure in a pre-technological, pre-bureaucratic world, is similar to Robert Duncan's idea of the poet as bard: 'They [Germanic and Celtic tribes] had their bards; they had to keep alive poetry, because poetry keeps the identity of the tribe alive.'[103] This insistence on the vitality of poetry arises not only from conviction, but from anxiety that the poet is steadily marginalized in an increasingly atomized society and competitive market. If the poet does not speak words of responsibility and

---
[103] Cited in Ginsberg, *Allen Verbatim*, 114.

integrity, she will be spoken for by alternative modes such as the media. The sense of unflinching and necessary integrity is central in Rich's poetry. The following exchange in an interview with David Montenegro in May 1987 indicates this quality of dedication:

> DM. So much of your work has been a struggle to speak honestly and openly, whether about poetry itself or about social issues, about racism, about lesbianism. What are the costs of doing so, as a poet, as a person?
>
> RICH. What would be the cost of *not* doing it? I feel as though it's for my survival, first and foremost. This is how I cope; this is how I survive. I have learned from my peers that this way of creating can be a way of surviving. I didn't invent that.[104]

The centre–margin conundrum raised in Nemerov's poems recurs here, but with the emphasis that 'marginality' does actually help. Poetry need not be 'the in thing' and saleable as entertainment. In fact, poetry is trivialized by the type of public spectacle and gimmickry Ginsberg often indulged in. Its value and effectiveness as subversive 'other' within a seemingly monolithic polity lies in its 'marginal' position. The bardic position of centrality may have changed, but Rich is convinced her voice is as valuable and necessary as ever. She is concerned with the identity and voice of the poet who will then speak/write the tribe/nation. The need for a radical rewriting of America was deeply felt during and after the Vietnam War and, while it has led to significant erasures, in Rich's poetry it is an attempt to accept the past and forge a new future.

Having briefly discussed some non-combatant poetry on Vietnam, I must consider some of the constraints and problems that characterize it. Some of the limitations such as a desire to prophesy and an oppositional monopoly on 'truth' have been mentioned earlier. The prophetic mode is connected to the problem of representation itself. Most of the poets were aware of the shifting, variable signification of language. Some, like Ginsberg, perceive the war as a pure perversion of language. They are also aware that representations, not 'truth', are circulated by cultural discourse. This awareness leads to the need to create oppositional and contesting representations. However, when these alternative

---

[104] David Montenegro, *Points of Departure: International Writers on Writing and Politics* (Ann Arbor: The University of Michigan Press, 1991), 20.

modes of apprehending the war are seen as absolute and neutral, the poetry is flat and takes on a shrill, denunciatory tone. As Evelyn Cobley, in her study of First World War narratives, points out, discursive productions of war cannot be neutral: 'These discursive productions are consequently motivated or interested rather than objective and neutral; they are the enunciation of a historically situated subject which not only speaks but is spoken by a contradictory cultural site.'[105] Cobley's observation is equally applicable to poetic narratives of Vietnam. As soon as the poet believes that she or he can abstract her/himself from 'a contradictory cultural site', the poet falls into a discursive mode not very different from government or military language. I have highlighted some aspects of the cultural sites to which the poets belonged, and it is not altogether surprising that the anxieties and contradictions of the 1960s and the protest movements are reflected in the poetry. What is surprising is the attempt to transcend one's context and historical location prophetically. Those poets who are most acutely aware of contexts are beset by instrumentalist anxiety, worried about the position and influence of their poetry. This might explain the element of didacticism, as well as the brittleness and stilted poetics of protest poetry.

The imbrication of poetry and history and contemporary culture is most obvious in representations of the 'other'. While the protest poets do highlight the horror of the war, the site of their representations is America. When Vietnam or the Vietnamese are presented, they are exoticized and pastoralized. The 'other' is written about and spoken for, but has no voice or agency. This attitude fits Edward Said's idea of the way in which Orientalist perception functions: 'Orientalism assumed an unchanging Orient, absolutely different (the reasons change from epoch to epoch) from the West.'[106] This absolutizing of the 'other' led to another perpetual divide fostered by poetry. Vietnam was transformed into an unchanging, beautiful, rural idyll populated by heroic revolutionary fighters and charming, self-sacrificing women. The transference of heroic virtues and ideals occurred due to the belief that America had betrayed its own ideal possibilities. As Todd Gitlin observes:

[105] Evelyn Cobley, *Representing War: Form and Ideology in First World War Narratives* (Toronto, Buffalo, and London: University of Toronto Press, 1993), 15–16.
[106] Edward Said, *Orientalism* (Harmondsworth: Penguin Books Ltd, 1978), 96.

We needed to feel that someone, somewhere in the world, was fighting the good fight and winning. . . . If the United States was no longer humanity's beacon—and if the movement was not building a new society itself—the light had to be found outside. The melodrama of American innocence was alive and well in the anti-American left.[107]

Some stateside anti-war poetry betrays a similar us–them mentality, except that it is now a reversal of political oppositions. The manichaean logic of the Cold War was reiterated by protestors and poets who projected America (often spelt with a 'k') as the fountainhead of all evil. This not only ignored the myriad reasons for and manifestations of the war, but it harked back to pristine originary myths and utopian impulses in US history. Acceptance of the idea of innocent origins and consequent decadence was a convenient way of ignoring historical complexity, a great temptation in a society consumed at some points by self-loathing and contradictions. This simplified opposition was, as Jean Elshtain points out, merely a reiteration of war language, not a real, viable alternative: 'Why should those opposed to war on one level reaffirm it at another, deeper level by embracing the paradigmatic narrative of war discourse, including figurations of heroes and villains, good guys and bad guys, wicked imperialists and noble peasants?'[108] In a society riven with fault lines the poets occasionally posited simplistic adversarial positions. In projecting the good society in Vietnam in the image of American ideals, protest language was sometimes a flip side of political rhetoric.

The problems of language, representation, prophecy, and solipsism are all intertwined. Solipsism, in its constant focus on American problems and anxieties, was most bizarrely and pompously articulated by Ginsberg, when he explained what he meant by 'I here declare the end of the war': '"I here declare the end of the war" is a fact, whether the war ends for everyone or not. I end the war in me and anyone who's affected by my gesture.'[109] While this might be an admirable form of private meditation and detachment, it constitutes what I would define as the aesthetics of denial. The idea of an entirely personal realm

---

[107] Gitlin, *The Sixties*, 262. It is interesting that Morris Dickstein's study of the period is titled *Gates of Eden*, harking back to the pristine possibilities in US history.
[108] Jean Elshtain, *Women and War* (New York: Basic Books, Inc., Publishers, 1987), 37.
[109] Cited in Hyde (ed.), *On the Poetry of Allen Ginsberg*, 311.

which banishes war is a comforting one, but it lacks the strenuous political and poetic insights we find in protest poetry. The karmic denial of the 'other' (be it war or the Vietnamese) is an extremely self-indulgent and naïve position. It seems necessary to highlight problems in the poems by non-combatants not only to focus on the complex terrain they create and inhabit, but also because there is a tendency to valorize and exempt protest poetry from critical scrutiny (much as the Vietnamese are valorized without qualification). For instance, James F. Mersmann has this to say about Ginsberg: 'A poet and a poetry that draw inspiration from the battle against Moloch, the heavy judger, may perhaps be granted the boon of our nonjudgement. They deserve attention and description, but are not illuminated by qualitative tags.'[110] While 'qualitative tags' may lead to critical simplification, 'nonjudgement' seems to be an invitation to critical anarchy and irresponsibility. It is not my contention that protest poetry was a purely solipsistic activity, dominated by the aesthetics of denial, but the quality of navel gazing has to be taken into account. The problems are integral to the poetry, as are the positive possibilities it created in a time of tribulation and chaos.

The problem of representation inevitably raises the question of whether non-combatants can write about war. Paul Fussell, in *Wartime*, seems to dismiss non-combatant opinions on the Second World War. W. D. Ehrhart, a Vietnam veteran and poet, mediates a complex response to the question. In an essay ' "Waiting for the Fire" ', he begins by dismissing anti-war poetry, particularly Walter Lowenfels's *Where Is Vietnam?* 'I'd turned down four colleges to volunteer for the war and I had no use for Lowenfels and his peacenik fellow-travelers.... The few poems I read about Vietnam after I came back only made me angry: What the hell did these people know about it, for chrissake?'[111] He then goes on to describe his shock of discovery at reading Philip Appleman's 'Waiting for the Fire' and W. S. Merwin's 'The Asians Dying': 'The two poems went a long way toward teaching me that people other than Vietnam veterans might have something worthwhile to say about Vietnam.'[112] This discovery was

---

[110] Mersmann, *Out of the Vietnam Vortex*, 63.
[111] W. D. Ehrhart, ' "Waiting for the Fire": An Essay on Vietnam War Poetry by Non-Vietnam Veterans', *Poetry East*, 9 and 10 (Winter 1982–Spring 1983), 112–17.
[112] Ibid. 113.

made in late 1975, and the rest of the essay, published in early 1983, analyses the positive aspects and problems of non-veteran poetry. Looking back on the body of protest poetry, Ehrhart writes:

> Those long, gut-wrenching years produced, among other things, a tremendous amount of poetry. And the anguish and frustration of those writers is as real and personal as anything experienced by the Vietnam veterans themselves, though the focus of the subject may differ. To make some kind of distinction between veterans and non-veterans is to set up one group of victims against another—a tactic used by Richard Nixon with devastating effectiveness—and if it took me years to understand that, I understand it now.[113]

The essay concludes with Ehrhart expressing a kind of solidarity with non-combatant poets and acknowledging their contribution to a saner world: 'In a world forever mad, and now facing extinction, it is and always has been the duty of thoughtful people to do what little they can to hold back the fire.'[114] Although the essay does stress the problems with stateside poetry, it is largely an endorsement of protest poetry in times of crisis such as the one represented by Vietnam. Since writing this essay, however, Ehrhart has modified his opinions. In an interview on 12 February 1997, he stated that poetry by Bly, Levertov, Ginsberg, and others, had 'served a political purpose', but it 'doesn't work' as poetry and is 'not durable'.[115] This is indeed the case with poems that are heavily contextualized and propagandist in their shrillness. On the question of whether non-combatants can portray war effectively in their poetry, the answer is that they seem ineffective and melodramatic. Yet their meditations on the horror of Vietnam are not without value since they articulate alternative viewpoints in a largely acquiescent culture. The focus is different and this indicates a different type of poetics that dwells on historical, political, cultural, moral, and linguistic implications of the war. These are poetic threads and concerns that recur in some veteran poetry as well, but they were explored first with passion and insight by stateside poets. In representing the reality of war and its terrible aftermath, veteran poetry is generally more accurate and moving, but for what it meant to be

[113] Ibid. 116.
[114] Ibid. 117.
[115] Interview with W. D. Ehrhart, La Salle University, Philadelphia, 12 Feb. 1997.

an intelligent dissenter and poet in a time of turmoil, the better non-combatant poems are a valuable testament.

Stateside poetry created and provided an alternative climate of opinion and conscience during and after the war. It attempted to revitalize the bureaucratized language that sustained the war. It helped to shift the linguistic parameters of perception, and hoped to alter 'the drift of modern history [that] domesticates the fantastic and normalizes the unspeakable'.[116] Poets focused not only on the destruction in Vietnam but on how the American agenda was related to its history. This, as contemporary and postwar revisionism was to highlight, was a vital act of poetic and historical inscription. The poets pointed to what had been erased from national, historical memory, through the establishment of connections between Vietnam and American history. Robert Bly's poems are a good example of this project of historical recovery. The recuperation of an often barbaric and unpleasant history was connected with the problem of memory and representation. I have mentioned a tendency in some war poetry—by Levertov, for instance—to aestheticize the horror of war, sanitize the insanity. While this is true, we need not condemn the 'aestheticizing strategy' (the term is Jameson's) in moral terms. We could, as Jameson does, see it 'as a strategy which for whatever reason seeks to recode or rewrite the world and its own data in terms of perception as a semi-autonomous activity'.[117] In the context of the Vietnam War there is a problem with a purely perceptual outlook, where individual impressions are everything, but Jameson's idea of recoding and rewriting the world underlines the importance of the aesthetic response. The aesthetic, as Herbert Marcuse observes, recalls and re-presents reality:

The medium of sensibility also constitutes the paradoxical relation of art to time—paradoxical because what is experienced through the medium of sensibility is present, while art cannot show the present without showing it as past. What has become form in the work of art has happened: it is recalled, re-presented. The mimesis translates reality into memory.[118]

---

[116] Fussell, *The Great War and Modern Memory*, 74.
[117] Fredric Jameson, *The Political Unconscious* (London: Methuen & Co. Ltd., 1981), 230.
[118] Herbert Marcuse, *The Aesthetic Dimension: Toward a Critique of Marxist Aesthetics* (London and Basingstoke: The Macmillan Press, Ltd., 1979), 67.

The problem with a reality as grotesque and varied as that of the Vietnam War has been translated into a critical position that stresses the unrepresentability of that war. Thus, for instance, John Carlos Rowe states: 'What is finally unrepresentable is the immorality of our conduct in Vietnam, and it is this unrepresentable fact, which is hardly ambiguous and certainly unequivocal, that is made presentable in every sentence we speak of "Vietnam".'[119] There are representations of the immorality of American actions in Vietnam that attempt to make it 'presentable'. The body of political discourse and some academic research (such as that by Richard Nixon and Guenter Lewy) would justify Rowe's castigation of the desire to 'speak of "Vietnam"'. The many poetic formulations seem to defy Rowe. With all their contradictions and problems, they have the courage to articulate the immorality of the war. In fact, Rowe's position represents a critical cul-de-sac: the war was so immoral that we cannot represent it, for if we do, we whitewash it and make it 'presentable'. The question raised by this impasse is: is it then best to maintain silence, since to speak the war is to misrepresent it? Rowe's implicit 'yes' to the question would align him, paradoxically, with revisionist historians and politicians, for the plea for silence is a plea for forgetfulness. The most singular contribution of the stateside poets was their refusal to be silent witnesses to Vietnam, to present (even if it was in hysterical, denunciatory terms) the moral problem of America's involvement. Their responses were mediated by television and *Time* and *Life* magazines, they were at a remove from the war (these are contributory factors to the inadequacies pointed out earlier), but they were convinced that the horror of the war had to be narrated. For, as Adrienne Rich points out, 'the imagining of a different reality requires telling and retelling the terrible true story: a poetry that narrates and witnesses'.[120] The retelling of 'the terrible true story' was the way in which protest poets created the basis of an alternative history. They were not only fashioning a climate of conscience, they contributed to the way/s in which Vietnam would be remembered.

---

[119] John Carlos Rowe, '"Bringing It All Back Home": American Recyclings of the Vietnam War', in Nancy Armstrong and Leonard Tennenhouse (eds.), *The Violence of Representation: Literature and the History of Violence* (London and New York: Routledge, 1989), 212.
[120] Adrienne Rich, 'What if?', *What Is Found There*, 247.

None of this, of course, either stopped the war or prevented further wars (for example, the Gulf War), and the instrumentalist agenda haunts poets, both stateside and combatant. The effective rewriting of the war by the dominant culture over the last twenty years seems to diminish further the 'effectiveness' of the poetic discourse. Nemerov's variation on Yeats's 'On Being Asked For A War Poem' is just one example of the problem. If the purpose of anti-war poetry was solely to propagandize (and some of it is in that vein), then it was a dismal failure. If, however, it was not simply another tool in the dominant political-power arena, then, with Frank Kermode, we can perceive alternatives. As he writes: 'The text . . . becomes the only existential platform on which it is possible to live, because it is possible to read without accepting official versions of reality.'[121] The world may not be absolutely reducible to the text, but the text–world relationship points to the real possibility of dissent, of perceiving new and different realities. Neither despair nor silence are then necessary or desirable responses. The glimmerings of a Rortyan solidarity seem possible, although it is a possibility somewhat stunted in the poetry analysed in this chapter. Rorty's idea of solidarity as a willed act provides a valuable context for my discussion of poetic representations:

It [solidarity] is to be achieved not by inquiry but by imagination, the imaginative ability to see strange people as fellow sufferers. Solidarity is not discovered by reflection but created. It is created by increasing our sensitivity to the particular details of the pain and humiliation of other, unfamiliar sorts of people. Such increased sensitivity makes it more difficult to marginalise people different from ourselves by thinking, 'They do not feel as we would,' or 'There must always be suffering, so why not let them suffer?'[122]

This idea of solidarity is present in some stateside poetry, but more effectively mediated in some recent poetry by veterans. The poets I have mentioned, however, do express a nominal awareness of suffering, pain, and humiliation. Ginsberg's eloquent line, 'Where are our tears? Who weeps for this pain?' written in response to the flood of East Pakistan refugees in Calcutta in 1971, could equally apply to the pain and anger expressed by

[121] Frank Kermode, 'The Art of Telling', cited in 'Introduction', *Poetry, Narrative, History* (Oxford: Basil Blackwell, 1990), 24.
[122] Rorty, *Contingency, irony, and solidarity*, p. xvi.

American poets writing on Vietnam.[123] Their witnessing prepared the way for the complex, experiential witness of the veteran-poet. Theirs was not the final voice, and there was no absolute stance that could be adopted and still claim to be true to the war. As Philip Beidler put it: 'There is no sense of commanding perspective, of some great and awful burden of remembrance imaginatively mastered and brought into the province of collective understanding in a way that might let it be put behind once and for all.'[124]

In fact any such possibility of imaginative mastering was shattered by veteran poetry with its particular anguish, anger, and horror. The stateside poets, however, did critically interrogate a contentious period in American history, and in this lies the value and relevance of their poetry.

[123] Ginsberg, 'September on Jessore Road', 573.
[124] Philip D. Beidler, *American Literature and the Experience of Vietnam* (Athens, Ga.: The University of Georgia Press, 1982), 202.

3
Veteran Poetry
Protest and Anguish—Bringing the War Home

In an advertisement in the *New York Times*, on Sunday, 19 November 1967, an organization of ex-soldiers, Viet-Nam Veterans Against the War (VVAW), spoke out against US involvement in Vietnam. Although protests against the war had become a part of the political landscape, this was significantly different in that first-hand witnesses and participants declared their opposition to the war, and the state that waged it. Their authority in protest 'carried the weight of tested patriotism, seeming to arise from the Vietnam conflict itself'.[1] As the first paragraph of the statement declared,

We are veterans of the Viet-Nam war. We believe that this 'conflict' in which our country is now engaged in Viet-Nam is wrong, unjustifiable and contrary to the principle of self-determination on which this nation was founded. . . . We believe that our policy in Viet-Nam supports tyranny and denies democracy. We believe this because of our experiences in Viet-Nam. We know, because we have been there, that the American public has not been told the truth about the war or about Viet-Nam.[2]

This emphasis on personal testimony as a sign of truth and authenticity echoes a public statement Siegfried Sassoon made in July 1917:

I am a soldier, convinced that I am acting on behalf of soldiers. I believe that this war, upon which I entered as a war of defence and liberation, has now become a war of aggression and conquest. . . .
    I have seen and endured the sufferings of the troops, and I can no

---

[1] Charles de Benedetti, *An American Ordeal: The Antiwar Movement of the Vietnam Era* (Syracuse, NY: New York University Press, 1990), 310.
[2] 'Viet-Nam Veterans Speak Out', *New York Times*, sect. 4, Sunday, 19 Nov. 1967, E 7.

longer be a party to prolong these sufferings for ends which I believe to be evil and unjust....

On behalf of those who are suffering now I make this protest against the deception which is being practised on them; also I believe that I may help to destroy the callous complacence with which the majority of those at home regard the continuance of agonies which they do not share, and which they have not sufficient imagination to realize.[3]

Sassoon's desire to protest and expose the reality of the Great War was repeated in the Vietnam context through endeavours such as the Winter Soldier Investigation. Organized by VVAW in Detroit, on 31 January and 1 and 2 February 1971, the investigation intended to publicize combat horror and atrocity in order to indicate the unjust nature of the war. Unlike some stateside protests, it refused to take absolute binary positions. William Crandell, a former 1/Lt., in the Americal Division, stated the aims thus:

The Winter Soldier Investigation is not a mock trial. There will be no phony indictments; there will be no verdict against Uncle Sam. In these three days, over a hundred Vietnam veterans will present straightforward testimony—direct testimony—about acts which are war crimes under international law. . . . We are here to bear witness not against America, but against those policy makers who are perverting America.[4]

The privileging of combat experience in the belief that 'direct testimony' would help to end the war, was both shrewd and naïve in its notion of effectiveness. For the first time in American military history soldiers publicly testified to the problems in a war, and their statements, along with symbolic gestures such as the returning of military honours and medals, contributed to the wider disenchantment with the war. Their involvement in protest may have hastened Nixon's 'Vietnamization' policy, the rapid withdrawal of US combat forces. The naïvety lay in the faith reposed in the power of 'direct testimony', as if a soldier's word would turn the nation and its politicians against this and perhaps future wars. While VVAW did have a political agenda, it did not always question some of the basic conditions and assumptions

---

[3] Cited in Jon Stallworthy, *Wilfred Owen: A Biography* (London: Oxford University Press and Chatto and Windus, 1974), 206.

[4] William Crandell, 'Winter Soldier Investigation', in Jan Barry (ed.), *Peace is Our Profession: Poems And Passages of War Protest* (Montclair, NJ: East River Anthology, 1981), 147.

that led to the war.⁵ In its indictment of 'policy makers who are perverting America' it implicitly contributed to the idea that a handful of policy administrators had led America astray. It maintained the sanctity and nobility of American intentions, of a war undertaken for heroic reasons but sadly perverted by the un-American few. The battleground for both the establishment and protester was America, and it is interesting that from the administrative point of view it was the protester who was un-American.

VVAW, and the Winter Soldier Investigation organized by it, represented a public genre of protest and witness, analogous to that of the anti-war movement at large, some stateside poetry, and to the earlier paradigm of witness, the House Un-American Activities Committee. While HUAC was a conservative, paranoid response to perceived internal threats, the other movements attempted to mobilize conscience against a war fought to preserve external interests. VVAW in its emphasis on testifying to the horror of war, its privilege, authority, and naïvety centred on combat experience, prefigured some of the concerns and problems of poetry by veterans. Like some of the poetry that was to follow, testimonies revealed the horror of war, the sense of betrayal and trauma both in Vietnam and back home, and the need to remember the past for a better future. As John Kerry concluded in his 'Testimony to Congress':

in thirty years from now when our brothers go down the street . . . without an arm, or a face, and small boys ask why, we will be able to say 'Vietnam' and not mean a desert, not a filthy obscene memory, but mean instead the place where America finally turned and where soldiers like us helped in the turning.⁶

More than twenty years after the end of the conflict, and America's effective recuperation of the war and its veterans in popular cultural memory, Kerry's hopes sound doubly naïve and ironic.

The rehabilitation of the Vietnam veteran, the transformation from baby killer and national scapegoat to neglected veteran and

⁵ It is important to remember that VVAW was not a monolithic organization, but almost an anarchic conglomeration of individuals and local chapters. It offered a broad range of viewpoints and sophistication of analysis, and certain elements within VVAW did question some of the assumptions underlying the war.
⁶ John Kerry, 'Testimony to Congress', in Barry (ed.), *Peace is Our Profession*, 157.

war hero, was initiated in the 1980s with the dedication of the Vietnam Memorial in Washington in 1982 and the Welcome Home parade in New York on 7 May 1985. Both events stressed the need for healing and reconciliation, conceding that the war had been an honest error, and the soldiers who fought in it were blameless. This process, as Walter Höbling notes, was a problematic one, since 'there is a tendency, in rehabilitating the Vietnam veterans, to present the war itself in a more positive light.... There is a great temptation to confuse means and ends, and to sanction the Vietnam War by doing justice to those who had to fight it.'[7] Healing and reconciliation involved a concurrent obliteration of uncomfortable and nationally unacceptable memories and histories. As W. D. Ehrhart stated in a Vietnam Veteran Writers Symposium,

> I've been hearing the terms healing and reconciliation for, I don't know, fifteen years. And ... by healing they mean, stop disturbing us by talking about this, stop giving us nightmares. We thought that the nightmares had stopped when the war ended. By reconciliation, do they mean that I'm supposed to embrace Henry Kissinger or Robert McNamara?[8]

Ehrhart's rhetorical question highlights the problems of a bland, unquestioning 'healing' process, and some of the veteran poetry I discuss disrupts this politically desired project.

The sombre, black granite Vietnam Memorial similarly encodes ideas of catharsis and healing. The roll call of the engraved dead, the lack of any triumphant upward thrust (in a city commemorating other glorious events and persons), is seen as a salutary reminder of the folly of Vietnam. Yet the Wall says nothing about the whys and wherefores of the war, it raises no questions about what happened in Vietnam to the Vietnamese, it seeks to erase particular historical detail in exchange for an existential, therapeutic experience. In that sense the Memorial serves the traditional purpose of all such memorials, reaffirming the valuable sacrifices of the soldier. The Memorial then becomes 'a sign of national expiation'. 'The Vietnam War is normalized in

---

[7] Walter Höbling, 'Literary Sense-Making: American Vietnam Fiction', in Jeffrey Walsh and James Aulich (eds.), *Vietnam Images: War and Representation* (Basingstoke and London: The Macmillan Press Ltd., 1989), 135.
[8] Cited in Robert M. Slabey (ed.), *The United States and Vietnam from War to Peace: Papers from an Interdisciplinary Conference on Reconciliation* (Jefferson, NC, and London: McFarland & Company Inc., Publishers, 1996), 226.

terms consistent with American political ideology, the deaths are made rational, and the veterans are whole again, stronger for their expiated guilt.'[9] Harry Haines's comment is apposite within the larger context of cultural amnesia and rewriting of the war to fit in with a notional democratic pluralism where errors are acknowledged and reparations made to the 'victims' of Vietnam, the veterans. This kind of all-encompassing pluralism, as Fredric Jameson points out, is dubious: 'Pluralism is one thing when it stands for the coexistence of methods and interpretations in the intellectual and academic marketplace, but quite another when it is taken as a proposition about the infinity of possible meanings and methods and their ultimate equivalence with and substitutability for one another.'[10] This is arguably a ubiquitous condition, but exacerbated in the context of Vietnam where disembodied facts are bandied about without any moral discrimination, and any set of facts can be counterbalanced by another. One person's fact is another's fiction, and the war and its aftermath can be mired in post-modern ambiguity and free-play of meaning. The best of the veteran poets, while asserting personal perceptions of the war, are wary of participating in a morally indiscriminate pluralism. They are aware of particular and undeniable historical and political facts, their own complicity in types of morally reprehensible actions, and they attempt to inscribe what has been and is being steadily edited from public memory and history. For the sake of clarity and organization I will discuss veteran poetry under three broad categories: the poetry of combat experience, conveying the immediacy of war and the need to witness the horror; the aftermath poems reflecting the sense of exile, mourning, trauma, and betrayal; and more recent poetry which gestures towards healing, comprehension, and solidarity with the former enemy. By and large, veteran poetry is one of anger and protest, personal anguish, pain, and terrible memory. It hopes that hard-earned witness and knowledge will not be lost upon the nation that sent them to war. Before considering this large and varied body of poetry, it seems worthwhile and necessary to dwell briefly on some pro-war poems. Vietnam aroused

[9] Harry Haines, 'Disputing the Wreckage: Ideological Struggle at the Vietnam Veterans Memorial', *Vietnam Generation*, 1: 1, (Winter 1989), 141–56.

[10] Fredric Jameson, *The Political Unconscious* (London: Methuen & Co. Ltd., 1987), 31.

strong and often vehement opposition, both in the activist and poetic sphere (the latter is manifest in the large body of stateside poetry), and it is the anti-war voice that is almost always privileged. While this study is party to that privileging, pro-war poetry provides us with a counterpoint to the anger of the anti-war poet. More vitally, it indicates the extent to which dominant ideological positions on the war were internalized by those fighting it, and this manifests itself as a loss of innocence trope in some protest poetry by veterans.

The *Pacific Stars and Stripes* published a collection of poems by soldiers in Vietnam titled *Boondock Bards*. Forest Kimler, the editor and compiler, provides an insight into the genesis of the collection, and the rationale behind it:

Pacific Stars and Stripes began a BOONDOCK BARDS column composed of these poems on November 5, 1965, and since then the newspaper has run 3,000 or more. Almost from the first printing of the poems in the Vietnam/Thailand daily edition of the paper, there were requests for *Pacific Stars and Stripes* to publish a collection of the GI verse in book form. A Vietnam-based officer wrote that such a project was a 'must' since 'the poems convey an unusual insight into the thoughts and attitudes of men of all ranks engaged in this war.'[11]

In a further piece of self-adulatory publicity the same page has a 'Comment' section, with the opinions of combat soldiers. For instance, Airman E.J., USAF, wrote: 'These poems really communicate. They tell it like it is. . . .' and Pvt. J.B.K., US Marines, 'Please put my mother down for a copy (address enclosed) so she can really understand the Vietnam War.'[12] The poems are primarily doggerel, and they detail the need to fight for freedom and democracy. American ideals and stated mission are accepted without question. PFC Thomas W. Piper's 'Why Am I Here?' states an unambiguous sense of righteous mission:

> Here I am so far from home,
> Here I am where the hostiles roam;
> I'm here to fight for freedom
> That lies so close at hand.
> To end the sadness and grief
> War brings to every man;

---

[11] Forest L. Kimler (compiler and ed.), *Boondock Bards* (APO San Francisco 96503: *Pacific Stars and Stripes*, 1968), no page number indicated. Subsequent references are indicated as *Bards* after the quotation.   [12] Ibid.

> To help conquer a common foe to people everywhere,
> A foe that threatens the happiness all people should share.
> To end a war that should not have started . . .
>
> *(Bards, 2–3)*

While expressing absolute resolve, the poem sees war as a necessary means to achieve peace. The line 'To end a war that should not have started' is a continuation of this idea, but it also offers a paradoxical, if unconscious, insight into the contradictions of the American involvement. Without American intervention and support for the sabotaging of the 1954 Geneva Accord, there might have been no war, at least not on the scale waged by US forces. PFC Piper is oblivious of this dimension; in his frame of reference the war started because of communist greed and it was his job to snuff it out.

The rallying call for freedom was often combined with a diatribe against protesters back home, as in PFC Pilarsky Harley's 'The Soldier's Call':

> Freedom, Freedom is the soldier's cry.
> We cherish it, we love it—
> And for it we may die.
>
> Show no pity on the draft-card burners back home
> For they are the unloyal
> That threaten the land we own.
>
> *(Bards, 3)*

It is interesting that PFC Pilarsky is aware of the influence of the protest movement and sees them as traitors. He also expresses absolute support for President Johnson who was responsible for the massive influx of US troops in 1965 (the year in which *Pacific Stars and Stripes* started the *Boondock Bards* column):

> LBJ carries the burden
> Of every nation and race.
> Please support him; he is doing his best.
>
> *(Bards, 3)*

This is the official rhetoric of the 'free world' and its burdens, the idea of manifest destiny on the move, reiterated in a soldier's verse. The combination of patriotism and hatred for one's dissenting countrymen is a theme often repeated in *Boondock*

Bards. SP4 Donald R. Sack, in 'To My Wife Lynne', worries about his wife in a country overrun by hippies and draft-dodgers. He offers these un-American specimens a choice:

> If they think our country is so unfair,
> Send them to China and see how they like it there.
> I'm an American and glad that I am.
> I'm doing my part for Uncle Sam....
>
> (*Bards*, 82)

While love of one's country is comprehensible, Sack displays and mirrors the official and national intolerance of dissent, a designation of China (and communism) in stereotypical terms of un-freedom as compared to the States. Yet the very distaste for opposition gives the lie to the claim of freedom back home being defended abroad. The idea of the USA as global protector of the peace was bolstered by its role in the 'good war', the Second World War. Stephen D. Slipich, in 'A Seabee', makes the usual claims for freedom, and ends with the couplet:

> World War II we won our fame,
> And here in Vietnam we prove the same.
>
> (*Bards*, 34)

A survey of *Boondock Bards* reveals a complex intertwining of national myth and personal belief, a combination of naïvety, bravado, and prejudice. The absolute certainty and clarity of pro-war poetry has a certain unreal and quaint air about it. Most of the poems are stilted and declarative, and Stephen Sossaman, reviewing 'American Poetry From the Indochina Experience', dismisses them completely: 'While the pitiable verse published daily in the Pacific edition of STARS AND STRIPES during the war invariably spoke either of the greatness of defending democracy or the anticipated joys of going home to one's girl knowing that one did his job, that poetry was simply not believable.'[13] Sossaman is right about the 'pitiable verse', but the pro-war sentiment is often suppressed and underestimated in the clamour against the war. From a post-Vietnam point of view, these poems are anachronistic and unpersuasive, but they do express

---

[13] Stephen Sossaman, 'American Poetry From the Indochina Experience', *Long Island Review*, 2 (Winter 1973–4), 30–3.

and retrieve a sentiment often forgotten. They reveal the extent to which the soldiers, especially in the 1965–7 period, believed in their mission, and in that expression of belief lay real feelings. There has been a tendency in post-Vietnam studies of the war to downplay the innocence of early combatants. W. D. Ehrhart, Vietnam veteran, poet, editor, and memoirist, enlisted in the US Marines: 'I believed in my country and its God-given role as leader of the Free World—that it was the finest nation on earth, that its political system and its leaders were essentially good, and that any nation or people who opposed us must be inherently bad.'[14] Although Ehrhart has no pro-war poems, his retrospective awareness of innocence destroyed is an important aspect of his and other veterans' poetry. The actual loss of innocence and betrayal of pristine impulses suffered by many veteran poets was very different from the cultural and societal pretence of a loss of innocence (mentioned in Chapter 1). As Ehrhart wrote, 'Certainly, I as a 17 year-old Marine volunteer did not know anything about my country except the national myths I had been taught, and thus the loss and betrayal are not tropes in poetry, but hard and bitter reality.'[15] The loss of innocence, a sense of betrayal and anger are aspects of some veteran poetry which I discuss in later chapters. The continuing thrall in which national myths hold the individual is evident in some poems published in the 1980s in a journal devoted to veteran poetry, *DEROS*. This was published between December 1981 and September 1987, and although it printed poems of various political persuasions and varying quality, there are a significant number of jingoistic, pro-war poems. If *Boondock Bards* reflected the euphoria and commitment of the early war years, *DEROS* partially reflects the power of national and war myths, particularly in an era of aggressive nationalism under Ronald Reagan.

Robert L. Parker, in 'The Gallant Men', valorizes the Green Berets, immortalized in John Wayne's film of the same name, and symbol of the early pioneering spirit in Vietnam. This spirit was connected with the ideals of compassion and freedom:

---

[14] W. D. Ehrhart, 'Learning the Hard Way', *In the Shadow of Vietnam: Essays, 1977–1991* (Jefferson, NC, and London: McFarland & Company Inc., Publishers, 1991), 47.
[15] W. D. Ehrhart, personal communication, 23 May 1997.

> The enemy they fought, the sick they would treat,
> Compassionate were they, knowing not defeat.
> Their job was tough, to free the oppressed,
> They wanted nothing more, accepting nothing less.[16]

The emphasis here is on a rugged, idealistic individualism that would fight the good fight and extend the frontiers of freedom and civilization. It was an ideal embodied in President Kennedy's exhortation to do what one could for one's country, and the initial enthusiasm was closely tied to his charismatic personality. The Kennedy administration believed that, through counter-insurgency, 'all we were going to have to do was send one of our Green Berets out into the woods to do battle with one of their crack guerrilla fighters and they would fight a clean fight, and the best man would win and they would get together and start curing all villagers of smallpox'.[17] The freedom pioneered by the Green Berets is an apolitical concept and deeply, if unconsciously, desired by the enemy. Such a concept in the early, less bloody and contentious years of the war, is perhaps comprehensible. To see it reiterated by a veteran in 1982 is to be placed within a disturbing time warp, and a reminder of the power of politico-mythic concepts deeply embedded in American history and culture.

The all-encompassing and imminent threat of communism was a primary political motivation for US involvement, and helped to consolidate a domestic consensus. Fred Dougherty's 'Simple Truth' repeats a familiar theme:

> In these times of war and strife
> Let this simple truth ring clear
> If we quit the battles over there
> We may have to fight them over here.
>
> (*DEROS*, 3: 2 (Mar. 1984), 5)

The idea that Vietnam posed any threat to the USA is and was preposterous, but it had a powerful currency in the States. The only way to eliminate the threat was to destroy the enemy, to preserve sanctuaries of freedom at any cost. This involved, as in

---

[16] Robert L. Parker, 'The Gallant Men', *DEROS*, 2: 1 (Dec. 1982), 9. Subsequent references are indicated after the quotation.

[17] John Hellman, *American Myth and the Legacy of Vietnam* (New York: Columbia University Press, 1986), 51–2.

any war, the diabolization of the enemy, and Robert Raulerson's 'Rule of Thumb' sums up a part of this process:

> Any living Asiatic
> May be a Viet Cong
> Any dead Asiatic was definately [sic] a Viet Cong.
> (*DEROS*, 1: 4 (Sept. 1982), 34)

This 'Rule of Thumb' harks back to the Indian killings where the only good Indian was a dead one. As Loren Baritz notes, the Indian massacres informed the language of the war: 'Everyone in Vietnam called dangerous areas Indian country. Paraphrasing a bit of Americana, some GIs painted on their flak jackets THE ONLY GOOD GOOK IS A DEAD ONE. They called their Vietnamese scouts who defected from the Communists Kit Carsons.'[18] Massacres such as My Lai were justified on similar grounds of terror and vengeance, an inability to come to terms with the intractable nature of guerrilla warfare. The Indian parallel also underlines the racist tenor of the war. Vietnam was not the good and clean war conceived by military strategists, and counter-insurgency was not effective in dealing with committed guerrillas. Since the guerrillas mingled with civilians, and they all looked alike to the American soldiers, the safest bet seemed to be to shoot first and ask questions later. Raulerson baldly summarizes the cynicism of military operations, particularly the 'body counts', and there are poems by veterans—Ehrhart's 'Guerrilla War', for example—that offer disturbing insights into the question of genocide.[19]

W. J. Walsh's 'The Veteran' moves from the immediacy of war to its remembrance, in particular, the position of the veteran in a context of national amnesia:

> I am the Veteran!
> Light a candle there for me!
> Remember me eternally!
> I fought for what was good.
> (*DEROS*, 5: 4 (Sept. 1986), 26)

---

[18] Cited in Vince Gotera, *Radical Visions: Poetry by Vietnam Veterans* (Athens, Ga. and London: The University of Georgia Press, 1994), 33.

[19] For an analysis of the Vietnam War as a genocidal one, see Jean-Paul Sartre, 'Vietnam: Imperialism and Genocide', *Between Existentialism and Marxism* (London: Verso, 1983), 67–83.

There is a desire to universalize 'the Veteran', to make connections with veterans of the Second World War, the heroic, acceptable ones. The desire for memorializing was granted at the Vietnam Memorial and the parade in New York, and it is significant that in breaking national silence, the events recuperated the war and its veterans: 'I fought for what was good.' Walsh's poem, along with the others cited from *DEROS*, is indicative of immediate responses and subsequent revisions, in particular poetic responses to Vietnam. The veteran poetry I discuss subsequently lacks the naïve certainty of *DEROS* and *Boondock Bards*, but these two collections provide valuable contexts and subtexts for some of the more sophisticated responses. They represent a bedrock of pro-war sentiment that resurfaced in the 1980s and contributed to the recuperation of Vietnam.

The transition from the *Boondock Bards* and *DEROS* poets to the more mature veteran poetry marks a progression from innocence to experience. This pattern, evident in First World War poetry, is not a simple linear movement towards greater anger, cynicism, maturity, or insight. The responses are often ambiguous, and well-known veteran poets such as Steve Mason often recapitulate dominant ideological positions. The pattern seems clearer in letters and retrospective testimonies. These indicate a broad shift in attitudes towards the war, a movement from euphoria to cynicism, akin to the difference between *Boondock* poets and later veteran poets.

Mark Baker's *Nam: The Vietnam War in the Words of the Men and Women Who Fought There* is a collection of anonymous testimonies dealing primarily with attitudes towards combat and life in Vietnam. Occasionally a veteran reflects on motivations that led to participation: 'I wanted to go to war. . . . It was a manhood test, no question about it. . . . some part of me knew that Vietnam was the event of my generation.'[20] In an ironic sense Vietnam was indeed 'the event of [a] generation', and more, in its reverberations through subsequent generations. The speaker is totally unaware of that irony, and depoliticizes and decontextualizes the war. War is seen, as it traditionally was, as a *rite de passage*, an initiation into the mysteries of manhood. The macho mystique was deliberately played up by the Marines in particular

---

[20] Mark Baker, *Nam: The Vietnam War in the Words of the Men and Women Who Fought There* (London: Abacus, 1981), 27.

(only a Marine was a 'real' man), and the astounding naïvety mirrors the enthusiasm with which hundreds marched off to the First World War. Letters written by soldiers between 1965 and 1967 (occasionally even later) reflect a total absorption in dominant political and cultural myths. Writing on 12 December 1965, PFC Richard E. Marks stated he did not like being in Vietnam, 'but I am doing a job that must be done—I am fighting an inevitable enemy that must be fought—now or later. I am fighting to protect and maintain what I believe in and what I want to live in—a democratic society.'[21] Captain Rodney R. Chastant, passing American graveyards in the Philippines and recalling US graves in other theatres of war, wrote to his brother: 'I was proud to be an American, proud to be a Marine, proud to be fighting in Asia. I have a commitment to the men who have gone before me, American men who made the sacrifices that were required to make the world safe for ice skating, department stores and lamp shades.'[22] Captain Chastant has no doubt that the American way of life is not only worth fighting for, but that the world must be made safe for such a lifestyle (a metaphor, perhaps, for making the 'world safe for democracy'). As the war progressed, however, some soldiers were more sceptical about American war aims, and some expressed admiration for a worthy enemy. Writing on 27 March 1968 (soon after the Tet Offensive), a soldier, Mike, stated:

I'm extremely impressed by almost every report I've heard about the enemy . . . He is a master of guerrilla warfare and is holding his own rather nicely with what should be the strongest military power in the world. But it is mostly his perseverance that amazes me. He works so hard and has been doing so for so long.[23]

This is a remarkable insight about an enemy who was commonly reviled as a communist and a 'gook'. While there were stateside protesters and poets who were often exaggeratedly and naïvely pro-Vietnamese, Mike assesses their military strengths accurately. It is a type of solidarity and mature awareness of the 'other' that manifests itself in veteran poetry many years later.

---

[21] Cited in Bernard Edelman (ed.), *Dear America: Letters Home From Vietnam* (New York and London: W. W. Norton & Company, 1985), 123.
[22] Ibid. 211.
[23] Ibid. 40.

Viet-Nam Veterans Against the War, *Boondock Bards*, *DEROS*, and the letters cited provide different kinds of witness, ranging from the nationalistic to the critical. They express hope, illusions, anxieties, and anger that were emblematic of the times, and were to reverberate through the nation's politics, poetry, and cultural memory. In poetic terms the first detailed, immediate, anguished witnessing of Vietnam was a collection titled *Winning Hearts and Minds*, and Michael Casey's *Obscenities*. Both were published in 1972, the former by a veteran's co-operative, the 1st Casualty Press. Its initial success led to McGraw-Hill reissuing the collection the same year. Casey was awarded the Yale Younger Poets Series title for his collection.

PROLOGUE: WITNESS AND ANGUISH

Winning Hearts and Minds is an uneven collection in which the need to tell the tale and an element of didacticism accompanies the telling, often smothering the verse in angry detail. As W. D. Ehrhart noted in his review on the importance of the collection in 1987: 'Most of the poems in *Winning Hearts and Minds* are carried by raw emotion alone, and most of the soldier-poets were not really poets at all but rather soldiers so hurt and bitter that they could not maintain their silence any longer.'[24] This is true of most of the poems which concentrate on the immediate and occasionally brutal details of the war, and its effect on the soldier's mind. The latter is not fully articulated, since the soldier-poets were too close to the events to write about them with any composure or much insight. The hurt and bitterness that Ehrhart refers to arose out of the trauma of participation in a war, and the often confused sense of horror and betrayal at what they actually witnessed on the battleground. The chasm between innocent expectation and political mythology on the one hand, and the actual horrible details of war, on the other, seemed unbridgeable and furthered the desire to tell the 'true' story. The poems in this collection are fine examples of a deep, almost pathological desire to bear witness, a desire reflected in later veteran poetry as well. This phenomenon is not unique to the Vietnam War. Evelyn

---

[24] W. D. Ehrhart, 'Soldier-Poets of the Vietnam War', *The Virginia Quarterly Review*, 63: 2 (Spring 1987), 246–65.

Cobley notes a similar imperative in First World War narratives: 'The main impulse of those who had witnessed the First World War was to set the record straight, to tell it as it had been. The suspicion of First World War writers was that official accounts distorted what the soldiers knew to have happened.'[25] If this was a suspicion in the First World War, the almost absolute incongruity between reality and report in Vietnam was a shocking truth. Michael Herr writes about the soldier's need for truthful witness: 'And always, they [the grunts] would ask you with an emotion whose intensity would shock you to please tell it, because they really did have the feeling that it wasn't being told for them, that they were going through all of this and that somehow no one back in the World knew about it.'[26] Early poetry by soldier-poets dwelt obsessively on detail, as if by capturing external realities they would be able to reverse the absurd world of hyper-reality created by the military and the government. Implicit in this agenda and in Cobley's comments on First World War narratives, is the idea that first-hand soldier narratives are repositories of truth, 'they tell it as it had been'. The privileging of veteran accounts tends to ignore contingent factors such as individual bias, politics, and perception that shape those accounts as any other. This is not to imply a free-play of meaning but an awareness of contingency is necessary. The witness of the veteran poet is valuable and moving but it is not beyond history, a factor sometimes overlooked in analysis of the poetry.

W. D. Ehrhart's 'Fragment: 5 September 1967' is precisely that: a fragment of the reality of war:

> We lay in mud, struggling
> While the waves of death broke over us,
> Swallowed us,
> And cast us loose on a sea of madness.
>
> Eighteen—
> And the blood felt like tears
> On the blade of my bayonet;
>
> And youthful dreams lay dead
> Amid spent cartridges and broken bodies
> Littering the earth.

[25] Evelyn Cobley, *Representing War: Form and Ideology in First World War Narratives* (Toronto, Buffalo, and London: University of Toronto Press, 1993), 6.

[26] Michael Herr, *Dispatches* (New York: Alfred A. Knopf, 1978), 206.

After that, there was no innocence;
And there was no future to believe in.²⁷

The poem conveys some of the immediacy of war, but its stilted language gives the poem an archaic quality. There were soldiers in Vietnam holed out in the trenches, particularly during the siege of Khe Sanh, but the image of 'waves of death [breaking] over us' belongs to the Great War, as does the bayonet dripping with blood. This is an important connection evident in Ehrhart's early war poetry ('Christ' has some obvious First World War typology), and one that he acknowledged in a recent interview:

> The main thing that happened in the early writing when I was trying to figure out how to write about the Vietnam War, was the influence of other writers I read—some of Sassoon, but everything of Owen when I was in high school. I knew his work very well. . . . so when I began to write about my war, that was my reference point, that was what war poetry was for me. . . . So, early on, you find me completely missing all the rich imagery of my own war and, instead, inserting images about blood dripping like tears from the blade of a bayonet.²⁸

The appropriation of language is indicative of the immature soldier-poet trying to write his war, and the difficulty of finding one's own language and idiom. Trying to come to grips with the peculiar reality of Vietnam through the language of another war creates the distanced, set-piece quality of the poem. Even this deliberate literariness, however, does not negate themes and emotions that recur in Ehrhart's more mature poems: the loss of innocence, a numbing sense of betrayal and alienation. The last stanza sums up a personal, moral, and political wilderness that Ehrhart inhabited (as did many other veterans) for many years, a sense of exile that still remains. This loss of innocence is, perhaps, paradigmatic of all wars, and the earlier citation from an Ehrhart essay provides an insight into this psychology. An excerpt from a letter he left for his parents on 6 January 1967 (to be opened only

---

²⁷ W. D. Ehrhart, 'Fragment: 5 September 1967', in Larry Rottmann, Jan Barry, Basil T. Paquet (eds.), *Winning Hearts and Minds: War Poems by Vietnam Veterans* (New York and London: McGraw-Hill Book Company, 1972), 33. Subsequent references are indicated as *WHAM* after the quotation.
²⁸ 'A Conversation With W. D. Ehrhart', *War, Literature, & the Arts: W. D. Ehrhart: A Special Issue*, 8: 2 (Fall/Winter 1996), 149–57. Ehrhart also acknowledges the influence of Stephen Crane's writing in the course of this conversation.

after his death) indicates the mindset that was shattered by the war:

> Be proud that I died for my country. I am happy in death for I have been given the chance to die for a cause, the cause of freedom. Whether this war is right or wrong I do not know. But my country is engaged in it and I believe in my country, and so am willing to die for these United States.[29]

This absolute conviction was soon to be replaced by disillusionment—'Fragment' represents the beginning of the process—and followed by an equally strong desire to reform the country and its politics. The messianic zeal and desire to witness are evident in poems I consider later, as they mark a transition towards a quieter, maturer poetic voice.

Basil T. Paquet's 'Morning—A Death' conveys the numbing reality of war from the perspective of a medic. Like Ehrhart's 'Fragment' it inscribes ideal possibilities that are distanced by contemporary experiences:

> I grow so tired of jostled litters
> Filling the racks, and taking off
> Your tags and rings, pulling out
> Your metal throats and washing
> Your spittle down with warm beer at night,
> So tired of tucking you all in,
> And smelling you on me for hours.
> I'd sooner be in New England this winter
> With pine pitch on my hands than your blood,
> Lightly fondling breasts and kissing
> Women's warm mouths than thumping
> Your shattered chests and huffing
> In your broken lips or aluminum windpipes,
> Sooner lift a straying hair from her wet mouth
> Than a tear of elephant grass from your slack lips
> I'd much rather be making children,
> Than tucking so many in.
>
> (*WHAM*, 23)

As a medic, Paquet sees himself as nurturer, protector, and preserver of life. Yet that role has now been subsumed in dull

---

[29] Cited in Ronald Baughman (ed.), *Dictionary of Literary Biography, ix. American Writers of the Vietnam War* (Detroit and London: Gale Research Inc., 1991), 7.

routine, in the mindlessness of mass death which obliterates the individuality of his patients. The death principle, a Freudian thanatos, is contrasted with the life principle embodied in New England nature ('pine pitch') and women, a fulfilling eros. Stephen Sossaman believes that this 'perfunctory ministration to the dying, without desperation and without rage, without fear and without horror, is chilling in its implications of a cauterized humanity'.[30] There is certainly an attempt to desensitize oneself to daily death, but the calm cataloguing of medical duties is deceptive. The recollection of New England, the desire for 'Women's warm mouths', the contrast of sensuality with 'shattered chests' and 'aluminum windpipes', gives the lie to an idea of 'cauterized humanity'. The speaker actively recalls all that is lovely and life-sustaining and this memory is an attempt to negate the numbing nature of his work. New England is projected as a type of pastoral to offset the war which is anti-pastoral. This is an idea available during the First World War where England was seen as an ideal landscape. For instance, Lt. C. C. Carver wrote in a letter to his brother on 27 February 1917 that he always felt that he was 'fighting for England, English fields, lanes, trees, English atmospheres, and good days in England'.[31] Carver's Brookean eulogy is more emphatic than Paquet's evocation of New England, but it is a precursor to a pattern of fond, idealized remembrances of peacetime existence. It is an evocation of an Arcadian archetype that both heightens and ameliorates the horror of war. As Paul Fussell comments in his classic study, *The Great War and Modern Memory*: 'Since war takes place outdoors and always within nature, its symbolic status is that of the ultimate anti-pastoral. In Northrop Frye's terms, it belongs to the demonic world, and no one engages in it or contemplates it without implicitly or explicitly bringing to bear the contrasting "model world" by which its demonism is measured.'[32] Through his sensual, sensitive remembrance of New England Paquet attempts to keep despair at bay, but the poem seems to end in despair and suppressed rage. 'I'd much rather be making children, | Than

---

[30] Sossaman, 'American Poetry From the Indochina Experience', 31.
[31] Cited in Hilda D. Spear, *Remembering We Forget* (London: Davis-Poynter Limited, 1979), 35.
[32] Paul Fussell, *The Great War and Modern Memory* (New York and London: Oxford University Press), 231.

tucking so many in' points not only to the literal youth of US combat soldiers, but to the pointless waste of their lives, and his own death-in-life existence.[33]

Herbert Krohn, a doctor in Military Assistance Command Vietnam (MACV) IV Corps, presents Vietnam in his poem 'Can Tho' as a pastoral idyll, one that totally ignores and eludes the American troops:

> I love the gentle people of this city
> Fragile as birdsong, flexible as rice ...
> I love this race of farmers and musicians
> With a love that no more needs reciprocation
> Than my love for bread and songs. ...
>
> (WHAM, 81)

While Paquet projects New England as a type of pastoral, Krohn perceives a world seldom seen by the American soldier, and often mutilated by his presence. The pastoralizing of Vietnam is a sign of sympathy for the 'other', an implicit condemnation of the war machine, and yet it furthers a stereotype. The 'gentle', 'fragile' people portrayed here were also revolutionaries and freedom fighters, and capable of great sacrifices and barbarities in their quest of political goals. Epithets such as 'gentle', 'fragile', 'flexible' tend to place the people in ahistorical contexts and infantilize them. The sympathy is real, the desire for comprehension is genuine, but the images are opaque: they do not give us a sense of a real, palpable existence. They are frozen within the framework of the poet's perception and desire. This is not surprising given the dominant culture of war and hate, and 'Can Tho' is an important beginning on the road to solidarity. Krohn's style of portraying Vietnamese people and nature finds its apotheosis in John Balaban's poems, discussed in a subsequent chapter.

Serigo, pen-name of Igor Bobrowsky, reverses the impulse to empathy available in Krohn's poem and paradoxically reveals its resurgence in the midst of conflict. In 'I Hate You ...', he presents a stark, radical opposition as if, through sufficient hatred, the involvement in war would seem more justifiable:

---

[33] The average age of US combat personnel in Vietnam was 19 as compared to 27 in the Second World War. Source: *Vietnam Online: The American Experience Website*.

> I hate you
>   with your yellow wrinkled skin—
>   and slanted eyes,
>   your toothless grins . . .
>   Always when the time is wrong;
>   while friends are moaning
>   through tight-clenched teeth
>   and bitter eyes . . .
>   (WHAM, 86)

The actuality of hatred (rather than brittle solidarity), racial stereotyping, and a sense of bonding created by the death of friends, actualize the conditions of combat. The need to hate, to construct the 'other' as enemy was a process ably directed by the political and military establishment, and constituted a basic mode of sustaining the war. Yet this hate has a curious backwash, a subtext deeper than the mere 'gook syndrome' where all Vietnamese were characterized as subhuman slime. It is an expression of submerged guilt, similar to that expressed by a veteran in Mark Baker's *Nam*: 'I began to hate them, because I couldn't stand the idea that we were coming into these people's lives and totally disrupting them.'[34] The mesmeric intonation of 'I hate you', with which every section begins, is a sort of ritual incantation to exorcize the guilt and justify the involvement. Also, paradoxically, the transparency of the opposition indicates a desire to reach out to the 'other', move beyond the parameters of stereotyped hate. The poem ends with despairing awareness that if the 'other' responded as an enemy ought, was indeed a diabolical presence, it would make the war easier to fight:

> Why
>   do you not respond,
>   resist or fight?
>   It would make hating you
>   so very much easier . . .
>   (WHAM, 86)

Herbert Marcuse's idea that language creates the enemy not 'as he really is but rather as he must be in order to perform his function for the Establishment', is borne out by the manner in

---

[34] Baker, *Nam*, 144.

which the poet attempts to maintain, and simultaneously realizes the futility of maintaining, the oppositional framework.[35] The reasons for hatred are clichéd and, by revealing the desperate construction of that hatred, Serigo articulates the futile basis of the Vietnam conflict.

Winning Hearts and Minds in its title and poetry questioned the US involvement in Vietnam. It was published not only to voice private anger, anguish, and disillusionment, but was activist in its editorial exhortation that the poems should be read aloud and passed around. The money from the McGraw-Hill edition was channelled to a Quaker relief fund for Vietnamese civilian casualties of the war. The collection is valuable in that it serves as a prologue to the body of poetry that follows. Its poems adumbrate themes that are repeated and refined by later veteran poets. These range from delineating the immediacy of war to the complexity of hate, from the trauma of memory to the desire for solidarity with one's former enemy. The poems in *Winning Hearts* are of varying quality, but the best of them give 'voice', as Stephen Spender wrote in a review of the collection, 'to a particular infinite agony packed into a transitional moment'.[36] It was, for many veterans, an 'infinite agony', a lifetime of traumatic memories, that arose from a 'transitional moment' of combat. It is to this poetic rendition of combat that I will now turn.

---

[35] Herbert Marcuse, *An Essay on Liberation* (London: Allen Lane The Penguin Press, 1969), 74.
[36] Stephen Spender, 'Poetry of the Unspeakable', *New York Review of Books*, 20: 1 (8 Feb. 1973), 3–6.

4
Veteran Poetry
Combat Experience—The Actuality and the Need to Bear Witness

Combat training, even in the élite Marine Corps, did not (could not?) prepare soldiers for the reality of death, and initial poetic responses dwelt on the fact in minute detail. The close proximity to arbitrary and immediate annihilation or grave injury heightened one's sense of mortality and, according to some veterans, provided an adrenalin rush and excitement, that made life after war seem pallid and boring. William Broyles Jr. served as a Marine in 1969 and 1970, and his article, 'Why Men Love War', attempts to explain its allure:

Part of the love of war stems from its being an experience of great intensity; its lure is the fundamental human passion to witness, to see things, what the Bible calls the lust of the eye and the Marines in Vietnam called eye fucking. War stops time, intensifies experience to the point of a terrible ecstasy. . . . if you come back whole you bring with you the knowledge that you have explored regions of your soul that in most men will remain uncharted.[1]

Broyles's article is disturbing not only because he avers that men love war (undoubtedly some do, as is evident from poems and statements nostalgic about combat in Vietnam), but because he valorizes and essentializes that love, implying that it is human nature to love war. He attempts to convey the palpable excitement and glamour of war, a project not dissimilar from that of the journalist Michael Herr's *Dispatches*. Herr turns Vietnam into a rock-'n'-roll war, fought by wired-up, tripped-out, angst-ridden American teenagers. The Vietnamese are almost totally absent from his macho bonding with these children of destruction and

---

[1] William J. Broyles Jr., 'Why Men Love War', in Walter Capps (ed.), *The Vietnam Reader* (New York and London: Routledge, 1990), 71–2.

existential ennui.² Most of the sensitive veteran poetry on this subject is less excited by the prospect of war and death.

Jack Kelley, a Marine, presents a numb sense of dislocation and horror in the poem 'Flak Jacket'. The first two sections emphasize the terrible reality of a 'first kill'.³ The term 'first kill' makes war out to be a barbaric hunt, and the hunter is obsessed with his prey. The reality of war death is contrasted with the rituals of death in civilian life, the ceremonies of death that dignify it, 'some powdered floral bouquet | of a stiff viewed contemptuously' ('Flak Jacket', 29). There is no dignity in war death (a theme emphasized by several poets, most effectively in Michael Casey's 'On Death'), and the collocation of life ebbing away with a life-affirming symbol—'his intestines like a bridal train'—reiterates the shocking nature of war. Having described the 'first real dead man', the next three sections dwell on 'the killer['s]' worries about his own safety. Death has indeed heightened his sense of mortality, but it provides no adrenalin rush, no insight into unexplored regions of his soul. Instead, he desires protection in techno-terms, 'a thick molybdenum chest, | titanium arms and legs, . . .' ('Flak Jacket', 29). This vulnerability is ironic in the context of America's immense technological superiority, but it is a recurring theme comprehensible in the context of the foot-soldier, the 'grunt' who felt exposed to varied dangers. The enemy was more at home in the jungle and, paradoxically, his death heightens the insecurity of 'the killer'. It is significant that the soldier is addressed through the poem as 'the killer': an actual designation, rather than the socially sanctioned heroic connotations that the word 'soldier' has. 'The killer' turns to nature for protection, but is forced to face up to the consequences of his deed in the last section. There is no escape from the reality and the thought of death which 'the killer' internalizes. The soldier as

---

² For an analysis of problems in Herr's portrayal of the war, see Philip Melling, *Vietnam in American Literature* (Boston: Twayne Publishers, 1990), 70–82. Melling writes: 'As a cultural text *Dispatches* is agoraphobic. The only spaces that excite the narrator are the ones inhabited by Westerners and, in particular, by the "radical, wigged-out" crazies of Vietnam, the grunts and the correspondents that the narrator describes as "authentic subculture"'(82). For a journalist's account more sensitive to the effect of US policies on Vietnamese lives, see Jonathan Schell, *The Village of Ben Suc* (London: Jonathan Cape, 1968).

³ Jack Kelley, 'Flak Jacket', in Barbara Menghini Frohman (ed.), *Incoming: Poems by Vietnam Veterans* (Islip, NY: Island Poets, 1993), 29. Subsequent references are indicated after the quotation.

killer returns home to 'the attic of his | mind' ('Flak Jacket', 29), an isolate from the rest of society, whose taboo against killing he has violated in participating in the socially sanctioned act of war. This is a warp, a contradiction that all veterans face, but a particular problem for Vietnam veterans, who returned as pariahs rather than war heroes. This marked the beginning of a process of alienation that Robert Jay Lifton outlines: 'Sent as intruders in an Asian revolution, asked to fight a filthy and unfathomable war, they return[ed] as intruders in their own society, defiled by that war in the eyes of the very people who sent them as well as in their own.'[4] Alienation and exile are powerful realities articulated in many poems by veterans and remain a fact of existence for some despite the cultural rehabilitation of the veteran.

David Connolly, who fought as an infantryman with the 11th Armored Cavalry Regiment, chronicles the life of a 'grunt' with accuracy, a dry humour, and a relentless awareness of the pointless horror of war. For instance, in a prose poem 'Incident Near Ap Bac Ba Ria', included in his poetry collection *Lost in America*, Connolly describes a 'sweep':

I hated sweeps. The name implies swift movement, armor charging across an open plain. In Vietnam, it more often meant sneaking fearfully through the daylight darkness of the jungle, a soaking, leech-filled trek through the breathless oven of a mangrove swamp, or a ball-breaking, inching climb, sometimes under fire, up the side of a mountain.[5]

The incongruity between the word and the actuality harks back to the idea that Vietnam, the war itself, was a betrayal of expectation. For a generation raised on the stories of the Second World War, the films of John Wayne, and the charisma of John F. Kennedy, Vietnam came as a cruel disappointment. The landscape itself seemed hostile, something evil that provided refuge to the Vietcong, and had to be destroyed. Large-scale defoliation was justified on these grounds and in this context, heroism and the love of war were redundant. Connolly's 'After the Firefight'

---

[4] Robert Jay Lifton, *Home From the War: Vietnam Veterans, Neither Victims Nor Executioners* (London: Wildwood House, 1974), 100.

[5] David Connolly, *Lost in America* (Woodbridge, Conn.: Viet Nam Generation Inc. & Burning Cities Press, 1994), 28. Subsequent references are indicated after the quotation. Larry Heinemann refers to 'the wretched soul-deadening dread, the grueling, *grinding* shitwork of being a grunt' (*Paco's Story* (London and Boston: Faber and Faber, 1986), 73).

portrays the aftermath of a fight in a more sombre light than Broyles might have:

> Afterwards, with the gunfire
> still ringing loudly in our ears,
> but not so loudly
> that it drowned out the screams.
> And afterwards,
> still blinded by the tracers' flashes,
> but not blinded enough
> by the pumping or sucking or gaping wounds;
> we'd come to our senses,
> what senses were left.
>
> When the rush of adrenaline,
> and the haste to stop the life
> from spilling out of a Brother,
> and the hesitancy to touch
> what was human,
> was over,
> we'd strut and brag and bluster
> for each other.
> Later, we would weep,
> separately,
> for the little
> that was left of us.
> Much later
> we would weep together,
> when it appeared
> there would be nothing left.
>
> (*Lost in America*, 11)

Connolly acknowledges the adrenalin rush Broyles mentions, but he does so in a context of wounds, death, and horror. It is the aftermath that is the centre of the poem, the disturbing supra-awareness with which the combatant is left, that leaves no room for ameliorative thoughts. If one were 'blind enough', then one could be saved from the perpetual agony of life after the war. The movement from bluster and bragging to weeping is a transition from what the soldier was trained to be (masculine, manly with its connotations of not showing emotion, of male bonding that Marine training inculcated) to a more vulnerable, feminine awareness of feeling and loss. The terms 'masculine' and 'feminine' function here as stereotypical gender differentials, and the cult of super-masculinity promoted by the armed forces, the 'bogus manhood, the "tough guy" mythos of the warrior cult', are deconstructed by Connolly.[6] Chaim Shatan goes on to write that militarized mourning is a denial of grief. Connolly, however, presents an individual and collective acceptance and immersion in grief: 'Much later, | we would weep together.' This 'much later' is transformed into a perpetual now as the memories of war do not fade. At the end of the battle there is 'nothing left' except the awareness that one has lost everything; the long, lonely nightmare of life after war has just begun. W. D. Ehrhart, reviewing Connolly's poetry, writes that the poet 'is peerless at bringing to life the ruthless drudgery of battle'.[7] The portraits are moving and disturbing precisely because grief and perpetual loss are part of that 'ruthless drudgery of battle'.

Bryan Alec Floyd was a Marine during the Vietnam era, stationed at Quantico, Virginia, as the chaplain's assistant. Since there was no chaplain, returning and decommissioned Marines often turned to him for solace and told him their tales. Thus, although he has no first-hand experience of combat, he represents a unique voice in Vietnam poetry, a witness to, and narrator of, war from a very different perspective. His collection, *The Long War Dead*, is subtitled 'An Epiphany Ist Platoon, USMC', and the poems are all named after specific people. The specificity gives the sense of a roll call, of individual stories recollected in anguish. This is part of the artifice since Floyd has translated and transcribed their stories into his poems. That is not to imply that he misrepresents the veterans' stories, only that he fashions them into a particular collection of poems.

Floyd is deeply sceptical about US air power. In 'Sergeant Brandon Just, U.S.M.C.', he portrays the horror and agony of indiscriminate violence, particularly that visited on children:

> He was alive with death:
> Her name was Sung
> and she was six years old.

[6] Chaim F. Shatan, 'Happiness is a Warm Gun: Militarized Mourning and Ceremonial Vengeance: Towards a Psychological Theory of Combat and Manhood in America, Part III', in Jacqueline Lawson (ed.), *Vietnam Generation*, special issue: *Gender and the War: Men, Women, and Vietnam*, 1: 3–4 (Summer–Fall 1989), 127–51.
[7] W. D. Ehrhart, '"What Grace Is Found In So Much Loss?"' *Virginia Quarterly Review*, 73: 1 (Winter 1997), 99–111.

> By slightest mistake of degrees
> on an artillery azimuth,
> he had called for rockets and napalm.
> Their wild wizardry of firepower
> expired her mistake of a village,
> killing everyone except her,
> and napalm made her look
> like she was dead among the dead[8]

He implicitly condemns this brutality without adopting a hysterical or binary tone. Sergeant Just is a figure of sympathy, tortured by his act of calling for air support. 'He was alive with death' conjoins the idea of being alive as a result of killing others, and aware of the constant presence of death, a type of death-in-life existence. The correlation between 'mistake' and death is a devastating one, and it is one that haunts the child and the Sergeant through the poem. Except that the child is innocent, and it is this innocence that sears Just's soul:

> And as he would come in,
> Sung would hobble up to him
> in her therapeutic cart,
> smiling even when she did not smile, lipless,
> her chin melted to her chest
> that would never become breasts.
> He would stand
> and wait for her touch upon his hand
> with her burn-splayed fingers
> that came to lay a fire upon his flesh.
>
> (*Long War Dead*, 14)

Napalm returns to haunt Sergeant Just, 'lay a fire upon his flesh'. The horror of the 'mistake' is constantly reiterated in the body of the child left to live a pointless existence. Her touch, actual physical and psychological contact, was something that a pilot was spared. Fighting a technologized war allowed for convenient distancing, as Jon Floyd, a Marine Corps pilot, testified at the Winter Soldier Investigation: 'Sometimes you get shot down, but you don't see any of the explosions. You look back and see 'em,

---

[8] Bryan Alec Floyd, 'Sergeant Brandon Just, U.S.M.C.', *The Long War Dead: An Epiphany Ist Platoon USMC* (Sag Harbor, NY: The Permanent Press, 1976), 13. Subsequent references are indicated after the quotation.

but you don't see any of the blood or any of the flesh. It's a very clean and impersonal war.'⁹ This detachment allowed for killing without conscience, but as an infantry officer responsible for an air attack this is not true for Sergeant Just. He must live with his deeds just as Sung lives with its consequences:

> Sung was child-happy
> that he came and cared,
> and when he would start to leave,
> she would agonize her words
> out of the hollow that was her mouth.
> Her tongue, bitten in two while she had burned,
> strafing his ears,
> saying without mercy,
> I love you.
>
> (*Long War Dead*, 15)

Sergeant Just is a tortured, sympathetic figure, yet Floyd never allows the tone to meander into sentimentality. As representative of an invasive power, Just is responsible for the annihilation of a village, and the particularization of Sung's predicament highlights the peculiarly human and touching aspect of life being wiped out by US jets. As a child Sung bears no grudge, can barely comprehend her state, and her love for Just completes the merciless circle of responsibility and memory that he must live with. The lack of a binary consciousness gives the poem a complex and sad dimension missing in many articulations of war atrocities by stateside poets. As a Marine in the Vietnam era and a non-combatant privy to combatant confessions, Floyd was both an insider and observer, and these viewpoints coalesce in his poems.

While Floyd dwells on the effects of bombing, Walter McDonald's 'Caliban in Blue' conveys the disturbing pathology of air combat from a pilot's perspective. The pilot and his craft are fused in a kind of sexualized power-bonding:

> For this, I trained to salivate
> and tingle, target-diving,
> hand enfolding hard throttle
> in solitary masculine delight.[10]

---

[9] Cited in Lifton, *Home From the War*, 348.
[10] Walter McDonald, 'Caliban in Blue', *Caliban In Blue* (Lubbock, Tex.: Texas Tech Press, 1976), 11. Subsequent references are indicated after the quotation.

McDonald, who served briefly as an Air Force pilot in Vietnam, portrays the thrill of combat in a masturbatory image that encapsulates an infantile, particularly masculine urge to power and control. The connection between war and sex is, as William Broyles points out, another disturbing reason why men love war: 'The love of war stems from the union, deep in the core of our being, between sex and destruction, beauty and horror, love and death . . . It is, for men, at some terrible level, the closest thing to what childbirth is for women: the initiation into the power of life and death.'[11] It is this 'initiation into the power of life and death' that McDonald's pilot is thrilled by, an initiation that probably allowed and abetted the techno-war in the sky. A total of 8,000,000 tonnes of bombs were dropped over Vietnam (north and south), Cambodia, and Laos primarily to 'pacify' the south Vietnamese and destroy the northern insurrection. American air superiority was overwhelming in its presence and destructive capacity, signifying the arrogant domination that the USA desired. Paradoxically, it did not affect the north Vietnamese war effort in any significant manner, as the efficacy of the Ho Chi Minh trail and underground bunkers proved. McDonald dwells on the psychology of power that believes it is invincible:

> Focused on cross hairs,
> eyes glazing, hand triggers switches in
> pulsing orgasm,
> savage release;
> pull out
> and off we go again
> thrusting deep
> into the martial lascivious blue
> of uncle's sky.
>
> (*Caliban in Blue*, 11)

The collocation of flying and sexual, masturbatory images continue re-emphasizing the paradoxical power–insecurity framework. The Caliban paradigm provides a context of domination and colonization. Quite clearly the skies are colonized by US air power, but the individual colonizer, the pilot, is a type of Caliban, slave to his techno-sexual urges and desires. The aircraft and what it represents have a complete hold over the individual, just

---

[11] Broyles, 'Why Men Love War', 74.

as the hierarchy of the Air Force would reinforce the control of the state over the pilot. The Caliban-pilot has internalized the destructive and insecure urges of his masters, and is now imposing destruction on nameless others. 'Uncle's sky' is deliberately ambiguous: most obviously it is the USA—Uncle Sam's territory that nurtures the pilots; it could also refer to north Vietnam—Uncle Ho's territory that faced the wrath of Uncle Sam's minions. Broyles's linking of the terrible reality of war with childbirth attempts to imbue war with a regenerative halo, as if war were an equally fulfilling experience. McDonald's poem conveys the excitement of flying, but it does so in contexts and images that underline its destructive, sterile, and pathological nature.

Richard E. Baker's 'Hoedown' marks a return to the war on the ground fought by 'grunts' and explores the meaning of life in that environment:

> The bodies hang on barbed wire like slum laundry
> and Homer, (who is not quite so blind as is said)
> sails by our bunker singing another lie. Soon,
> he is accompanied by the bodies which dance
> in the wind and play the concertina wire
> with a fineness only the dead possess.
>
> Soon, we too are taken with a need to dance
> and our canvas boots slap about the bunker.
>
> Meanwhile, Homer, now a giant fly, plucks
> out the eyes of the band. But we do not notice
> as we are too far into the rhythm of killing.
> All too soon, wind blows through the empty skulls
> and makes a lullaby as we dance to that weird siren.[12]

The poem mediates effortlessly between the real—'The bodies hang on barbed wire like slum laundry'—and the hallucinatory aspects of the war—Homer flitting about, 'singing another lie'. 'The bodies hang[ing] on barbed wire' refer to a fairly common and grisly occurrence during the war. Most American bases, terrified of Vietcong incursions, were fortresses ringed by concertina wire. Vietcong volunteers would often attempt to sneak in at night, their bodies greased and virtually naked to make the passage easier. If discovered, they were sitting targets and were

---

[12] Richard E. Baker, 'Hoedown', *Shellburst Pond* (Tacoma, Wash.: Vardaman Press, 1982), 25.

'wasted' (to use GI terminology). Homer is seen here as an archetypal writer, the poet of war stories in antiquity, fuelling the grand myths of war. That he 'is not quite as blind as is said' could be an indication either of his perspicacity, or, as the next line suggests, his duplicity; he sings about war knowing better. The presence of Homer could be a self-referential one: outlining the role of the poet in his attempt to delineate the war, the need to tell the tale. If this is so, the poet and the dead are conjoined in a grotesque dance, accompanied by the music of 'the concertina wire'. The perimeter fence was supposed to demarcate lines between 'inside' and 'outside', safety and danger, us and them, but here the distinctions are blurred. The facts of war and death transgress artificial boundaries, and Homer's violence—'plucks | out the eyes of the band'—implicates poet and soldier in his later incarnation as soldier-poet. The poem is a surrealistic meditation on 'the rhythm of killing', as if that rhythm were a drug-induced hallucination: frightening and beautiful at the same time. The lullaby at the end, 'as we dance to that weird siren', is a type of lyrical madness. The 'siren' could be an echo of the Sirens in *The Odyssey* that Odysseus and his men were warned against. Odysseus, tied to the mast, heard the forbidden Sirens and the soldiers in Vietnam have done so too, except that theirs is a music of despair; they are not restrained, and they have no home to return to. Their 'empty skulls' are at one with the ones hanging on the barbed wire (the two are interchangeable) and they have to live with the song of the 'weird siren' for the rest of their lives. They may not feel the adrenalin rush that Broyles writes about, but their souls have indeed been transformed by the war.

'Hoedown' moves beyond the physical description of combat, to the ambiguity of war, a feature evident in Yusef Komunyakaa's poetry. Komunyakaa, as Steven Cramer notes, 'fires off present tense communiqués directly from the front'.[13] These dispatches, however, are meditations on combat, not merely descriptions of war, although they begin and are rooted in the physical aspects of battle. 'Maps Drawn in the Dust' represents the radical 'otherness' of the combat landscape in Vietnam:

> We went into the bush
> young men, pushing

---

[13] Steven Cramer, 'Facts and Figures', *Poetry*, 156: 2 (May 1990), 100–15.

> silhouettes of trees
> ahead of us like shields,
> thinking we were moving
> with cat feet. No one could tell us
> we didn't have what it takes:
> superior firepower & artificial
> illumination, search & destroy
> missions down to a science.[14]

The image of soldiers 'pushing | silhouettes of trees | ahead of us like shields' is reminiscent of Birnam Wood moving to Dunsinane in Shakespeare's *Macbeth*. Whereas in *Macbeth* the illusion worked as a military strategy, in Vietnam the combatants are snared into a false sense of protection and power. This was a shadowy war with an elusive enemy, very different from the Second World War, where most of the theatres of war had demarcated fronts. The paradox of 'superior firepower' in a guerrilla war was that it did not make a difference. Technology was at a loss when confronted by the tactics of the guerrilla warrior. As a Mrs Ba, who was in charge of Vietcong infrastructure and lived underground for five years, told Tim O'Brien after the war: 'You had the daylight, but I had the earth.'[15] The idea of US soldiers as an alien presence in a hostile landscape is a common theme in Komunyakaa's poems, and outlined in section II:

> But in the green confusion
> ten steps were a mile.
> We studied the ground
> till black vines & spiderwebs
> grew into tripwires. . . .
>
> ('Maps Drawn', 13)

Nature seems to conspire to defeat the American enterprise. Although the delineation of combat conditions is superb, there are stereotypes inherent in the description: the Vietcong are a shadowy absent presence, the landscape is menacing (which was true, but used to justify large-scale defoliation), and the poem

---

[14] Yusef Komunyakaa, 'Maps Drawn in the Dust', *Colorado Review*, NS 15: 1 (Spring–Summer 1988), 13. Subsequent references are indicated after the quotation.
[15] Cited in Tim O'Brien, 'The Vietnam in Me', *New York Times Magazine* (Oct. 1994), 48–57.

remains self-obsessive. Despite the accuracy of the description, we are aware of the contingency of one point of view and the underlying justification for indiscriminate violence. This justification coexists with an implicit questioning of America's presence:

> We weaved in & out of
> brain fog & effusion,
>
> back to places & people
> that followed maps in the dust—
> sleepwalkers moving toward
> some forgotten outpost;
> apparitions we couldn't set free
> & remain alive ourselves. We were
> no longer young,
> no longer innocent:
> with the circle now complete,
> we were wired to our trigger fingers.
>
> ('Maps Drawn', 13)

Komunyakaa transcribes the classic cycle of vulnerability and paranoia, fear and guilt available in an earlier history of genocide. Richard Slotkin in his study of the Indian massacres notes a particular pathology of violence that emphasizes certain cultural-mythic continuities:

Their sense of guilt for the deaths of the comrades and the victimization they have come to avenge or prevent is the product of their terror, their fear of a jungle whose laws of survival they do not know, and an enemy whose ways, motives, endurance and intentions are incomprehensible and therefore terrifying—and their terror of themselves, of their own capabilities for 'strange' or 'alien' thoughts and actions under these conditions.[16]

Slotkin is referring here to the colonizers in America, but their predicament and attitudes were mirrored in Vietnam. 'Maps Drawn in the Dust' is an accurate metaphor for the involvement: a presence based on unreal and exaggerated political fears, fuelled by unreal expectations, and mired in hyper-real projections so that reality in Vietnam was totally at odds with any

---

[16] Richard Slotkin, 'Dreams and Genocide: The American Myth of Regeneration Through Violence', *Journal of Popular Culture*, 5: 1 (Summer 1971), 38–59. Robert Bly draws connections between Indian killings and Vietnam in some of his writing. See Chapter 2.

other reality, particularly back in America. Cartography was a means by which MACV sought to impose order on an unknown and hostile landscape. The clarity of the generals clashed with confusion on the ground.[17] General Westmoreland's 'Light at the end of the tunnel' pronouncement, a few months before the Tet Offensive, was a good example of differing perspectives. Whereas the war managers worked out a clear mode of war, and represented it in clinical language, the footsoldier perceived no such order.[18] 'We weaved in & out of | brain fog & effusion' accurately sums up the chaos of combat, which is also reflected in the abrupt break of lines and syntax. Komunyakaa also stresses the loss of innocence, and although the poem does not deal with actual violence, it prepares us at the end for its inevitable outbreak: 'with the circle now complete, | we were wired to our trigger fingers'. The poem describes the regression into, and the conversion to, pathological violence. Combat is seen here as a ghastly psychological state arising from the perception of a terrible reality.

'A Greenness Taller Than Gods' reveals a similar obsession with a hostile environment and the need to name and order that preoccupied military commanders:

> When we stop,
> a green snake starts again
> through deep branches.
> Spiders mend webs we marched into.
>
> . . . . . .
>
> The lieutenant puts on sunglasses
> & points to an X circled
> on his map. When will we learn
> to move like trees move?
>
> . . . . . .

---

[17] J. G. Ballard writes about a similar dilemma in *Empire of the Sun*. One character asks Jim, the protagonist, 'The Japanese have captured so much ground they've run out of maps. Doesn't that mean they're lost?' Jim's response is 'Not really. They just haven't captured any maps.' And his companion replies: 'Good—never confuse the map with the territory.' J. G. Ballard, *Empire of the Sun* (London: Victor Gollancz Ltd., 1984), 97.

[18] John Keegan differentiates between the 'comparatively stable environment' of the commanders and the soldiers who lack this 'clear-cut vision'. *The Face of Battle* (London: Jonathan Cape, 1976), 47. Tim O'Brien conveys a similar confusion in Alpha Company: 'They did not have targets. They did not have a cause. They did not know if it was a war of ideology or economics or hegemony or spite.' *Going After Cacciato* (London: Collins, 1988), 255.

> We move like a platoon of silhouettes
> balancing sledge hammers on our heads,
> unaware our shadows have untied
> from us, wandered off
> & gotten lost.[19]

Nature reclaims its own domain once the soldiers clump by, and the 'X' on the lieutenant's map is an arbitrary signifier, a desperate attempt at controlling one's existence in the forest. While the American presence was loudly declared through its military strength (particularly the Huey helicopter for platoon missions), the Vietcong moved like wraiths, seemingly invisible lords of their own land:

> The point man raises his hand *Wait!*
> We've just crossed paths with VC,
> branches left quivering.
>
> (*Dien Cai Dau*, 11)

The Vietcong are at home in the forest and their power is heightened by their ability to choose the time and place for an encounter. They seldom engaged in direct combat, and the poem, like 'Maps Drawn in the Dust', conveys the tripwire tension of jungle patrols. This was a basic fact of guerrilla warfare that US leaders such as Thomas J. Dodd never grasped:

If the United States, with its unrivaled might, with its unparalleled wealth, with its dominion over sea and air, with its heritage as the champion of freedom—if this United States and its free-world allies have so diminished in spirit that they can be laid in the dust by a few thousand primitive guerrillas, then we are far down the road from which there is no return.[20]

Both poems, however, contribute to the process whereby the Vietcong are nameless 'others', dangerous in their cunning invisibility. Simultaneously they convey the disturbing ambiguity of American perspectives in Vietnam.

---

[19] Yusef Komunyakaa, 'A Greenness Taller Than Gods', *Dien Cai Dau* (Middletown, Conn.: Wesleyan University Press, 1988), 11. Subsequent references are indicated after the quotation.

[20] Cited in Marcus G. Raskin and Bernard B. Fall (eds.), *The Viet-Nam Reader: Articles and Documents on American Foreign Policy and the Viet-Nam Crisis* (New York: Random House, 1967), 35.

With 'Starlight Scope Myopia' Komunyakaa moves towards a vision that actually perceives the Vietcong as human, while acknowledging the tunnel vision of US soldiers. The second section highlights this myopia:

> Making night work for us,
> the starlight scope brings
> men into killing range.
>
> *(Dien Cai Dau, 8)*

The idea here is to see only to kill, a notion partially reversed by the rest of the poem. He does peer down the sights of his M-16 in the last section, but the fact that he does not shoot indicates a kind of silent solidarity. That is all that is possible: the poet is too strongly anchored in his own world totally to abandon it and perceive an absolute otherness. The more he looks at his enemies, however, the more they are individuated and humanized:

> Caught in the infrared,
> what are they saying?
>
> Are they talking about women
> or calling the Americans
>
> *beaucoup dien cai dau?*
> One of them is laughing.
> You want to place a finger
> to his lips & say 'shhhh.'
> You try reading ghost talk
> on their lips. They say
> 'up-up we go,' lifting as one.
> This one, old, bowlegged,
> you feel you could reach out
> & take him into your arms. . . .
>
> *(Dien Cai Dau, 8–9)*

Individuation begins in curiosity—'what are they saying?'—and ends in tenderness—'reach out | & take him into your arms'. 'Dien Cai Dau' was Vietnamese slang for American soldiers and literally meant 'crazy', summing up the American presence in Vietnam. The articulation of that phrase in the poem is an awareness of other points of view, and the depiction of the old, bowlegged man he wants to 'reach out' to is a trope that we come across in other war poetry, recognizing the humanity of the enemy. It reveals the futile loneliness of soldiers on both sides. To take one's enemy into one's arms would assuage that sense of estrangement, but the moment of tenderness is denied almost immediately by the framing reality of war:

> You
>
>   peer down the sights of your M-16,
>   seeing the full moon
>   loaded on an oxcart.
>
>   (*Dien Cai Dau*, 9)

The M-16 shatters the reverie of empathy and also indicates the civilizational and military gulf separating the two sides. Thus while solidarity is indicated, the dominating images occur earlier in the poem:

> Viet Cong
> move under our eyelids,
>
> lords over loneliness
> winding like coral vine through
> sandalwood & lotus,
>
> inside our lowered heads
> years after this scene
>
> ends. . . .
>
>   (*Dien Cai Dau*, 8)

Once again the Vietcong is seen as being at one with his world, while the Americans blunder around. The Vietcong and the war are inscribed in one's brain and memory forever, and the later vision of them as human does not radically alter perspectives. The poem is an act that inscribes the Vietcong as well as attempting to reach out to them. That attempt, along with its attendant futility, highlights the moral ambiguities of the war, the problems of vision and re-visioning. The infra-red scope both reveals and, in its revelation, complicates the simplistic binary oppositions that sustained the war.

Komunyakaa's poetry is rooted in the jungle, conveying the paranoia of everyday existence amidst a hostile environment. Whereas he hints at the moral quicksands underlying American involvement, Bruce Weigl plunges into the literal and metaphysical horror of Vietnam. 'The thing that I can't forget about Nam was the smell of it. The smell. You smelled the napalm and you smelled the human flesh burning. That will live with me to the end of my days.'[21] Weigl adds the smell of burning shit to the smells catalogued by the anonymous veteran, in the poem 'Burning Shit at An Khe'. The poem is a literal depiction of the speaker going about organizing the burning of fellow soldiers' shit:

> Into that pit
> I had to climb down
> with a rake and matches; eventually,
> you had to do something
> because it just kept piling up
> and it wasn't our country...[22]

This was, as another veteran testifies in Mark Baker's *Nam*, a standard and necessary practice: 'What do you do if you've got 500,000 men and no plumbing facilities? What do you do with all the human shit? The Army's answer to that was to collect it in barrels, then drag them someplace where they soaked all that human waste in fuel oil and set it on fire.'[23] Weigl's poem dwells on the process in unpleasant detail and the speaker finds himself mired in the shit while the war carries on around him:

> I'd grunted out eight months
> of jungle and thought I had a grip on things
> but we flipped the coin and I lost
> and climbed down into my fellow soldiers'
> shit and began to sink and didn't stop
> until I was deep to my knees. Liftships
> cut the air above me, the hacking
> blast of their blades
> ripped dust in swirls so every time
> I tried to light a match
> it died
> and it all came down on me, the stink
> and the heat and the worthlessness
> until I slipped and climbed
> out of that hole and ran

---

[21] Cited in Mark Baker, *Nam: The Vietnam War in the Words of the Men and Women Who Fought There* (London: Abacus, 1981), 48.
[22] Bruce Weigl, 'Burning Shit at An Khe', *Song of Napalm* (New York: Atlantic Monthly Press, 1988), 36. Subsequent references are indicated after the quotation.
[23] Baker, *Nam*, 28.

>   past the olive-drab
>   tents and trucks and clothes and everything
>   green as far from the shit
>   as the fading light allowed.
>
>   (*Song of Napalm*, 37–8)

The contrasts are deliberately ignominious: he refers to having survived eight months as a 'grunt' and to the liftships as if they were positive aspects of the war. In comparison to his present task, being a soldier seems almost heroic. Personal valour and technology are now replaced by the basic need to maintain hygiene, stay clear of human excrement. The speaker's predicament epitomizes the US position in Vietnam, at least 'the stink | and the heat and the worthlessness' that many soldiers felt. The pit into which the 'I' climbs down is an allegory of Vietnam: a filthy, meaningless, worthless, degrading enterprise.[24] The scatological counterpoint seriously diminishes any notion of war as a heroic enterprise. The need to escape is imperative, but the war is embedded in one's system:

>   Only now I can't fly.
>   I lay down in it
>   and fingerpaint the words of who I am
>   across my chest
>   until I'm covered and there's only one smell,
>   one word.
>
>   (*Song of Napalm*, 38)

If the shit that he attempted to burn is a metaphor for life in Vietnam, it overwhelms and defines everyone and everything. Identity, experience (including the eight months of 'grunt' life), and memory are now subsumed in the ultimately degrading product of human existence. The problem is that the shit is not burned, the memories cannot be erased, the past is smeared forever in horror and degradation. 'Burning Shit at An Khe' is not an obvious delineation of combat, but a meditation on what combat meant and did to its participants. In a larger sense it

---

[24] Tim O'Brien's 'In the Field', where Kiowa dies in a shit field, and 'Field Trip' convey a similar degradation. Returning to Vietnam after the war, O'Brien writes: 'For twenty years this field had embodied all the waste that was Vietnam, all the vulgarity and the horror.' *The Things They Carried* (London: Harper Collins Publishers, 1990), 186.

allegorizes the nation that sent them to Vietnam, that left its veterans with no place to run to, no solace from the existential horror of the war.

Kevin Bowen's 'Incoming' is a detailed portrait of a firefight, the sounds and the sensations of mortars bringing imminent death and, in its conclusion, presents the continuity of that memory in civilian life (a theme available in Weigl's 'Burning Shit at An Khe'). It begins by demythologizing war as seen in films:

> Don't let them kid you—
> The mind no fool like the movies,
> doesn't wait for flash or screech,
> but moves of its own accord,
> even hears the slight
> bump the mortars make
> as they kiss the tubes goodbye.
> Then the furious rain,
> a fist driving home a message:
> 'Boy, you don't belong here.'[25]

Preconceived notions of war are quickly jettisoned in the face of the reality of combat. 'The mind' develops an innate, instinctive, minute awareness of death in the air and 'moves of its own accord'. The message communicated to the soldier—'Boy, you don't belong here'—gives the lie to Broyles's thesis that war taps into some innate aspect of every man. It is a message emphasizing the disjunction between man and war, the totally alien nature of the war world. Bowen highlights the negative aspect of any identification that war may arouse:

> You wait for them to fall,
> stomach pinned so tight to ground
> you might feel a woman's foot
> pace a kitchen floor in Brownsville;
> the hushed fall of a man lost
> in a corn field in Michigan;
> a young girl's finger trace
> a lover's name on a beach along Cape Cod.
>
> (*Playing Basketball*, 22)

---

[25] Kevin Bowen, 'Incoming', *Playing Basketball With the Vietcong* (Willimantic, Conn.: Curbstone Press, 1994), 22. Subsequent references are indicated after the quotation.

The fear that a mortar attack creates leads to an intimate connection with the earth. The ground is the only referent that is solid and immovable in a world churned upside down. This moment of fear, need for protection and empathy, leads to a sympathetic connection with geological tremors elsewhere. That elsewhere is what is familiar and normal, the quotidian and therefore comforting. In fact there is a reiteration of pastoral impulses and motifs noted in earlier veteran poems. A moment of fear and trembling is contrasted with moments of growth and love: the man may be lost, but his fall is amongst benign life-sustaining corn; the lover's name may be obliterated by the waves, but there exists the young girl to reinscribe her love. These are transitory moments, but they may be extended into a future that could be positive. These positive connections are, however, overwhelmed by post-war recollections:

> In a moment, it's over.
> But it takes a lifetime to recover,
> let out the last breath
> you took as you dove.
> This is why you'll see them sometimes,
> in malls, men and women off in corners:
> the ways they stare through the windows in silence.
>
> (*Playing Basketball*, 22)

The poem encapsulates a moment that seems a lifetime and lasts for one, an endless continuum of memory and trauma. Stephen Spender's comment about veteran poetry 'giving voice to a particular infinite agony packed into a transitional moment' is very apposite here. The memory of war alienates the combatant, and breaks the thread of empathy with the normal and daily round of life. It marks the beginning of a long, stark silence and, in the case of Vietnam veterans, a silence matched by a deafening lack of sympathy from the world outside. The poets fill that void, not only to retrieve and represent their memories, but to come to terms with them, to give them shape and meaning.

Stephen Sossaman, in the review cited earlier, asserted the angry, truth-telling function of poetry in *Winning Hearts and Minds*: 'As if in desperation at the failure of words and in frustration at American moral cowardice, many of the poets in the 1st Casualty Press book seem to hurl their truths like bloody severed heads in the reader's lap.'[26] The element of anger and didacticism in these poems is undeniable, as if only through relentless reiteration could the 'truth' of war be told. The anger and bewilderment are comprehensible within a context of innocence and its subsequent betrayal. The progression from innocence to experience, traceable from pro-war poems in *Stars and Stripes* and *DEROS*, to poems of anguish and horror, is not as simplistic as it may seem. Just as 'American moral cowardice' is not a monolithic, easily identifiable and therefore destructible entity, so too the poets are not unencumbered tellers of uncomplicated truths. Their first-hand witness gives them a unique insight into combat, and resultant authority to narrate the war. That narration, up to the point discussed, has its shortcomings: it is self-obsessed, didactic, often simplistic, and occasionally naïve in its assumption of moral truth (or the moral truth assigned to it by critics such as Sossaman). None of these problems invalidate the poetry, but overlooking them gives the poetry greater stature than it deserves. Given their experiences, and circumstances after the war, it is remarkable that soldiers who were not poets, as Ehrhart points out, wrote poetry at all. While it would be futile to examine original motivations, it is useful to hypothesize what the poetry was doing (not in a crudely instrumentalist sense) for the poet. The innocence-to-experience paradigm offers a clue: having been placed in an alien, hostile, often incomprehensible environment, and having undergone experiences that undermined deeply held values and ideas of the way the world functioned, the soldier-poet had to rewrite his world. The poetry discussed in this chapter is a desperate attempt to narrate, order, and place in perspective deeply traumatic events. It is, to use Richard Rorty's phrase, an attempt to weave 'a coherent web of belief and desire', since the war seems to have unravelled the web that constituted the 'self'.[27] The process is a painful one and does not imply a linear reconstruction of the 'self', since the excavation of terrible memories is traumatic in itself. The second clue to the imperative 'need' for poetic expression lies in the paradoxical desire to remember in order to forget. 'Forget' not in the sense of obliterat-

---

[26] Stephen Sossaman, 'American Poetry From the Indochina Experience', *Long Island Review*, 2 (Winter 1973–4), 33.

[27] Richard Rorty, *Contingency, irony, and solidarity* (Cambridge and New York: Cambridge University Press, 1989), 178.

ing memory (that, as poetry discussed in the next chapter testifies, is impossible), but the belief that a minute, honest recollection would help to place the war events in some comprehensible scheme. Repression of war memory would be more traumatic, perhaps, than facing up to it. John Felstiner writes that 'Memory, which can work with a saving grace in lyric poetry, works in these poems like a burning fuse.'[28] It is the obsessive dwelling on combat detail and its remembrance that constitutes a link between the poems discussed in this chapter. The recollections may seem masochistic, a constant dwelling on unpleasant memory in order to exorcize its horror. As Evelyn Cobley notes in her study of First World War narratives: 'Strongly motivated by both the impulse to remember and the impulse to forget, the war narratives illustrate Derrida's contention that the memoir has a double source, namely "Mnemosyne/Lethe: source of memory, source of forgetting." '[29] Derrida's 'Mnemosyne/Lethe' paradigm is equally applicable to veteran poetry, with the added dimension and responsibility on the soldier-poet's part for rigorous remembrance in a climate of deliberate amnesia. The poems discussed in this and the previous chapter are important initial testaments towards personal and cultural memory. The poems in the next chapter, the 'aftermath' poems, share some of the qualities discerned in these chapters. They too are bound by anger, anguish, bewilderment, occasional stridency, and are centred mostly within America. The passage to empathy and solidarity with the 'other', to a poetry that gestures towards healing and comprehension, lies through the trauma and alienation of the next stage in Vietnam veteran poetry.

[28] John Felstiner, 'Bearing the War in Mind', *Parnassus: Poetry in Review*, 6: 2 (Spring–Summer 1978), 30–7.

[29] Evelyn Cobley, *Representing War: Form and Ideology in First World War Narratives* (Toronto, Buffalo, and London: University of Toronto Press, 1993), 9.

5
Veteran Poetry
The Aftermath

POETRY OF ALIENATION, MEMORY, AND RESPONSIBILITY

The transition from Vietnam to America, from 'in country' to 'the World' was a swift, often bizarre and almost incomprehensible process for many veterans.[1] In thirty-six hours they were transported from the immediacy of war to the sometimes hostile, but mostly pleasant and placid environment of 'home'.[2] The most common response to returning veterans was a stolid, uncomprehending silence: an absolute refusal to know. This, combined with the hostility of anti-war protesters, contributed to the veterans' sense of alienation. Just as the war had betrayed stereotyped expectations, so did the homecoming. The gap between expectation and reality is portrayed by W. D. Ehrhart in *Passing Time*, his memoir of the post-Vietnam period:

I'd enlisted in the Marines in the spring of 1966 with visions of brass bands, victory parades, free drinks in bars, and starry-eyed girls clinging to my neck like so many succulent grapes. But by the time I got back to the States from Vietnam, I considered myself lucky to get out of San Francisco Airport without being assaulted by bands of rabid hippies armed with snapdragons and daisies, and carrying placards reading Baby Killer.[3]

Homecoming was not only literally traumatic in the dislocation of locale and expectation, but a goal or possibility that seemed

---

[1] 'In country' was Vietnam and America 'the World' in soldier slang.
[2] The swift transition and ambiguous reception at home for Vietnam veterans may be contrasted to the homecoming of soldiers from the Second World War. They had a considerably longer transit period, returning in their troopships with their comrades. They returned as heroes to a tumultuous welcome and were recipients of national gratitude. Vietnam veterans returned alone (because of the 365-day tour of duty) to a country deeply divided by the war, and dismissive of the veteran.
[3] W. D. Ehrhart, *Passing Time: Memoir of a Vietnam Veteran Against the War* (Jefferson, NC, and London: McFarland & Company, Inc., Publishers, 1986), 7.

(and still does to some veterans) totally out of reach. This, as Kali Tal explains, was because homecoming is not only spatial, but psychological: 'Such a homecoming as they [veterans] might wish for is always unreachable, because it is based on returning not only to a place, but to a time where they were innocent of war— the pre-trauma state.'[4] The loss of innocence and living in a post-trauma state—later diagnosed as Post Traumatic Stress Disorder—exacerbated the veterans' sense of isolation and angst. A related factor that contributed to the sense of alienation was the absolute disjunction between war experience and civilian life. While a lot of the 'grunt' work was tedious, tiring, and terrifying in turns, many veterans testify to a sense of power, of a lack of restraint that society imposes, in their combat life in Vietnam. In Tobias Wolff's recollection, power takes on a tone of benign paternalism, an unconscious identification with the imperium that his country represents:

My special position did not make me arrogant, not at first. It made me feel benevolent, generous, protective, as if I were surrounded by children, as I often was—crowds of them, shy but curious, taking turns stroking my hairy arms and, as a special treat, my mustache. In My Tho I had a sense of myself as father, even as lord, the very sensation that, even more than all their holdings here, must have made the thought of losing this place unbearable to the French.[5]

Wolff offers a delicate insight into the psychology of imperialism and the desire for overlordship that animates the imperial mind. It is significant that he recalls French imperialism in connection with his own position, since this was a parallel vigorously denied by official America. Despite the disturbing condescension of his account, it is a self-aware portrait of his position and attitudes. Another veteran conveys a more brutal (equally real) account of power:

I had a sense of power. A sense of destruction. See, now, in the United States a person is babied. He's told what to do. You can't carry a gun, unless you want to go to jail. . . . But in the Nam you realized that you

---

[4] Kali Tal, *Worlds of Hurt: Reading the Literatures of Trauma* (New York: Cambridge University Press, 1996), 87.

[5] Tobias Wolff, *In Pharaoh's Army: Memories of a Lost War* (London: Bloomsbury Publishing, 1994), 12–13.

had the power to take a life. You had the power to rape a woman and nobody could say nothing to you. That godlike feeling you had was in the field. It was like I was a God. I could take a life, I could screw a woman. I can beat somebody up and get away with it.[6]

This testimony expresses a deeply disturbing pathology of war, collating freedom with violence and power, whether it be to kill or rape. The raping of Vietnamese women (to kill the raped woman was to be a 'double veteran', a distorted appellation of valour) represented the need to assert power in a situation that daily reminded the veteran of his insecurity and impotence. That killing and rape were not visited by social sanctions and reprisals contributed to 'that godlike feeling'. It is entirely unsurprising that such an individual would find it difficult to settle back into civilian life, but Ehrhart's and Wolff's disappointments and recollections highlight the liminality of the veteran. As Eric J. Leed points out in *No Man's Land: Combat and Identity in World War I*:

He [the veteran] derives all of his features from the fact that he has crossed the boundaries of disjunctive social worlds, from peace to war, and back. He has been reshaped by his voyage along the margins of civilization, a voyage in which he has been presented with wonders, curiosities and monsters—things that can only be guessed at by those who remained at home.[7]

Veterans from Vietnam returned with memories and monstrous recollections that they could not share with a society that had undergone its own upheavals, but was unprepared to face the people it had sent to fight its battles. They were cooped up in their memory warp, unable to reach out to non-veteran society.

The poetry of this period represents, in part, a desire to break the silence, force people to take notice. It is possible to see a progression from poems that are nostalgic about the war, to poems of political anger and alienation, to a more mature remembrance and sense of responsibility. The pathology of war, in terms of the disjunction between the war world and peace back home, is most

---

[6] Mark Baker, *Nam: The Vietnam War in the Words of the Men and Women Who Fought There* (London: Abacus, 1981), 134.

[7] Eric J. Leed, *No Man's Land: Combat and Identity in World War I* (Cambridge: Cambridge University Press, 1979), 194.

fully expressed in poetry that revels in the excitement and beauty of combat. Jim Nye's 'Chimaera' is one such graphic portrait:

> fabulous fire-breathing monster.
>
> There is something dark in my soul
> That casts its crimson eyes
> Into the smoke.
> Its heart pulses heavily
> And it inhales deliciously the
> Bitter cordite, coppery smell of blood.
> That revels in the fear,
> Watching the tracers stitch
> Across into the brush,
> The body dropping, heavily, limp.
> Jamming home another magazine,
> Panting, gasping,
> Nourished and feeding,
>
> My God, I love it.[8]

The poem begins by acknowledging the 'dark in my soul' that leads to the 'panting, gasping' appreciation of combat and death. That confession only deepens the disturbing edge that the rest of the poem conveys. The epigraph could be a reference to the soldier, or to Puff the Magic Dragon, 'a converted twin-engine propeller-driven C-47 (the military version of the DC-3) with three sophisticated Vulcan cannons mounted along one side of the fuselage'. Each gun could fire 6,000 rounds per minute and Ehrhart ends his description with, 'Really it was quite beautiful.'[9] Puff the Magic Dragon approximates and imitates the mythological Chimaera, who had the head of a lion, the body of a goat, the tail of a dragon, and 'vomited forth horrible flames'.[10] She was the personification of the storm cloud, in opposition to the regular winds ruled over by Aeolus. War unleashes all that is horrible and primeval in human nature and the incongruous use of words such as 'deliciously', 'revels', 'nourished', and 'feeding', in the context of destruction, further highlights the repugnance. It is a horror that must be acknowledged because there are men who seem to love war. Broyles writes that 'one of the most troubling

[8] Jim Nye, 'Chimaera', *After Shock* (El Paso, Tex.: Cinco Puntos Press, 1991), 45.
[9] W. D. Ehrhart, 'What's In a Name? The Snake', *WIN* (Nov. 1979), 13–14.
[10] Robert Graves (introd.), *New Larousse Encyclopedia of Mythology*, (London and New York: Hamlyn, 1974), 146.

reasons men love war is the love of destruction, the thrill of killing'.[11] His contention is borne out by this poem, and by some veteran testimonies, such as this one: 'I enjoyed the shooting and the killing. I was literally turned on when I saw a gook get shot. ... A GI was real. American get killed, it was a real loss. But if a gook got killed, it was like me going out here and stepping on a roach.'[12] 'My God, I love it' is a summation of this warped mentality, and in part the poem reinforces the baby killer stereotype that dogged the veteran in post-war America. The speaker is one with the chimaera, a fabulous monster unable to make the transition to civilian life.[13]

Horace Coleman's 'D-Day + 50; Tet + 25' is a more ironic and critical look at the problems of survival, trauma, and nostalgia. He begins by charting a generational connection that inspired 18 year olds to volunteer for Vietnam:

> It's been all my life since Normandy
> and half my life since Tet.
> And the scars my father and I
> share in our minds are half-healed.
> The shock of survival can be
> worse than other wounds.
> We didn't know there would be
> seams on our souls.[14]

It is crucial that Coleman mentions a bonding of survival and trauma with his father who fought the 'good war', the war that sustained myths for generations to come. Second World War veterans did not lay bare their souls in the same way their children were to do later, and their silence helped to nurture the 'good war' myth. The emphasis on 'we' in 'We didn't know there would be | seams on our souls', is both an empathic reaching out—father and son suffered through similar innocence and ignorance—and

---

[11] William J. Broyles Jr., 'Why Men Love War', in Walter Capps (ed.), *The Vietnam Reader* (New York and London: Routledge, 1990), 75.

[12] Baker, *Nam*, 51.

[13] Eric Leed observes that 'The encounter with the home, paradoxically enough, could lead to a counter-idealization of the war that had just been fought, to an idealization of "comradeship," military life, and the simplicities of war' (*No Man's Land*, 189). Vietnam war novels such as James Webb's *Fields of Fire* reiterate this notion of bonding and community in war.

[14] Horace Coleman, 'D-Day + 50; Tet + 25', *In the Grass* (Woodbridge, Conn.: Viet Nam Generation Inc. & Burning Cities Press, 1995), 43. Subsequent references are indicated after the quotation.

a reproof. 'We' could refer to the community of Vietnam veterans who now suffer because their fathers did not/would not tell them the horrors of war. It is not only a generational connection, but a culpability that Coleman is indicating here. As Lorrie Smith observes: 'One way to view the Vietnam War is as a grotesque form of child abuse, abandonment and betrayal by parents who repressed and lied about their own earlier traumas of World War II and Korea.'[15] Smith's essay examines fatherhood poems by John Balaban, Bruce Weigl, and Ehrhart, a tenderness, vulnerability, and concern evident in recent veteran poetry. Her comment on parental repression and its effect on the next generation is, however, appropriate for Coleman's poem. He is aware that blaming his father's generation does not change anything, and that the mesmeric cycle of war will continue:

> But we'd still do it again, even if we know
> the stories before their 10th syllable
> or the second spilled drink
> at the VA, Legion Hall, AMVETS,
> Vet Centers, VFW, parks,
> parking lots or at The Wall.
> It beats being bored.
>
> *(In the Grass, 43)*

In post-Vietnam America nothing fundamental has changed: the military myth might have taken a beating, but war is still a cynical positive: 'It beats being bored.' This last statement is ironic, but it reveals a psychology common to veterans of every war, so that even as divisive and terrible a war as that in Vietnam has been reclaimed for national purposes and mythologies.

Dale Ritterbusch's 'Better Dead Than Boring' expounds on a similar theme: the attractiveness of the armed forces (most of the poem is about a recruitment drive in a university), the complicity of universities in the larger military scheme, and, implicitly, the inevitability of war. He takes up the socio-

---

[15] Lorrie Smith, '"What Shall We Give Our Children?" Fatherhood Poems by Veterans', in Robert M. Slabey (ed.), *The United States and Vietnam From War to Peace* (Jefferson, NC, and London: McFarland & Company Inc., Publishers, 1996), 163.

economic aspect of war, a factor not often mentioned in veteran poetry, which is as compelling as any psychological reason:

> There's the usual bitching about
> the role of the university in military affairs
> but hell, for some it's the only way out—
> the only way out of a trailer park
> on the edge of some cornfield—either that or be
> a shit kicking farmer, or work for a potato chip
> factory and come home smelling like overused grease—
> better to die in Lebanon or Grenada than live in Ohio...[16]

The ideal of heroism inherent in war furthers an individual's self-image. Lebanon and Grenada were post-Vietnam forays to bolster national self-esteem: the former was a disaster, the latter a hollow victory. Yet they provided, for some at least, a way out of actual or perceived lives of degradation. Social class and poverty were important contributory factors for the large number of blacks and Puerto Ricans who enlisted and fought in Vietnam. During the Vietnam War, the Selective Service System meant that working-class people were more likely to be drafted and placed in active combat positions. Student deferment was linked to socio-economic status, so that those wealthy enough to go to college could stay out of the war. Ironically it was precisely this class that chose to protest against the war, while their poorer compatriots died in it. As Leslie Fiedler remarked, with some hyperbole, Vietnam was turning into 'the first war of which it can be said unequivocally that it is being fought for us by our servants'.[17] If not 'by our servants', it was fought by a disproportionate number of the poor, the disenfranchised, and therefore the powerless. Ritterbusch leaves little space for nostalgia and raises uncomfortable questions.

The shift from nostalgia to political anger and occasional stridency is best embodied in W. D. Ehrhart's polemical poems. 'A Relative Thing' is a poem of witness and responsibility addressed to an apathetic public. He wishes to connect the

---

[16] Dale Ritterbusch, 'Better Dead Than Boring', *Lessons Learned: Poetry of the Vietnam War and its Aftermath* (Woodbridge, Conn.: Viet Nam Generation, Inc. & Burning Cities Press, 1995), 112.

[17] Cited in Milton J. Bates, *The Wars We Took to Vietnam: Cultural Conflict and Storytelling* (Berkeley, Los Angeles, and London: University of California Press, 1996), 95.

experiences of the veteran to the nation that sent him there, so that in collective remembrance, rather than amnesia, people may awake to the consequences of war:

> We have been Democracy on Zippo raids,
> burning houses to the ground,
> driving eager amtracs through new-sown fields.
>
> We are the ones who have to live
> with the memory that we were the instruments
> of your pigeon-breasted fantasies.
> We are inextricable accomplices
> in this travesty of dreams:
> but we are not alone.
>
> We are the ones you sent to fight a war
> you did not know a thing about—
> those of us that lived
> have tried to tell you what went wrong.
> Now you think you do not have to listen.
>
> Just because we will not fit
> into the uniforms of photographs
> of you at twenty-one
> does not mean you can disown us.
>
> We are your sons, America,
> and you cannot change that.
> When you awake,
> we will still be here.[18]

The poem describes a community of experience, memory, and betrayal that bestows on the veteran an identity that seems utterly separate from that of the non-veteran. While some war experiences may be untranslatable, Ehrhart categorizes well-known occurrences such as Zippo raids, and moves beyond them to political and cultural responsibility. Like Coleman, he makes a generational connection, and refuses to be ostracized because he and his fellow veterans do not fit into mythologized pictures of war heroes. Underlying the bitterness is the loss of innocence of an entire generation and, ironically, the generation that sent them to war clings on to a pre-war type of innocence. Ehrhart stresses

[18] W. D. Ehrhart, 'A Relative Thing', *Beautiful Wreckage: New & Selected Poems* (Easthampton, Mass.: Adastra Press, 1999), 9–10. Subsequent references from the collection are indicated as *Wreckage* after the quotation.

the past and continuing complicity of both generations who are 'inextricable accomplices', and the last section of his poem is not only a warning, but voices trauma and a conscience that America did not and does not want to hear. Although the hope throughout the poem is one of collective awareness and responsibility, it is framed by the insistent we–you dialectic, the voice of betrayed innocence and belated wisdom haranguing the ignorance and silent culpability of the nation at large. The insistence on the 'you' is implicitly an evasion of personal volition and represents a politics of blame that coexists uneasily with Ehrhart's desire for strenuous responsibility. Despite its undeniable truth and power, 'A Relative Thing' is a strident activist poem that requires particular contexts (or knowledge thereof) for a fuller understanding. As historical and political contexts have changed in the way the war is now perceived, so too the last section of the poem has been appropriated by the right wing (and this includes Vietnam veterans) to conform to the POW/MIA myths.[19] With the rehabilitation of the veteran, 'We are your sons, America' becomes a clarion call for a new nationalist identification. In fact, this appropriation by the conservative right seems to validate the need for more vigilant and accurate remembrance, and much of Ehrhart's poetic career has been devoted to this end. He has pursued public and private hypocrisies in American public life with messianic zeal, and although the idealism may now be tempered, the convictions have not: 'I no longer believe that even all of us together are going to change the world. But I do believe that we have to keep trying because if our voices fall silent, the only voices left will be those of people like Elliot Abrams and Oliver North.'[20]

The desire for strenuous remembrance is embodied in 'The Invasion of Grenada' which cites a contemporary event, revisioning the greatness of America, to reflect on the Vietnam Memorial,

[19] This reinterpretation by conservative veterans was pointed out by Ehrhart during an interview at La Salle University, Philadelphia, on 6 Feb. 1997. A Veterans Administration Study in 1980 reflected the reinstatement of the war: 'Looking back, 71 percent of those polled said that they were "glad" to have gone to Vietnam; 74 percent claimed to have "enjoyed" their tour there; 66 percent expressed a willingness to serve again.' Cited in Stanley Karnow, *Vietnam: A History* (London: Pimlico, 1994), 480.
[20] W. D. Ehrhart, 'Stealing Hubcaps', *In The Shadow of Vietnam: Essays, 1977–1991* (Jefferson, NC, and London: McFarland & Company Inc., Publishers, 1991), 127.

and the way/s in which a political establishment has appropriated the war:

> I didn't want a monument,
> not even one as sober as that
> vast black wall of broken lives.
> I didn't want a postage stamp.
> I didn't want a road beside the Delaware
> River with a sign proclaiming:
> 'Vietnam Veterans Memorial Highway.'
>
> What I wanted was a simple recognition
> of the limits of our power as a nation
> to inflict our will on others.
> What I wanted was an understanding
> that the world is neither black-and-white
> nor ours.
>
> What I wanted
> was an end to monuments.
>
> (*Wreckage*, 75)

The Memorial is, in a sense, an acknowledgement of the defiant call to memory voiced by Ehrhart at the end of 'A Relative Thing'. War memorials such as the Wall perpetuate the heroic paradigms that were desired by many veterans and debunked by some. They highlight official sanction and acceptance: individual, 'marginal' histories are now subsumed within a state-sponsored history. This acknowledgement constitutes what Harry Haines defines as 'hegemony's therapeutic strategy': the ghosts of the war can finally be laid to rest now that the state has recognized the encounter as an honest error, and the veterans as long-neglected heroes.[21] This is precisely the position that the poets resist, and Gerald McCarthy's 'The Hooded Legion' is an appropriate companion piece to Ehrhart's poem. The first section points to what the Wall edits from collective memory and history:

> There are no words here
> to witness why we fought,
> who sent us or what we hoped to gain.[22]

The epigraph to the poem, Joseph Brodsky's 'let us put up a

---

[21] Harry Haines, 'Disputing the Wreckage: Ideological Struggle at the Vietnam Veterans Memorial', *Vietnam Generation*, 1: 1 (Winter 1989), 144.

[22] Gerald McCarthy, 'The Hooded Legion', *Shoetown* (Bristol, Ind.: Coverdale Corporation, 1992), 27.

monument to the lie' underlines the idea that the Wall merely papers over the complex history of the war. In contrast, Ehrhart posits a personal negation: 'What I wanted | was an end to monuments', along with a desire that the nation will learn the lessons of Vietnam. However, such 'simple recognition[s]' are not the way of history and politics, and there is an underlying naïvety in the poetic protest. The title indicates a nationalist resurgence and the subject of the poem gestures to a simultaneous acknowledgement of, and convenient closure to, the war. For the veteran poet, however, there is no easy closure and the angry protest in Ehrhart's poems is an indication of disturbing insights that will not disappear. They are also an index of alienation, a theme common to veteran poetry. As he stated in an interview in 1997: 'One of the great sadnesses of my life is that I feel an outsider in my own country. I cannot ever feel fully a part of this society anymore. And that's too bad.'[23] Ehrhart's poetry and prose writing remain uncompromising in their delineation of what he considers to be the hypocrisy and lies in post-Vietnam America. A part of the anger and stridency of his political poetry arises out of this sense of betrayal, awareness, and outrage, as he traversed the path from innocence to knowledge. Former complicity, the awareness of the power of unquestioning belief, and exile combine to create a consciousness and poetry that is riven with the desire to bear witness so that another generation is spared his personal and generational trauma. As events have unfolded over the two decades since the war, Ehrhart has had deep cause for disillusion (particularly the triumphalism after the Gulf War), but he has chosen not to give up his project. The Vietnam experience underlines most poems, but there is a corpus of poetry which displays a calmer, more mature tone.

The new tone and idiom is available in 'Dancing' which has none of the harshness and bewilderment of his combat poems, nor the stridency and anger of later poems. It is a poem troubled by memory and truth, yet poised in a type of serenity not always available in Ehrhart's work:

> Having been where contrasts meet,
> I perceive reality to be
> Whatever looms largest in the mind.

[23] Interview with W. D. Ehrhart, 6 Feb. 1997.

> Thus truths are never absolute;
> Nebulous, they never lose the shifting
> Beat of music changing time.
>
> Books I read, and faces seen
> In sunlight tell me where I am;
> At night this truth melts away;
>
> An older truth looms within
> And I submit, take my rifle,
> Rejoin comrades on patrol
>
> Until the sun returns the books,
> And faces, and the other truth
> I dance with to a kinder beat.
>
> (*Wreckage*, 3)

The first stanza, with absolute economy of expression, delineates the binary consciousness of the veteran, both during and after the war. The reality of war looms large in memory, yet there is a possibility of ameliorating that state. The second stanza opens the path towards reconciliation by acknowledging the contingency of truth, which is likened to 'the shifting | Beat of music changing time'. A sense of place, identity, rootedness is located in books and faces, words and people; the poet through his craft fashions a new world of potential healing. If this were the only truth, then healing would have been complete, but it is not as 'An older truth looms within'. The continual, subliminal existence of war memory is perceived as an ur-memory, older and more basic. This reiterates the earlier idea of war as a fundamental experience, one that irretrievably recasts and haunts one's soul. Yet in this stanza the contrasts coalesce, so that the 'older truth' coexists with a kinder memory of books, friends, sunshine. The latter constitutes the 'other truth' that the last stanza mentions. The veteran poet's consciousness is fractured in that he is aware of a before and after difference, and of war as a type of bedrock experience, but the combining of the two provides for a more balanced perspective: 'the other truth | I dance with to a kinder beat'. Dancing and the rhythms of music are woven into the poem as a metaphor for changing perceptions and rhythms of life, for harmony, and for passionate remembrance. There is none of the glib overload of healing wounds and reconciliation that gained wide currency in the 1980s. Instead, there is a delicate interweaving between war memory and everyday life, a recovery of memory to reconstruct and reconsider positive possibilities. There is no shallow optimism, only a strong and calm perception of the world and the self.

Walter McDonald's 'Black Granite Burns Like Ice' is a more direct and less consolatory recollection of the war. In contrasting the expiation and closure ostensibly represented by the Vietnam Memorial with his own searing memories and with life after the war, McDonald opens up the fractured psychological territory of trauma:

> Watching the world from above,
> all fallen friends applaud
> in blisters on our backs.
> Wherever I go, there's fire.
>
> My dreams are napalm.
> I've been to the wall
> and placed my fingers on their names.
> Black granite burns like ice
>
> no lips can taste. Sad music's
> on my mind, a war on every channel.
> After the madness of Saigon
> flew back through California
>
> to the plains, hardscrabble fields
> with cactus and the ghost of rattlers.
> I feed the hawks field mice and rabbits.
> I'm no Saint Francis,
>
> but even the buzzards circle,
> hoping whatever I own keeps dying.
> My wife's green eyes count cattle
> all week long, saving each calf,
>
> each wounded goat ripped open
> by barbed wire. After dark
> we rock on the porch
> and watch the stars,
>
> wondering how many owls dive
> silently per acre, how many snakes
> per grandchild, how many wars
> before all dreams are fire.[24]

[24] Walter MacDonald, 'Black Granite Burns Like Ice', *Where Skies Are Not Cloudy* (Denton, Tex.: University of North Texas Press, 1994), 58.

The poem traverses the memory landscape of the past, and through the present links up with a vision of an apocalyptic future consumed by violence and fire. Fire dominates the beginning and the end, as a metonym for the war (available to the civilian public through photographs of napalmed children and villages) and for existence after the war: 'My dreams are napalm.' The black granite surface of the Wall is charged with the transmutation of actuality (the war and those who died in it) into remembrance that cannot be assuaged. In an interview in June 1991, McDonald, dividing Vietnam poems into three groups, said that the third and largest group 'focuse[d] on the fact of survival. How does one cope? How does one go on?'[25] The poem outlines the actuality of survival in the 'hardscrabble fields' of Texas. The desire, in sharp contrast to involvement in the war, is to create and sustain new lives, with the farm as a possible locale for this renewal. Regeneration, however, is a mirage as the dominating images are those of threat, violence, and death: rattlesnakes, hawks, buzzards, 'goat[s] ripped open | by barbed wire'. The incongruity and irony of the disclaimer, 'I'm no Saint Francis' is fairly obvious in a hostile natural environment. There is no redemption through nature in the poem. In fact, west Texas and Vietnam are entangled, they are both landscapes of hardship and violence, of preying, killing, and desolation. This sparseness, a sense of a spiritual and physical wasteland, is further emphasized by the 'lean, uncluttered, precise' language and imagery of the poem, 'almost as stark and arid as the desolate West Texas landscape'. The poem is a 'record of human endurance in hard times and harsh places'.[26] It is also a chronicle of the harsh continuity and possible cyclicity of war and its trauma. The poem that begins with an individual notion of perpetual horror, ends with husband and wife calculating, almost anticipating, a future broiled in violence and war that will affect a collective consciousness. Perhaps 'the madness of Saigon' is not merely an individual pathology, it encompasses and envisions a collective and doomed future.

[25] Ronald Baughman, interview with Walter McDonald, 26 June 1991, in Ronald Baughman (ed.), *Dictionary of Literary Biography*, ix. *American Writers of the Vietnam War* (Detroit and London: Gale Research Inc., 1991), 268.
[26] Thomas Zigal, 'Prizes for a Plains Poet', in Baughman (ed.), *Dictionary of Literary Biography*, 244.

The move towards a more resilient remembrance, the burden of responsibility in post-war America, are perhaps best embodied in the poetry of John Balaban. He occupies a unique position in that he did not go to Vietnam as a soldier, but spent two years, 1967–9, as a conscientious objector, working as an instructor at the University of Can Tho in the Mekong Delta, and then as a field representative for the Committee of Responsibility to Save War-Injured Children. He was in Vietnam during the Tet Offensive and witnessed the devastating effect of war on civilians, particularly children. In his memoir, *Remembering Heaven's Face: A Moral Witness in Vietnam*, he consciously distances himself from his fellow Americans: 'I was after all a conscientious objector to military service. Somehow I wanted Vietnamese to know this, as if they would appreciate the moral difference between my presence and that of 500,000 other young Americans who were pouring into the country: I had come not to bear arms but to bear witness.'[27] There is an element of naïvety in his attitude as a CO, but his work with the Committee of Responsibility (an agency that did excellent work with injured Vietnamese children), his genuine empathy with the Vietnamese, their culture, and language (he is one of the few veteran poets who knows fluent Vietnamese, and has translated their oral folk poetry, the *ca dao*) allow him to write poems of sympathy and quality about a sad, brutal period of history. As Jeffrey Walsh observes: 'Historical inclusiveness, an equal sympathy for American and Vietnamese alike, distinguishes Balaban's work. His poems are also characterized by a feeling for Vietnamese culture and are thus not marred by an ethnocentric narrowness of perspective: he has no burden of personal guilt to escape, for example.'[28] Although Balaban was not personally responsible for acts of killing or destruction, he does feel a 'burden of personal guilt' at what his country was doing to Vietnam. In his memoir he recalls watching a wounded toddler shriek with pain, 'until I was ashamed to be alive, to be human, let alone to be an American,

---

[27] John Balaban, *Remembering Heaven's Face: A Moral Witness in Vietnam* (New York and London: Poseidon Press, 1991), 17. In his refusal to bear arms Balaban moves beyond the archetypal witnessing of war offered by Wilfred Owen and Sassoon.
[28] Jeffrey Walsh, '"After Our War": John Balaban's Poetic Images of Vietnam', in Jeffrey Walsh and James Aulich (eds.), *Vietnam Images: War and Representation* (Basingstoke and London: The Macmillan Press Ltd., 1989), 145.

to be one of those who had brought the planes to this sad little country ten thousand miles away'.[29] His poems are marked by the need for accurate remembrance and moral witnessing.

'After Our War' dwells on the problems of existence and language in post-war America. It begins with images of physical dismemberment:

> After our war, the dismembered bits
> —all those pierced eyes, ear slivers, jaw splinters,
> gouged lips, odd tibias, skin flaps, and toes—
> came squinting, wobbling, jabbering back.
> The genitals, of course, were the most bizarre,
> inching along roads like glowworms and slugs.
> The living wanted them back but good as new.[30]

This grotesque parade of disembodied limbs is a metaphor for political, national, and psychic fragmentation. For a nation nurtured on the heroism of war, and for the individual soldiers trained into the masculine, macho myths of the Army and Marines, defeat and physical disablement was the worst type of disillusionment. 'The genitals . . . | Inching along roads like glowworms' symbolize the emasculation of the soldier, his deep fear of castration most vividly brought home by the Bouncing Betty mines deployed by the Vietcong. 'The living wanted them back but good as new' points to the desire for refurbished myths centred around freedom and democracy, a return to innocence. Such a turning back was not possible and many veterans protesting against the war displayed their mutilated bodies to emphasize the actuality of war damage. This was not a simple airing of war injuries. As Michael Bibby writes, 'More than testifying to atrocity, however, this attention to the mutilated body subverts the authority of the military and the body politic.'[31] The parade of injured Vietnam veterans, condemning the war, throwing away

---

[29] Balaban, *Remembering Heaven's Face*, 104.

[30] John Balaban, 'After Our War', *Locusts at the Edge of Summer: New and Selected Poems* (Washington: Copper Canyon Press, 1997), 41. Subsequent references from this collection are indicated as *Locusts* after the quotation.

[31] Michael Bibby, 'Fragging the Chains of Command: GI Resistance Poetry and Mutilation', *Journal of American Culture*, 16: 3 (Fall 1993), 29–38. Kali Tal makes a similar observation in her 'Feminist Criticism and the Literature of the Vietnam Combat Veteran', in Jacqueline Lawson (ed.), *Vietnam Generation*, special issue, *Gender and the War: Men, Women, and Vietnam*, 1: 3–4 (Summer–Fall 1989), 190–201.

their medals and commendations in protests in Washington, was a powerful statement against the entire structure and masculinist ideology fostered by the military. It brought the war home in a way stateside protesters could not have done. Violence and its aftermath returned home:

> Since all things naturally return to their source,
> these snags and tatters arrived, with immigrant uncertainty,
> in the United States. It was almost home.
>
> (*Locusts*, 41)

Balaban makes a connection here between violence perpetrated in Vietnam and reflected in the USA. In fact the USA is the source of the violence. This is an idea available in stateside poetry, that of Ginsberg and Bly, for instance, but Balaban articulates it without their hysterical binarism. The mutilated perpetrators and victims of war return 'with immigrant uncertainty' because their country is unable to deal with defeat. The estrangement—'It was almost home'—is mutual, but Balaban stresses the need to deal with consequences. He echoes Ehrhart's challenge in 'A Relative Thing': 'When you awake, | We will still be here.' Balaban's tone, however, is less strident, and the poem ends with troubled and troubling questions:

> After the war, with such Cheshire cats grinning in our trees,
> will the ancient tales still tell us new truths?
> Will the myriad world surrender new metaphor?
> After our war, how will love speak?
>
> (*Locusts*, 41)

The Cheshire cat image, harking back to the absurd, nonsense world of Alice in Wonderland, underpins the poetic anxiety: will the new revelations and truths be faced up to, or will they conveniently disappear? Published in 1982, this poem anticipates some of the problems that would soon arise with the aggressive rehabilitation of the veteran, and the revisioning of his role in Vietnam. While stressing the connections with the past, Balaban is concerned about whether one can rely on 'ancient tales' to 'tell us new truths'. Vietnam reflected a continuing strand in American history, but it also dislocated the apparently teleological progression of that history, revealing many of the 'ancient tales' that had sustained America to be a sham. The war discredited notions of American innocence, goodness, and manifest destiny, if only for a few years. Balaban's concern, as revealed by the last line, goes beyond the immediately political to the poetic and the metaphysical. He wonders whether there can be any healing and reconciliation without acknowledging pain and suffering. Can poetry deal with love and beauty after the war? Can love find a new language? Is language an adequate mode for representing the war? Balaban's answers to these questions are available in later poems where he meditates on possibilities. The questions invoke a harsh, difficult world, which the poet faces and evokes with courage, insight, and hope.

In 'Saying Goodbye to Mr. and Mrs. My, Saigon, 1972', Balaban expounds the poet's role as teacher and comforter:

> Nowadays, when 'poems are cased in steel,' poets know
> that literary words only limit and lie,
> that fine words only tug at the ear.
> A poet had better keep his mouth shut, we say,
> unless he's found words to comfort and teach.
> Today, comfort and teaching themselves deceive
> and it takes cruelty to make any friends
> when it is a lie to speak, a lie to keep silent.
> Wise to this, most men talk too much.[32]

'Poems are cased in steel' is a self-referential quotation from the first stanza of Balaban's 'For Mrs. Cam, Whose Name Means "Printed Silk"', and refers also to Ho Chi Minh's 'On Reading *The Ten Thousand Poets*', which is an epigraph to Balaban's poem. Ho Chi Minh contrasts the ancients who 'liked to write of natural beauty' with the moderns whose 'poems are cased in steel'.[33] The contrast points to the dilemma of the war poet who finds himself increasingly marginalized, 'unless he's found words to comfort and teach' (an echo of the healing and reconciliation

---

[32] John Balaban, 'Saying Goodbye to Mr. and Mrs. My, Saigon, 1972', *After Our War* (Pittsburgh: University of Pittsburgh Press, 1974), 80. 'A poet had better keep his mouth shut, we say', echoes W. B. Yeats in 'On Being Asked for a War Poem'.

[33] John Balaban, 'For Mrs. Cam', *Blue Mountain* (Greensboro, NC: Unicorn Press Inc., 1982), 41. The lines vary slightly in another translation, where Ho's poem is titled 'On Reading *Anthology of the Thousand Poets*' and 'The ancients [who] liked to hymn the glories of nature' are contrasted with contemporaries whose poems are 'armed with steel'. Maurice M. Durand and Nguyen Tran Huan, *An Introduction to Vietnamese Literature*, trans. D. M. Hawke (New York: Columbia University Press, 1985), 154.

agenda). In a situation where neither silence nor utterance seems adequate, the poet is caught in a bind, and some 'talk too much' (a verbosity and excess of outrage evident in some stateside poetry). Balaban's forte is his ability to combine 'cruelty' and 'natural beauty', a refusal to lie, and an abhorrence of extremes.

'In Celebration of Spring' exemplifies this fine, committed balance. The first two sections deal with decay and the deathly pall of the past, including the POW/MIA question that haunts the nation:

> Our Asian war is over; others have begun.
> Our elders, who tried to mortgage lies,
> are disgraced, or dead, and already
> the brokers are picking their pockets
> for the keys and the credit cards.
>
> In delta swamp in a united Vietnam,
> a Marine with a bullfrog for a face,
> rots in equatorial heat. An eel
> slides through the cage of his bared ribs.
>
> (*Locusts*, 108)

The end of the war marks a beginning as the cynical cyclicity of war is perpetuated by the power brokers (or their descendants) who led America into Vietnam. The idea of the older generation as an embodiment of evil, sacrificing lives of the young and innocent, is a familiar theme in First World War poetry, and recurs in section IV of this poem. Balaban is not interested, however, in apportioning blame, since that allows one set of participants (veterans, for example) to position themselves as victims, and thereby evade responsibility. In a war without conventional heroism or heroes, returning prisoners of war were feted by the nation, and the 'missing in action' became the great absent-presence of the war. The poem employs imagery that deconstructs the MIA myth: the equatorial heat and the eel dominate a landscape partially disturbed by the American presence. Sections III and IV move beyond stagnant memory and disgraced elders to a desire and need for renewal. The flat, low-key language and imagery change to that of hope:

> And today, in the simmer of lyric sunlight,
> the chrysalis pulses in its mushy cocoon,
> under the bark on a gnarled root of an elm.

> In the brilliant creek, a minnow flashes
> delirious with gnats. The turtle's heart
> quickens its taps in the warm bank sludge.
> As she chases a frisbee spinning in sunlight,
> a girl's breasts bounce full and strong;
> a boy's stomach, as he turns, is flat and strong.
>
> (*Locusts*, 108)

Sections I and II are dominated by words such as 'lies', 'disgraced', 'dead', 'swamp', and 'rots'. Contrast this with 'lyric sunlight', 'chrysalis pulses', 'flashes', 'delirious', 'quickens', 'bounce'. Language itself, in the lyrical celebration of new life and health, is revitalized and new possibilities are inscribed. There is a sense of plenitude and, in the figure of the young boy and girl, a turning away from generational decrepitude. It is a sensual celebration of beauty, delicacy, strength, and virility. The contrast with the first two sections is startling, but these are not the final words of the poem. The fourth section is a sombre reminder of responsibilities:

> Swear by the locust, by dragonflies on ferns,
> by the minnow's flash, the tremble of a breast,
> by the new earth spongy under our feet:
> that as we grow old, we will not grow evil,
> that although our garden seeps with sewage,
> and our elders think it's up for auction—swear
> by this dazzle that does not wish to leave us—
> that we will be keepers of a garden, nonetheless.
>
> (*Locusts*, 108–9)

The exhortatory 'Swear' which opens the section sets the tone for the rest of the lines. Images of transience dominate: 'the locust' (with a biblical resonance of righteous destruction), 'dragonflies', 'the minnow's flash'. The exuberance of the previous section is tempered by the need for a new sanctity and conscience in a world menaced by evil and senescence. While acknowledging the inevitability of decay, Balaban stresses the necessity of conscientious renewal. The hope embodied in section III can and indeed must be fulfiled: 'swear | by this dazzle that does not wish to leave us—'. The threat of dissolution is real, and so is the hope 'that we will be keepers of a garden, nonetheless'. The garden image harks back to America's notion of itself as a new Eden and also echoes the aspirations of some of the protest movements in the

1960s. The impulse towards utopian communities (mentioned in Chapter 2) is an attractive and powerful one, and thought to be worth pursuing. Unlike the protest movement, however, Balaban maintains a balance between possibility and betrayal. In holding contraries together he achieves a finer vision of post-Vietnam America, one that is 'cased in steel' and yet 'write[s] of natural beauty'.

The veteran poetry discussed in this section dwells primarily on the travails of homecoming and the trauma of post-war existence. Most such poems are tied to the immediately personal, the inextricability of war memory from a civilian life. The insistence with which this memory obtrudes on daily routine is a classic instance of lives dominated by a traumatic event. As Cathy Caruth observes: 'The pathology consists . . . solely in the structure of its experience or reception: the event is not assimilated or experienced fully at the time, but only belatedly, in its repeated possession of the one who experiences it. To be traumatized is precisely to be possessed by an image or event.'[34] The shutting out of unpleasant experiences is what Ehrhart refers to when he talks of 'put[ting] on blinders', when the 'questions were too disturbing, the answers terrifying'.[35] All these poems are 'possessed' by particular events or images, and poetry is one mode of 'belatedly' attempting to come to terms with that experience. The poems range from political anger and alienation to the resilient remembrance of John Balaban. The poems are still rooted in American problems and dilemmas, and the existential focus heightens the inward-looking bias. Vietnam remains a moral landscape for working out individual traumas, but this section marks the beginning of a move to alternate perceptions. In their representation of memory and trauma, the poets highlight the loss of innocence, the transition from belief in a certain set of values, to loss of belief. There is a movement towards creating new

[34] Cathy Caruth (ed.), *Trauma: Explorations in Memory* (Baltimore and London: The Johns Hopkins University Press, 1995), 4–5.

[35] Interview with W. D. Ehrhart, 6 Feb. 1997. Michael Mok, writing about an amphibious landing in 1965, quotes a Marine: ' "Sometimes I feel like one of the bad guys. I mean in World War II it was more clear-cut. You know, the Nazis on one side and us on the other. But when we go into these *villes* and the people look at you in that sad kind of way they have, it's pretty hard for me to imagine I'm wearing a white hat and riding a white horse." ' Mok's authorial comment is indicative of suppression: 'These are troublesome thoughts, but they are not entertained for long.' Michael Mok, 'Reality of Vietnam', *LIFE*, 59: 22 (Nov. 1965), 50–74.

values and possibilities in some poems I discuss in the following section. The values are expressed tentatively and often overridden by despair, but they do open up and occupy a new moral space. Most significantly, some veteran poems express a desire to reach out to the former enemy, a solidarity that is both personal and political. Old and recurring traumas, the persistence of memory, the contradictions of healing and reconciliation recur in the poetry, but there are visions of alternative worlds.

LIFE AFTER VIETNAM: GESTURES TOWARDS HEALING AND SOLIDARITY

The transition from a poetic inscription of traumatic memories to an awareness of other lives, particularly lives affected by the American presence in Vietnam, is available in Walter McDonald's 'The Food Pickers of Saigon'. The deprivation and degraded lives of refugees in Saigon, particularly the plight of children, are the thematic concern of the poem. It begins with a description of ragpickers:

> Rubbish like compost heaps burned every hour
> of my days and nights at Tan Son Nhut.
> Ragpickers scoured the edges of our junk,
> risking the flames, bent over,
> searching for food. A ton of tin cans
>
> piled up each month, sharp edged, unlabeled.
> Those tiny anonymous people could stick
> their hands inside and claw out whatever
> remained, scooping it into jars, into their
> mouths. No one went hungry. At a distance,
>
> the dump was like a coal mine fire burning
> out of control, or Moses' holy bush
> which was not consumed.[36]

The poetic gaze is still one of distanced observation, and the Vietnamese remain 'tiny anonymous people'. The shift towards a more humanized perspective occurs later in the poem, although even at this stage the picture is suffused with irony. 'No one went

---

[36] Walter McDonald, 'The Food Pickers of Saigon', *After the Noise of Saigon* (Amherst, Mass.: The University of Massachusetts Press, 1988), 5. Subsequent references are indicated after the quotation.

hungry' is a damning reflection of the reality underlying American rhetoric of an economic revolution in south Vietnam. The popular iconography of GIs handing out candy to Vietnamese kids and the economic miracle promised by US advisers is clearly a sham. The scene described is a direct result of American policies that drove south Vietnamese out of their villages (so that they would not support the Vietcong), and into Strategic Hamlets, or Saigon. These programmes disrupted civilian lives in a way and to an extent that Americans could barely imagine. As Frances Fitzgerald points out:

An American in Vietnam observes only the most superficial results of this sudden shift of population: the disease, the filth, the stealing, the air of disorientation about the people of the camps and the towns. What he cannot see are the connections between the mind and the spirit that have been broken to create this human swamp. The connections between society and its product, between one man and another, between the nation and its own history—these are lost for these refugees.[37]

McDonald's poetic observation of the 'human swamp' is, in Fitzgerald's terms, a superficial one, dwelling primarily on externalities. However, in the image of the dump as 'Moses' holy bush / which was not consumed', he conveys an insight of profound disruptions. The 'holy bush' recalls the presence of God, of salvation for a people, the Israelites, held in slavery. The disorientation of bondage under the Pharaoh is an archetype of the dislocation of the Vietnamese held in thrall by US advisers. The image of the 'holy bush' is even more resonant in this context since there is no Moses to lead the Vietnamese out of servitude. The total absence of a redemptory framework makes the Vietnamese position more grim and hopeless. It is this vision and insight that remains with McDonald as he tries 'to think of something good to write my wife', and the poem makes a transition to the present:

> Now, when my children
> eat their meat and bread and leave
> good broccoli or green beans
> on their plates, I call them back
> and growl, I can't help it.

[37] Frances Fitzgerald, *Fire in the Lake: The Vietnamese and the Americans in Vietnam* (Boston: Little, Brown and Company, 1972), 429.

> I never tell them
> why they have to eat it. I never say
> they're like two beautiful children
>
> I found staring at me one night
> through the screen of my window,
> at Tan Son Nhut, bone-faced. Or that
> when I crawled out of my stifling monsoon
> dream to feed them, they were gone.
>
> (*After the Noise*, 6)

In comparing his children, with their access to a comfortable life, to the 'bone-faced' but beautiful Vietnamese ones, McDonald collapses memory and the present. The present represents a life of comfort and privilege, at least a standard of living taken for granted by a majority in the USA. The connection is a clichéd one, a gesture of solidarity that is more self-consolatory than practically useful, but it is the beginning of a vision that is not self-centred, that is aware of his past and, in the recollection of children, acknowledges responsibility for the cruelty meted out to the war's most innocent victims. Vietnamese children were sometimes participants when they were used as messengers and, occasionally, to plant bombs or booby traps. The majority, however, were innocent and bewildered spectators and victims of war frequently menaced by US soldiers. Veterans at the Winter Soldier Investigation testified to practices such as throwing a C-ration can to split a child's forehead. Gloria Emerson explains this behaviour by observing that children 'confront[ed] the soldiers with themselves', highlighting the 'suffering of being unable to love'.[38] McDonald's poem recollects this deficiency and imaginatively attempts to redress the lack of sympathy.

The transition to a point of view that encompasses Vietnamese experiences arose partly out of a desire to expiate guilt and partly out of a genuine solidarity. Several veteran poets, W. D. Ehrhart, Bruce Weigl, John Balaban, Kevin Bowen, among others, have been back to Vietnam, and memorialized those experiences. In a way, these veterans seem to be guided by Balaban's exhortation at the end of his memoirs: 'Go visit Vietnam, I'd tell the troubled vets. Go visit, if you can, and do something good there, and your

---

[38] Gloria Emerson, 'Writers and War', *The Writer in Our World*, highlights of *Tri-Quarterly* magazine's 1984 symposium, Northwestern University, audio cassette, Side B.

pain won't seem so private, your need for resentment so great.'[39] In the realization that their pain is not private in the claustrophobic sense they thought it was, that their enemy, the 'gooks', suffered from, and still live through, the trauma of war, American veteran poets begin to bridge a chasm of ignorance and pain. Some of the best poets sketch not merely a political solidarity (as was done so often and simplistically by the anti-war movement), but a human one, the ability, as Grace Paley puts it, 'to imagine the real—the lives of other people'.[40] This imaginative ability to reach out to the 'other' is often combined with a sense of guilt, a desperate need for reassurance. On his way to Vietnam, Larry Rottmann, veteran-poet, muses on the motivations for his journey back: 'I wanted to meet these folks. To hold them. Touch them. Smell their life and sweat. I want to know they are alive, especially the children. I need to be reassured that we didn't kill or poison them all.'[41] The return to Vietnam is for most veterans caught up with their individual experiences of war, post-war trauma, and desire for solidarity. In a country cut off from US aid and trade links till very recently and ruled by an orthodox Marxist government, the disappointments are aplenty and reassurances more complex than the ones desired by Rottmann. Solidarity is often thwarted by the realities and legacy of a brutal war, as in Ehrhart's poem, 'For Mrs. Na', where he begins with the hope that although he is sorry for the war, he can consign it to a dead past. Confronted with Mrs. Na, he realizes that it is a living presence, and that an apology is a pathetic substitute for loss:

> But here I am at last—
> and here you are.
> And you lost five sons in the war.
> And you haven't any left.
>
> And I'm staring at my hands
> and eating tears,
> trying to think of something else to say
> besides 'I'm sorry.'
>
> (*Wreckage*, 110)

[39] Balaban, *Remembering Heaven's Face*, 333.
[40] Grace Paley, 'Writers and War', *The Writer in Our World*, Side D.
[41] Larry Rottmann, 'A Hundred Happy Sparrows: An American Veteran Returns to Vietnam', *Vietnam Generation*, 1: 1 (Winter 1989), 113–40.

This poetic attempt to transcend a purely egocentric and ethnocentric view of the war represents an imaginative leap that would have been inconceivable during the conflict. Stephen Sossaman concluded his review of *Winning Hearts and Minds* and Casey's *Obscenities*, with the following observation: 'American veterans can probably never adequately assess the Vietnamese people's experience of that war; had we been sensitive enough to their culture much of the war would never have happened. It is enough that veterans begin to test and assay their own experience.'[42] Sossaman is accurate in his estimation of a dominant thread in US cultural ignorance and arrogance that led to the war. His analysis, published in 1973, could not have foreseen that the 'test[ing] and assay[ing]' of veteran poetics and experience would expand to acknowledge, if not include, Vietnamese perspectives.

John Balaban's 'The Book and the Lacquered Box' delves with imagination and empathy into the atmosphere of 'other' lives during the war. It begins with the speaker-observer and his companion being enticed by rare books:

> The ink-specked sheets feel like cigar leaf;
> its crackling spine flutters up a mildewed must.
> Unlike the lacquered box which dry-warp detonated
> —shattering pearled poet, moon, and willow pond—
> the book survived to beg us both go back
> to the Bibliothèque in the Musée at the Jardin in Saigon,
> where I would lean from ledges of high windows
> to see the zoo's pond, isled with Chinese pavilion,
> arched bridge where kids fed popcorn to gulping carp,
> and shaded benches, where whores fanned their make-up,
> at ease because a man who feeds the peacocks
> can't be that much of a beast.
>
> (*Locusts*, 5)

The book and 'lacquered box' as artefacts conjure a world of delicacy and refinement, yet they are threatened with violence and disruption. 'Crackling', 'detonated', and 'shattered' disrupt notions of civilization and peace normally associated with works of art. These words relate not only to the war at hand but, in the references to the 'Bibliothèque' and 'Chinese pavilion', to earlier

---

[42] Stephen Sossaman, 'American Poetry From the Indochina Experience', *Long Island Review*, 2 (Winter 1973–4), 33.

histories of occupation. Architecture and buildings provide a context of imperial domination from within which the poetic gaze turns outward to survey normal life in the guise of kids feeding popcorn and whores fanning themselves. The collocation of innocence and necessity, finesse and violence is extended in the last part of the poem:

> A boatride,
> a soda, a stroll through the flower beds.
> On weekends the crowd could forget the war.
> At night police tortured men in the bear pits,
> one night a man held out the bag of his own guts,
> which streamed and weighed in his open hands,
> and offered them to a bear. Nearby, that night,
> the moon was caught in willows by the pond,
> shone scattered in droplets on the flat lotus pads,
> each bead bright like the dew in Marvell's rose.
>
> (*Locusts*, 5)

The war is a perennial absent presence, and torture is coterminous with the 'crowds' who 'forget the war'. Torture, as Elaine Scarry observes, is 'Brutal, savage, and barbaric, ... and explicitly announces its own nature as an undoing of civilization, acts out the uncreating of the created contents of consciousness'.[43] The poem, while presenting the horror imposed by the client government in south Vietnam, is a conscious act of making. It names and inscribes terrors and deprivations within a context of placidity and beauty. The epigraph to the poem, from Andrew Marvell's 'On a Drop of Dew', emphasizes this context:

> So the Soul, that Drop, that Ray
> Of the clear Fountain of Eternal Day,
> Could it within the humane flow'r be seen.[44]

The poem entwines the lives of people with the pastoral which throws into sharp relief the contrast between the decay and torment of Saigon and a desire for normality and peace. Like

---

[43] Elaine Scarry, *The Body in Pain: The Making and Unmaking of the World* (New York and Oxford: Oxford University Press, 1985), 38.

[44] The next line, 'Remembering still its former height', inscribes the memory of a better world, just as Balaban outlines the possibilities of beauty and civilization. In Marvell's poem contraries are held in balance. See Andrew Marvell, 'On a Drop of Dew', *Complete Poetry* (ed.), George deF. Lord (London and Melbourne: J. M. Dent & Sons Ltd., 1984), 6–7.

Krohn's 'Can Tho', Balaban projects beauty and placidity in the midst of war. Unlike him, however, Balaban does not idealize the people or the landscape. The poignancy of the poem lies in the portrayal of beautiful possibilities and desires cohabiting with real and palpable traumas. The poetic gaze and voice are both engaged and balanced; there are no 'tiny anonymous people' here, neither are they valorized as heroic. Balaban's unique perspective as a conscientious objector allows for insight and empathy in a poem that inscribes comprehension of and solidarity with the 'other'.

Kevin Bowen's collection of poems, *Playing Basketball with the Viet Cong*, 'reinscribes the humanity of a former enemy'.[45] The title poem displays a genuine sympathy with the Gauloise-smoking, ex Vietcong, who comes to the poet's house in Boston, and shoots baskets. 'Graves at Quang Tri' dwells on the price of war from a Vietnamese point of view. The problem of soil erosion and the continuing menace of unexploded mines, some planted, ironically, by the 'liberation' forces from the north, are two facets of post-war Vietnam that Bowen mentions. 'A Conical Hat' offers a rare insight into what it was like fighting for the Vietcong:

> Across the table all night
> I watch the stories
> come alive in his eyes;
> I can almost see the bulb burning;
> a man pedals a bicycle underground,
> in the shadows of the bunker
> he makes power for lights and suction
> in the operating room.
> Lungs burn, he inhales
> fine red bits of earth.
> They are digging to expand the tunnels,
> make more room for the wounded.
>
> (*Playing Basketball*, 52)

The underground network of bunkers and tunnels that sustained the guerrillas was an amazing testimony to the tenacity of a people who would not give in. It was the only way they could have survived the technology unleashed on them. As recollected

---

[45] Carolyn Forché, 'Introduction' to Kevin Bowen, *Playing Basketball with the Vietcong* (Willimantic, Conn.: Curbstone Press, 1994), 7.

by the former guerrilla, the past is a set of stories for the listener-poet, but it is significant that the poet-speaker, the 'I', 'watch[es] the stories | come alive in his eyes'. There is a direct, empathic connection, a desire to know and understand:

> One day he walks
> straight off the earth,
> right into the brown, wrinkled
> hide of an elephant,
> carves meat for a starving platoon,
> takes machete and scalpel,
> makes cut after cut
> until he's covered
> in blood and muscle,
> fighting for air.
>
> (*Playing Basketball*, 53)

The digging of tunnels, the making of 'cut after cut', are analogous to the poetic endeavour of recovering a war that coexisted with the soldier-poet's past, but did not really exist in his consciousness. From a war point of view the tunnels were a dangerous military impediment, but the poet now perceives human lives sustained by and in the tunnels:

> Ten years, his wife
> slept in mountain caves,
> after bombs, repaired roads,
> made posters, paintings
> to record each detail.
> 'Ham Rong Bridge, 1970,' he shows me.
> A woodcut on rice paper.
> Two women in conical hats
> load rocks along a road.
>
> (*Playing Basketball*, 53)

These sections offer a memory of war from the Vietcong perspective, and the 'woodcut on rice paper' is a representation of history as artistic detail. Just as the poem records other war experiences for a primarily American audience, the artifice of the woodcut gives voice to the former enemy. At one level, however, the poetic representation veers towards a heroic mode available in some stateside poetry. While imperialist America bombs Vietnam, its heroic revolutionaries dig in, repair roads, and even have time to make woodcuts. It is the sort of image north Vietnamese propaganda posters presented without any sense of irony. The language of political rhetoric might have different referents, but on both sides it tended to simplify and exaggerate issues. Bowen's poem is redeemed from this tendency to valorize the enemy by the last section, where even the stereotypical conical hat has symbolic connotations not usually noticed by outsiders:

> His eyes burn as he looks
> through the woodcut.
> I thank him. I will need this hat,
> the cool circle of its shade.
>
> (*Playing Basketball*, 54)

For the former Vietcong soldier the woodcut is not merely an artifice: it is a symbol of sacrifice, war, loss, and, perhaps, hate. The waste and sorrow of war cannot be transcended easily, and while he meets his former enemy in amity, and offers the hat as a gift, the gesture is troubled by the past. The poet is aware of this: 'the cool circle of its shade' is what he needs to shield himself from what his countrymen did to the Vietnamese. The hat is a symbol of peace as well as a protection from searing memory. In accepting the hat the poet reaches out to the 'other' and enters another circle of memory with all its troubling associations. The poem inscribes an act of solidarity and responsibility, and in so doing represents 'a just and genuine reconciliation'.[46]

Going back to Vietnam helped many veterans to ameliorate the sense of exile they felt in the USA. It was in some ways an extension of the homecoming theme discernible in poetry discussed in the previous section, a projection of Vietnam as a redemptive landscape. The latter is a theme exaggeratedly presented in some stateside poems in their delineation of the loss of innocence trope. Veteran poets are much more cautious, and if they do valorize Vietnam, it is a qualified endorsement. In fact they are less interested in binary oppositions; they recognize problems in both countries. Their focus is on the possibilities of reconciliation and comprehension of the past. As Kevin Bowen put it, going back to Vietnam 'stirs the mind, rekindles the imagination, and reopens the heart to hope. It cannot change the past, but it can reconnect

---

[46] Carolyn Forché, 'Introduction' to Kevin Bowen, *Playing Basketball with the Vietcong* (Willimantic, Conn.: Curbstone Press, 1994), 7.

the past with the present.'⁴⁷ Some of Bruce Weigl's poems attempt to establish connections and rekindle hopes that the war had snuffed out.

In 'Dialectical Materialism', Weigl describes a Vietnam at peace, the kind of world Rottmann desired when he looked forward to his visit; people live everyday lives and have not all been bombed or poisoned out of existence:

> Through dark tenements and fallen temples
> we wander into Old Hanoi,
> oil lamps glowing in small
> storefronts and restaurants
> where those, so long ago my enemy,
> sit on low chairs and praise the simple evening.
> . . . .
> The people talk and smoke,
> men hold each other's hands again in that old way
> and children,
> their black and white laughter all around us,
> kick the weighted feather
> with such grace into the air
> because the bombs have stopped.⁴⁸

It is a sympathetic portrait of a city and a world that was heavily bombed, particularly during Nixon's Christmas bombing in 1972. The scene is a type of pastoral: peaceful, harmonious, simple. It not only contrasts with the frantic horrors of war, but with stereotyped notions of the enemy. The shift from cultural typecasting and ignorance to awareness is evident in the line, 'men hold each other's hands again in that old way'. In Vietnam the sight of men holding hands was common and not necessarily an indication of sexual preference. For American soldiers, raised in a dominant culture and trained in a military that emphasizes manly virtues, the Vietnamese were effeminate and, most likely, homosexual. Charles R. Anderson observed this cultural prejudice and shock amongst Americans in Vietnam:

there was still another characteristic about the Vietnamese which completely repulsed the grunts. Asian peoples are much less inhibited

---

⁴⁷ Cited in Jayne S. Werner and Luu Doan Huynh (eds.), *The Vietnam War: Vietnamese and American Perspectives* (New York and London: M. E. Sharpe, 1993), 267.

⁴⁸ Bruce Weigl, *Song of Napalm* (New York: Atlantic Monthly Press, 1988), 66. Subsequent references are indicated after the quotation.

than westerners about displaying their affection for friends of the same sex. Among Asians, holding hands or walking arm in arm in public does not arouse suspicions of homosexuality. The grunts, however, were shocked at such behavior. They needed to believe their allies and those whose freedom they were supposedly defending were better than 'a bunch of queers.'[49]

Weigl may not have shared this attitude during the war but he is aware of a climate of ignorant condemnation and reverses it here. The reversal of cultural stereotype and the obvious sympathy of the poet does not, however, conceal an element of voyeurism. The observer is an outsider, pleased and relieved that the former enemy is getting along so well. If Vietnam and the return to it are constructed as redemptive landscapes, it is necessary that the enemy should be at peace, that the hardships of war be concealed, since that will return the observer-poet back to responsibility. To Weigl's credit, the poem does not shy away from the troubling legacies and questions of the war. At the Long Bien bridge they meet a man taking water to his corn, and he is a more, though not sufficiently, individuated figure:

> When we ask our questions
> he points to a stone and stick
> house beyond the dikes
> one thousand meters from the bridge
> our great planes
> could not finally knock down.
> He doesn't say
> how he must have huddled
> those nights with his family,
> how he must have spread himself
> over them
> until the village bell
> called them back to their beds.
> There are questions which
> people who have everything
> ask people who have nothing
> and they do not understand.
>
> (*Song of Napalm*, 67)

---

[49] Cited in Jacqueline Lawson, 'She's a Pretty Woman for a Gook: The Misogyny of the Vietnam War', in Philip K. Jason (ed.), *Fourteen Landing Zones: Approaches to Vietnam War Literature* (Iowa City: University of Iowa Press, 1991), 23.

'He doesn't say' is a key line in that the poet is aware of life events, traumas, memories that he can only dimly imagine. He is the perennial outsider, and the reticence of the Vietnamese farmer outlines a world of terrible suffering and dignified perseverance, something from which the poet can learn. As a veteran and a poet, he is aware of a subtext of anguish that is concealed beneath the graceful surfaces. He is also conscious of difference, of an inability to bridge cultural chasms, and the last four lines encompass this lack of comprehension. These lines are self-reflexive: they mediate precisely the questions of voyeurism and placid, uninvolved observation that were raised in section I. At the end, the poet is aware of the contrary visions he and his enemy bring to the war. Perhaps these attitudes arise out of cultural difference: 'people who have everything | ask people who have nothing'. While Vietnam is projected in the USA as something that happened to America, there is a whole world that suffered the war as well, and Weigl attempts to inscribe that reality. The desire to 'imagine the real' is entangled with the poet's personal agenda: the need to be reassured, to expiate guilt. This does not undermine the credibility of the desire, but it does indicate the tangled, intricate web of memory, trauma, and exile that the poet translates on to the 'other' in his representation of that 'other' world. Some of these themes recur in 'Her Life Runs Like a Red Silk Flag'.

The poem offers a more intimate, person-to-person interaction and understanding than in 'Dialectical Materialism'. The point of view is neither distanced nor voyeuristic:

> Because this evening Miss Hoang Yen
> sat down with me in the small
> tiled room of her family house
> I am unable to sleep.
> We shared a glass of cold and sweet water.
> On a blue plate her mother brought us
> cake and smiled her betel black teeth at me
> but I did not feel strange in the house
> my country had tried to bomb into dust.[50]

---

[50] Bruce Weigl, 'Her Life Runs Like a Red Silk Flag', *What Saves Us* (Evanston, Ill.: TriQuarterly Books, 1992), 13. Subsequent references are indicated after the quotation.

The genuine sense of empathy coexists with an unease, an overstatement of feeling at home. Miss Yen's recollection in the next few lines about her childhood in Hanoi during Nixon's Christmas bombing has the force of personal testimony that disrupts the glib acceptance of responsibility on the poet's part. Her account of war reopens the wounds of trauma and conscience:

> She let me hold her hand,
> her shy unmoving fingers, and told me
> how afraid she was those days and how this fear
> had dug inside her like a worm and lives
> inside her still, won't die or go away.
>
> (*What Saves Us*, 13)

Her fear is analogous to veteran trauma whereby the war becomes a continuous living presence. For the veteran-poet who returns to Vietnam this account offers a unique perspective on his own troubles. Some veteran poetry in its portrayal of post-war trauma is, perhaps understandably, wrapped up in its existential angst and tends to project the war as a unique and very personal problem. In recent years, particularly since the official rehabilitation of the veteran, he has been reconstructed as a victim, first of the war and then of neglect on returning home. Soldiers were traumatized by the war, and bewildered, angry, and alienated on their return home (as is evident from the poetry discussed in the previous chapters), but to construe the soldier as victim elides certain other problems. As Kali Tal points out: '"Soldier as victim" representations depend upon the invisibility of the soldiers' own victims, namely Vietnamese soldiers and civilians.'[51] Weigl highlights the hitherto invisible, gives voice to the victim and, paradoxically, only the victim can offer real forgiveness:

> And because she's stronger, she comforted me,
> said I'm not to blame,
> the million sorrows alive in her gaze.
> With the dead we share no common rooms.
> With the frightened we can't think straight;
> no words can bring the burning city back.
>
> (*What Saves Us*, 13)

---

[51] Tal, *Worlds of Hurt*, 138.

The poet acknowledges a weakness arising from guilt, and although he was not personally responsible for the bombing of Hanoi, he takes on his country's burden. The absolution offered is not sentimentalized, and the 'million sorrows', the dead and the frightened permeate the present consciousness. A healing and reconciliation that buried or rewrote the past (as some of the official reconciliation does) would be inadequate and would fail to establish any sympathetic connection. The poetic reconciliation is open to the contradictions and pain of the past and its memory in the present:

> All night I ached for her and for myself
> and nothing I could think or pray
> would make it stop. Some birds sang morning
> home across the lake. In small reed boats
> the lotus gatherers sailed out
> among their resuming white blossoms.
>
> (*What Saves Us*, 14)

In the midst of pain and trauma, Weigl presents the lotus gatherers as a revitalizing vision. The 'resuming white blossoms' are emblematic of a pastoral that is sometimes evoked as a counterpoint to the blighting experiences of war. One wonders, however, whether the residue of horrible memories can be counterbalanced by the pastoral evocation. There is another problematic thread running through the poem: the constant emphasis on the 'I'. Although the poem articulates the pain of another, vulnerable being, that utterance is placed within the context of the speaker-poet's desire, almost imperative need, for forgiveness. Miss Yen, in her ability to forgive, seems to understand this need; she combines remembrance with forgiveness. Weigl expressed awareness of a culture of egotism in an interview, which also explains the self-centred nature of some of the poetry: 'they [the Vietnamese] don't take the war as personally as we took it. It's easier for them to forgive. Because ours is an egocentric culture whereas theirs is a much more selfless culture. If you're Vietnamese, you're always attached to some larger thing: a family, hamlet, village, et cetera. It's not just "I".'[52] Weigl generalizes and thereby simplifies the differences, but the lack of

---

[52] Cited in Eric James Schroeder, *Vietnam, We've All Been There: Interviews With American Writers* (Westport, Conn., and London: Praeger Publishers, 1992), 194.

Vietnamese egotism in the poem is striking. It may not be easier for Miss Yen to forgive, but she can because she transcends (if only for a moment) her world and reaches out to another one. In fact she displays greater strength of character and capacity for solidarity than the poet-speaker. The latter is egotistical, weak, and passive, but the poet inscribes the possibilities of hope and renewal. That he does so within uncompromising contexts of indelible pain and trauma, makes the poetic effort all the more resonant and valuable.

The path towards reconciliation and understanding that I have traced thus far might convey the impression that veteran poetry developed in an unproblematic and linear mode; that once veterans undertook the pilgrimage back to Vietnam, they were entirely convinced of the need for rapprochement. While the desire for solidarity is a strong one, there are disruptions that modify any simplistic notion of post-war brotherhood across borders. I have indicated some of the problems in the poems of McDonald, Bowen, and Weigl. In David Connolly's 'Another Chance', complex and violent impulses coexist with the stated desire of acknowledging the humanity of his former enemy. The poem begins with the latter sentiment:

> What I'd like, I guess,
> is another chance
> with those I know I killed.
> Perhaps to sit over a meal
> and talk, share cold beers,
> easy laughs, some fine smoke.
> I don't want to be friends.[53]

Although the section begins tentatively—'I guess'—in its cataloguing of things he could share, he seems confident that solidarity is indeed what he desires. The list of things he would like to do with an enemy now dead conveys a sense of regret, of opportunities for fellowship that were disrupted by the war. This is a theme common to the literature of other wars, reaching out to an enemy, acknowledging in Whitman's terms the divinity of the dead adversary. This idea is taken up in the following section:

---

[53] David Connolly, *Lost in America* (Woodbridge, Conn.: Viet Nam Generation Inc. & Burning Cities Press, 1994), 52. Subsequent references are indicated after the quotation.

> But I'd like, I guess,
> to show them
> that I know, though I killed them
> they were more like me than not.
>
> (*Lost in America*, 52)

These lines and stated sympathies are jeopardized by the statement that links the two sections: 'I don't want to be friends.' The coexistence of a desire for solidarity and its denial give the poem a yes–no dialectic, as if one were following the flow of thoughts and arguments in the speaker's mind. The final section tips the scales and ends in a desire for renewed violence:

> But I'm afraid I'd remember
> that those I killed
> each had their own dead
> who were my Brothers
> and I might wait
> for another chance
> to kill them all again.
>
> (*Lost in America*, 52)

The 'I don't want to be friends' that disrupted sections I and III, is now fully extended. He cannot be friends because he cannot forget or forgive. He cannot transcend the us–them paradigm that had sustained the war and its attendant hatred. Instead of reconciliation there is a recovery of violence, and the poem conveys the disturbing reality of a post-war vengeance fantasy. Paradoxically, the poem ends with a type of solidarity—the kinship the speaker feels for his 'Brothers'—that inverts the universal brotherhood nominally conceptualized in sections I and III. 'Another Chance' (the title is both ambiguous and ominous) encapsulates in its quiet, colloquial language, a contradictory and disturbing pathology of post-war desires, and disrupts any notion of a smooth transition to reconciliation.

The veteran, grappling with the intractable networks of personal involvement, history, politics, and memory, is often unable to perceive complexities and paradoxes in his situation. Steve Mason's poetry embodies some of these confusions, even as he is hailed as the 'Poet Laureate of Vietnam Veterans' (blurb on the back cover of his collection, *Warrior for Peace*), and goes around the country delivering poems at official ceremonies. His first collection, *Johnny's Song*, has many poems which were recited to commemorate veteran events. For instance, 'The Wall Within' was 'Delivered at the Commencement of the National Salute II in Washington D.C., on Nov. 19. 1984 as part of the official activities prior to the dedication of the Vietnam Veterans Memorial as a national monument'.[54] With Mason, the veteran-poet announces his presence at the site of the new veteran-political stage and he is a reincarnation of the counter-culture gurus in his public readings and activism. Vince Gotera characterizes him as 'an attractive, charismatic figure, a spokesman for Vietnam veterans, a cathartic presence'.[55] His voice and profile, as well as the media attention he has received, do provide a necessary corrective to the long neglect that the Vietnam veteran suffered. However, Mason has a propensity for sweeping, prophetic statements and, like some of his stateside predecessors such as Allen Ginsberg, he has been transformed into a cult figure. Lorrie Smith highlights the problems inherent in a poetry that is more of a roadshow than serious reflection:

> Hawking his work on the veteran's memorial circuit and sounding like a cross between Chuck Norris and Rod McKuen, Mason's lugubrious ramblings have little to offer the serious reader. His work is significant, however, because as a slick commodity of popular sentiment, it gives expression to some of our culture's inchoate anxieties about men, women, and war.[56]

The grand rhetorical flourishes in some of his poems reflect insights into the veteran's situation and a desire to be assimilated, without quite mediating political and historical quagmires.

In 'The Wall Within', Mason begins by expressing anger at various conceptual constructs that are mobilized to constitute the sense of a country:

> Sometimes, when I'm angry
> it seems as if I could start my own country

---

[54] Steve Mason, *Johnny's Song* (New York and London: Bantam Books, 1987), 18. Subsequent references are indicated after the quotation.

[55] Vince Gotera, *Radical Visions: Poetry by Vietnam Veterans* (Athens, Ga., and London: The University of Georgia Press, 1994), 220.

[56] Lorrie Smith, 'Back Against the Wall: Anti-Feminist Backlash in Vietnam War Literature', in Jacqueline Lawson (ed.), *Vietnam Generation*, special issue, *Gender and the War: Men, Women, and Vietnam*, 1: 3–4 (Summer–Fall 1989), 115–26.

> with the same twenty Spill and Spell words
> we shake out at the feet of our heroes
> . . . .
> Words like:
> peace and sacrifice, war and young
> supreme and duty, service and honor
> country, nation, men and men and men again,
> sometimes God and don't forget women!
> Army, Air Force, Navy, Marines and freedom.
>
> (*Johnny's Song*, 8)

The pairing of words like 'peace and sacrifice' are precisely the modes used by the state and its armed forces to mobilize for war. The catalogue is accurate in its Hemingwayesque awareness of the sham and obscenity that underpins the manipulation of these concepts.[57] The repetition of 'men' that breaks the pairing is like the cry of a victim: men have suffered from war and, paradoxically, upheld the very concepts that perpetuate their suffering. The list closes with 'freedom', the putative purpose of war, particularly the one in Vietnam. This awareness of contingency, of hierarchies of power that constitute the manufacture of consent, is an important as well as an uncomfortable one and Mason shies away from it:

> Then, just as quickly the anger passes
> and reverence takes its place.
> Those are good words, noble words, solemn
> & sincere
> It is the language of Death
> which frightens me
>
> (*Johnny's Song*, 9)

This is a startling recovery, as if Mason had looked into the abyss of new possibilities and meanings, and recoiled in terror. He reposes trust and 'reverence' (a term with loaded religious

---

[57] In *A Farewell to Arms*, Frederick Henry muses on the hollowness of such concepts: 'I was always embarrassed by the words sacred, glorious, and sacrifice and the expression in vain. We had heard them, sometimes standing in the rain almost out of earshot, so that only the shouted words came through, and read them, on proclamations that were slapped up by billposters over other proclamations, now for a long time, and I had seen nothing sacred, and the things that were glorious had no glory and the sacrifices were like the stockyards at Chicago if nothing was done with the meat except to bury it.' Ernest Hemingway, *A Farewell to Arms* (1929; London: Everyman's Library, 1993), 175.

connotations) in those very constructs he had condemned earlier. He overlooks the fact that political language, in so far as language is instrumentalist, is constituted partly of what he now calls 'the language of Death'. His desire for comforting moral categories is naïve, and the need to recover nationalist myths and locate the veteran within a more heroic cultural framework falls into the trap of revisionism. It is significant that Mason's poem in its context and manner of presentation is complicit with the politics of rehabilitation that the Wall represents. His poem does not interrogate the heroic-nationalist framework in any significant sense. In fact he seizes the occasion as an opportunity for national and community recuperation. The dubious aspect of this project lies in the simplifications and confusions of perspective, the eliding of disconcerting facts. Steve Mason and his poetry seem to benefit from a cultural phenomenon that values 'authentic', first-hand, experiential poetry as long as it raises no discomfiting questions, and promises absolution. Mason's popularity also coincides with the aggressive recuperation of the war by the political right in the USA. His is the poetic voice of pseudo-insight and his poetry helps to highlight the finer achievements of the better veteran poets.

W. D. Ehrhart is perhaps the most intense and committed chronicler of post-Vietnam America. The messianic mode and stridency, noted in poems in the previous section is still apparent, but there are new tones and voices as he has matured as a poet. These voices increasingly encompass the Vietnamese and his own family, particularly his daughter, Leela. There is a type of philosophical insight, an ability to perceive and live in contraries, a refusal to be silent in spite of all the disillusionment. I discuss a few of his poems to draw out this progression and to highlight the vision of a veteran-poet in a time of artificial reconciliation and healing.

'Letter', from the collection *Empire* published in 1978, begins with a deep sense of alienation, a 'death wish' that the aftermath seems to have heightened:

> But I lived,
> long enough to wonder often
> how you missed; long enough
> to wish too many times
> you hadn't.

> What's it like back there?
> It's all behind us here;
> and after all those years of possibility,
> things are back to normal.
> We just had a special birthday,
> and we've found again our inspiration
> by recalling where we came from
> and forgetting where we've been.
>
> (*Wreckage*, 29)

The first section refers to a north Vietnamese grenadier in Hué City who just missed killing him, and now survival seems worse than death. The sense of alienation:

> alive among a people
> I can never feel
> at ease with anymore...
>
> (*Wreckage*, 30)

is heightened by the general apathy in the country. The Bicentennial celebrations, coming hard on the heels of defeat in Vietnam and Watergate, were a conscious revival of the 'feel good' factor. It was as if the country had collectively decided to forget the traumas of the past decade and hark back to America's 'glorious' founding and subsequent history. 'Possibility' is a key word, since the poet feels that all the hopes of a new and better society, envisioned by both President Johnson and the peace movement, have been betrayed. It is this sense of betrayal that is the impulse behind the question, 'What's it like back there?' and the exhortation that follows:

> remember where you've been, and why.
> And then build houses; build villages,
> dikes and schools, songs
> and children in that green land
> I blackened with my shadow
> and the shadow of my flag.
>
> Remember Ho Chi Minh
> was a poet: please
> do not let it all come down
> to nothing.
>
> (*Wreckage*, 30)

The poet's sense of alienation in his own country, guilt at his complicity in the war, and a transference of hope coalesce in this plea for a better future in Vietnam. The problem of betrayal is a theme that recurs in Ehrhart's and other veteran writings. Part of the project of veteran poetry is predicated on betrayal: it begins by writing the disillusion of war where heroic paradigms are exposed as horror; it then castigates the nation for not living up to its stated ideals; and finally, a sense of impotence at the inefficacy of poetry in dominant contexts of revisionism and regeneration. Some of these anxieties are available in stateside poetry and explain the acute oppositional stances adopted by some poets. In its projection of hope on to an idealized Vietnam, 'Letter' echoes the binarism evident in stateside protest poetry. The formula is simple: since America, the fountainhead of all 'good', has now revealed itself as 'evil', the enemy must fulfil all these failed possibilities. It is a simplistic dichotomy that reveals the insecurities of the poet, and ignores the problems in post-revolution Vietnam.[58] Ho Chi Minh was, indeed, a poet and a beacon of hope for oppressed peoples everywhere, but he was also a ruthless politician. 'Letter' expresses a kind of solidarity, but it is marred by a projection of personal angst and idealized clichés. There is not much imaginative empathy and the images, in their projection of goodness and hope, are stilted. The overly public, exhortatory mode of 'Letter' marks a first step, however, towards a more genuine solidarity available in the poem 'The Distance We Travel'.

The title poem of a collection published in 1993, 'The Distance We Travel' marks the path Ehrhart has traversed since writing 'Letter'. The poet-speaker, referred to as 'The Strange American' or 'the stranger' throughout the poem, is plunged into the world projected in 'Letter' and seeks forgiveness:

> In silence he passes among them
> nodding agreeably, nodding in wonder,
> nodding at what he remembers was here,
> wanting to gather the heart of this place
> into himself, to make it forgive him.
>
> (*Wreckage*, 175)

There is no exhortation here and none of the public posturing

---

[58] For a more complex vision of post-war Vietnam see Ehrhart's 'The Perversion of Faith', *Wreckage*, 217, which portrays the extravagance, obscenity, and betrayal of 'pure' revolutionary ideals.

evident in 'Letter'. The poet moves in silence, he wishes to immerse himself in this strange and vivid world. The war exists as memory, but there is no need for imagery such as 'blackened with my shadow'. The desire to belong and the plea for forgiveness coexist, and contraries can be held in balance. The stranger's walk through a Vietnamese town leads him to two girls playing badminton. He plays with them and is then served a 'cool drink', and sits with the girls' father. To override the awkwardness he shows them a photograph of his daughter, Leela, and the man responds by showing him the scars he suffered at the hands of the Vietcong:

> The father lifts his shirt to reveal
> a scar on his chest. 'VC,' he says, then
> drops his shirt and lights a cigarette,
> offers one to the stranger. Together
> they smoke the quiet smoke of memory.
>
> Seven years the father spent in a camp
> for prisoners of war. The wife
> lightly touches her husband's knee.
> Lightly his hand goes to hers.
>
> The stranger considers the years he has spent
> wearing the weight of what he has done,
> thinking his tiny part important.
>
> . . . .
>
> The children are playing badminton again.
> The shuttlecock lands in the stranger's lap.
> 'Li-La,' the father softly says, touching
> the stranger's heart with his open hand.
>
> (*Wreckage*, 176–7)

The father, who suffered during and after the war, destroys any notion of a binary opposition between 'evil' Americans and 'good' VC. The situation was more complex and the re-education camps set up in post-war Vietnam (for unreconstructed non-communists) were as horrific as the penal systems in wartime south Vietnam. The father's experience enables the speaker to transcend partially his solipsistic attitude. Now he has some insight into the aftermath of what was also a civil war, a world of great suffering, perseverance, and finally, forgiveness. The transition from a world of violence and hardship to one of tenderness and concern, is reflected in the final act of solidarity: '"Li-La," the father softly says, touching | the stranger's heart with his open hand.' As in Weigl's 'Her Life Runs Like a Red Silk Flag' it is the victim, the formerly weak, who now has the strength to forgive. The bonds of solidarity are stronger and less ambiguous in Ehrhart's poem because the bridge is his daughter. The Vietnamese father reaches out to a sphere of innocence, in the hope that another father's memory will spare the world and its children the trauma of war.

One of the themes and concerns that animates Ehrhart's postwar poetry is the future of America, and he perceives this future in terms of its ability to learn from the past. He sees himself as a poet and teacher and invests a tremendous amount of hope in children. That hope is often shattered (as it was during the Gulf War when another generation of 17–18 year olds went to war), and Ehrhart's poems move from messianic protest to an occasional sense of futility, to the imperative need to carry on. 'The Teacher' is dedicated to his 'students at Sandy Spring Friends School' and translates the lessons he learnt into a zeal to pass that on:

> Hardly older then
> than you are now,
> I hunched down shaking
> like an old man
> alone in an empty cave
> among the rocks of ignorance
> and malice honorable men
> call truth.
>
> Out of that cave I carried
> anger like a torch
> to keep my heart from freezing,
> and a strange new thing called
> love
> to keep me sane.
>
> (*Wreckage*, 49)

The sense of betrayal and loss of innocence noted in earlier poems fuels the anger that Ehrhart brings back with him. The cave image and its collocation with 'ignorance' is significant in its echoes of Plato's simile of the cave in *The Republic*. Just as the denizens of Plato's cave lived in darkness and ignorance, until one ventured out to perceive a very different reality, so too Ehrhart sees his prewar state as mired in myth and non-knowledge. The simile 'anger like a torch' extends the idea of enlightenment dawning on the poet, and he brings 'light' not only out of the cave, but also back to the 'cave' that is post-war America. Teaching becomes not only a mode of communicating knowledge, but a personal and philosophical obligation. It is important that as a teacher he is sustained not merely by anger but by love, a genuine concern for a collective future. As he wrote in an article 'Why Teach Vietnam?' the purpose is not to foster divisions; even in opposition the love of country can be preserved:

I do not seek to turn the youth of America into leftist political activists or implacable opponents of the U.S. government. I still believe that we all owe something to our country. I do not believe, however, that what we owe our country is uncritical support for our government's policies or that young people owe military service wherever and whenever the government demands it. . . . What we owe our children is the opportunity to learn to think clearly and knowledgeably . . . I do not want my children and their generation to have to go through the fire that savaged me and my generation.[59]

This is a remarkably sober manifesto from a man and poet 'savaged' by Vietnam. It voices a vision and a desire that sustain him despite disappointments. At the same time there is an element of hubris in the projection of the poet as prophet. It is the assumption of this mantle, perhaps, that leads to inevitable despair. 'The Teacher', however, is redeemed as a poetic statement by its admission of vulnerability:

> It is a desperate future
> I cling to,
> and it is yours.
> . . . . . .
> I am afraid;
> I do not want to fail:
>
> I need your hands to steady me;
> I need your hearts to give me courage;
> I need you to walk with me
> until I find a voice
> that speaks the language
> that you speak.
>
> (*Wreckage*, 50)

[59] W. D. Ehrhart, 'Why Teach Vietnam?', *Social Education*, 52: 1 (Jan. 1988), 25–6.

Having lost his illusions and hopes, he hopes to instil knowledge that will sustain a future generation. The poem is animated by belief in the transformative possibilities arising from painful experiences. Robert Jay Lifton provides a psychological paradigm for such desires: 'The death imprint is likely to be associated not only with pain but also with value—with a special form of knowledge and potential inner growth associated with the sense of having "been there and returned."'[60] Ehrhart wishes to translate his encounter with 'the death imprint' into an ethical and collective future. It is a task he undertakes with fear, particularly of failure, and the reiteration of 'need' underlines his sense of inadequacy. It also emphasizes his alienation from a country he loved and cannot, indeed will not, entirely dissociate himself from. The need to communicate, to establish a connection with the most vulnerable section of his people, is both a task and a means of salvation. It represents a different mode of solidarity than the one in 'Letter' or 'The Distance We Travel', and is as important. 'The Teacher' is an amalgam of betrayal, anger, love, concern, and vulnerability. It ends with the tentative hope that he will find a voice that speaks a language that can communicate. It is a vision of enlightened and hopeful community that events in the 1980s and 1990s were to belie. Despite all the disincentives and despair, however, Ehrhart finds it impossible to maintain silence in the face of what he perceives to be lies and hypocrisy. As he wrote in 'Stealing Hubcaps': 'Nothing I do will make any difference, but to do nothing requires a kind of amnesia I have yet to discover a means of inducing.'[61] The messianic zeal and naïvety available in 'The Teacher' is modified in later poems by an awareness of futility and contradictions. Poetry, protest, and prophecy, the imperative need to tell the truth, now coexist with an awareness of contraries, and this maturer, quieter perspective is evident in poems such as 'The Farmer', 'Why I Don't Mind Rocking Leela to Sleep', and 'The Way Light Bends'.

'The Farmer' encapsulates some of the anxieties of earlier poems, but it does so in a more restrained manner:

---

[60] Robert Jay Lifton, 'Understanding the Traumatized Self: Imagery, Symbolization, and Transformation', in John P. Wilson, Zev Harel, and Boaz Kahana (eds.), *Human Adaptation to Extreme Stress: From the Holocaust to Vietnam* (New York and London: Plenum Press, 1988), 19.

[61] W. D. Ehrhart, 'Stealing Hubcaps', *In the Shadow of Vietnam*, 126.

> Each day I go into the fields,
> to see what is growing
> and what remains to be done.
> It is always the same thing: nothing
> is growing; everything needs to be done.
>
> . . . .
>
> I have sown my seed on soil
> guaranteed by poverty to fail.
>
> (*Wreckage*, 79)

The messianic desire to tell the truth is still evident although the terms of metaphorical reference have altered. While an earlier poem, 'The Teacher', employed Plato's simile of the cave to convey the need for truth-telling, here Ehrhart uses the parable of the sower. 'I have sown my seed on soil | guaranteed by poverty to fail' is from Christ's ministry and the biblical context recalls the prophetic mode. If the nation and its collective memory are the barren soil, Ehrhart as poet-prophet-Christ figure is one constantly faced by failure.[62] Yet the parable is one of possibility for the seed that fell on good soil did grow; there is hope that the poetic voice does not speak in a total wilderness, and the second section conveys some of this resilience:

> But I don't complain—except
> to passersby who ask me why
> I work such barren earth.
> They would not understand me
> if I stooped to lift a rock
> and hold it like a child, or laughed,
> or told them it is their poverty
> I labor to relieve. For them,
> I complain. A farmer of dreams
> knows how to pretend. A farmer of dreams
> knows what it means to be patient.
> Each day I go into the fields.
>
> (*Wreckage*, 79)

The need to bear witness is still the animating impulse behind

---

[62] The soldier-poet as a Christ figure is available in First World War poetry. Ernest Spencer comments on the paradoxical idea in his memoir: 'There isn't a Christian thing about war. If Jesus is supposed to be about love, then there is no way that he'd have a thing to do with war or violence.' *Welcome to Vietnam, Macho Man: Reflections of a Khe Sanh Vet* (Springfield, Oh.: Corps Press, 1987), 156.

poetic utterance, but it is not bound by anger or impatience. The allegory of the farmer of dreams envisions the poet as a type of practical visionary. It is a vision of isolation but it does address a potential future community. The poem does not hold out hope for an immediate solidarity in terms of experiences, and in that it is analogous to Ehrhart's own reactions after the war. He says that he has 'no sense of veteran solidarity', and that it is 'shared ideas that create a sense of community not the experience in Vietnam itself'.[63] This lack of veteran solidarity is perhaps furthered by right-wing veterans who have recreated community by warping history or ignoring its unpleasant aspects. Caught between different kinds of amnesia and revisionism the poet ploughs a lonely furrow, hoping his word will have currency some time in the future.

It is a bleak hope and in 'Why I Don't Mind Rocking Leela to Sleep' Ehrhart reverts to a sense of despair:

> What hurts most
> is the plodding sameness
> of cruelty, a circular world
> impervious to change,
> the grinding erosion of hope
> stripping the soul.
> These days, it almost seems enough
> just to accomplish the household chores
> and still be ready for work.
>
> (*Wreckage*, 115)

The poem is weighed down by anomie and failure, a loneliness that is ameliorated only by his family. Leela is a precious being he wants to shelter from the ravages of the world, but the world intrudes, and it is not one Ehrhart would like his daughter to inherit:

> What I want for my daughter
> she shall never have:
> a world without war, a life
> untouched by bigotry or hate,
> a mind free to carry a thought
> up to the light of pure possibility.

---

[63] Interview with W. D. Ehrhart, 6 Feb. 1997.

> She should be young forever.
> I could hold her here in my arms
> and offer her comfort,
> a place to rest,
> the illusion, at least, of shelter.
>
> (*Wreckage*, 115–16)

Out of despair and loneliness arises a vision of an ideal and impossible world, and that furthers the sense of hopelessness of the poet. The instinct for protecting and nurturing is aroused at the beginning of the poem by the connection drawn between a car backfiring and rifle shots. The war remains a constant memory and all attempts to fashion a future different from the past end in failure. This is a continuation of the loss of innocence theme: just as he lives in a post-lapsarian world, so too will Leela have to deal with a world of war, bigotry, and hate. Responsibility and vision provide insight and despair, and in 'The Way Light Bends' Ehrhart asks for a metaphorical blindness, the comfort of ignorance:

> A kind of blindness, that's what's needed now.
> Better not to know. Better to notice
> the way light bends through trees in winter dusk.
>
> What, after all, does knowledge bring? Cold rage,
> the magnitude of history, despair.
>
> . . . .
>
> what's possible, what is, what can't be changed
> is better left to dreamers, fools, and God.
>
> . . . .
>
>   Marvel at
> the way light bends through trees in winter dusk
> and don't imagine how the light will bend
> the way light bends through trees in winter dusk
> and burst forever when the missiles fly.
> A kind of blindness, that's what's needed now.
>
> (*Wreckage*, 147)

The dichotomy between a poetry of isolation and that of engagement is too neat and binary. It sets up a rhetorical argument that knowledge brings rage and despair, but it is an easy way out of the dilemma of responsibility and knowledge. To notice 'the way light bends through trees in winter dusk' is not necessarily an opting out of engaged poetry. In fact, while the rhetorical construction of the poem trumpets the efficacy of blindness, the poem is actually rooted in vision. It might be hubristic to try to change 'what can't be changed', but it is bad faith to know better and turn a blind eye. This can be construed as a poetry of despair and hopelessness, and at one level it is, but it implicitly projects hope, warmth, and integrity. In the act of writing the poem and raising the questions he does, Ehrhart refuses to be swamped by blindness and despair.

An underlying anxiety in 'Why I Don't Mind Rocking Leela to Sleep' and 'The Way Light Bends' is the ineffectiveness of poetry in a culture that has rewritten the Vietnam War, and rehabilitated the veteran. In this culture, Ehrhart projects himself as one of a minority group, and wonders whether dissent makes a difference. In an oft-quoted statement at the 1985 Asia Society conference on literature and the Vietnam War, he asserted an overly didactic and instrumentalist agenda:

> I find it extremely difficult to sit here and talk about the Vietnam War as art. I don't give a damn about art. I'm not an artist. I'm an educator, and my writing is a tool of education. . . . if I cannot affect the course of my country as a result of my experiences, then whatever I do as a writer is an utter failure.[64]

This artist–educator dichotomy is seldom evident in Ehrhart's best poems and to see his work in either-or terms is to simplify it. Lorrie Smith's response to this statement is more accurate than an analysis that eventually proves that Ehrhart is an artist despite his predilection for educating. She writes: 'It is more realistic, I think, to take this confession as a highly rhetorical indication of Ehrhart's distrust of art purely for art's sake and his deep commitment to writing which will reach the unconverted and bring about progressive social and political change.'[65] Ehrhart's poetic anxieties, particularly the transformation of Vietnam into pure

---

[64] Cited in Timothy Lomperis, *'Reading the Wind': The Literature of the Vietnam War* (Durham, NC: Duke University Press, 1987), 32. In the interview cited earlier, Ehrhart indicated that this statement had come at the end of a long academic discussion on the war which seemed to forget that it had been a brutal, bloody war, and that he was uncomfortable with discussing Vietnam 'bloodlessly'.

[65] Lorrie Smith, 'Against a Coming Extinction: W. D. Ehrhart and the Evolving Canon of Vietnam Veterans' Poetry', *War, Literature, & the Arts*, 8: 2 (Fall–Winter 1996), 1–30.

poesis, is expressed in his more didactic poems, as well as in the later poems of despair. Art and didacticism, impotence and power can and do coexist in a text (the poem) that interprets the aftermath of the war. Ehrhart's occasional sense of futility and committed desire to continue writing reflect, perhaps, the nature of the text itself. As W. C. Dowling comments, 'the paradoxical fact is that a text is both a symbolic *act* and a *symbolic* act: that is, it is a genuine act in that it tries to do something to the world, and yet it is "merely" symbolic in the sense that it leaves the world untouched'.[66] Thus Ehrhart's poetry (or any other veteran-poet's) may not have shaped US foreign policy or dominant cultural attitudes, but, for all those touched by their voices, there is the possibility of a new consciousness. In making their perceptions and memories available to readers, Vietnam veteran poets acknowledge both hope and futility. The value of the poems discussed, particularly in this section, lies partly in their courage to give expression to, and exist in, contraries.

In an unpublished poem, 'Loving You', Ehrhart expressed the coexistence of these contraries:

> For me, there has never been,
> Never can be a middle path.
> My mind is a complex vault of tempered wisdom.[67]

To the extent that he has remained steadfast in his opposition to the war and its underlying causes, there is no 'middle path' in his poetry. However, in the transition from angry, didactic early poems to more complex meditations on the aftermath, we perceive the 'tempered wisdom' of a sensitive poet and veteran, the development of a true 'warrior for peace'.[68]

I have discussed the complex and often contradictory trajectory of Ehrhart's poems and opinions because they are emblematic of the transitions I have plotted in this section. In a dominant culture that had initially construed the veteran as a scapegoat and then valorized him, there is the temptation to

---

[66] W. C. Dowling, *Jameson, Althusser, Marx: An Introduction to the Political Unconscious* (Ithaca, NY: Cornell University Press, 1984), 122.

[67] W. D. Ehrhart, 'Loving You', *More Recent Poems* (Imaginative Representations of the Vietnam War Archive, La Salle University: 1969 penciled in by author), typescript, no pagination.

[68] Steve Mason, *Warrior for Peace* (New York and London: Simon & Schuster Inc., 1988), 21.

accept the valorization with little or no questioning. Steve Mason's poetry is an example of this tendency. While Bowen, Weigl, and McDonald effect imaginative leaps to comprehend the 'other', they are still rooted in America and their recollections of war (Balaban is a worthy exception). This imbues the poetry with a certain self-referential tone that is disturbing. The ideological perception of, and sympathy with, the 'other' is often mired in personal trauma and guilt. That solidarity is not a simplistic or linear apprehension of the 'other' is most dramatically illustrated in David Connolly's 'Another Chance'. In Ehrhart's poems there is the desire to reach out not only to the Vietnamese, but to his own countrymen who will fight its future wars. In the midst of silence and rejection, he finds solace in his daughter and his wife, and a significant number of non-war poems are addressed or dedicated to them. However, a large number of 'personal' poems are underlined by the experience of Vietnam, and this is true of the other poets mentioned. The war remains the central animating event and trauma of the lives and poetry of the best veteran poets. Perhaps, as Ehrhart said in an interview in 1991, that is an inevitable thread in post-war poetry on the Vietnam conflict: 'I think that those poets who are going to be durable are those who have managed not to transcend Vietnam but to incorporate it into the experience of their lives.'[69] While it may be too soon to pass judgement on literary longevity, it is certainly true that the best veteran poetry is valuable precisely because of its meditations on Vietnam and what it means in individual and collective lives in the 1980s and 1990s.

This brief survey of veteran poetry (it is brief if one takes into account the prolific amounts of poetry written by Vietnam veterans!) raises some issues about representation, witness, and memory to which I will now turn. As may be evident throughout Chapters 3, 4, and 5 there are connections, continuities, and significant differences between this poetry and the body of stateside protest poetry discussed in Chapter 2. The question of whether the war can be represented is raised again by commentators. For instance, Don Ringnalda asks rhetorically, 'How can you write about the unspeakably horrifying without somehow

---

[69] Interview with Ronald Baughman, in Baughman (ed.), *Dictionary of Literary Biography*, ix. 72.

domesticating it and making it non-threatening to rugs?'[70] Ringnalda echoes an earlier debate in American poetry between 'raw' and 'cooked' poetry, between that which soils rugs and maintains their cleanliness. Just as John Carlos Rowe had averred that the immorality of the Vietnam War was not representable, so too Ringnalda questions the possibility of poetic renditions of the war. As stated in Chapter 2, this argument implicitly favours silence and is at one with a body of revisionist history. While it is true, as James Aulich and Jeffrey Walsh point out, that representations tend to mediate the war, make it 'harmless' so that 'it frightens no longer and can be quite literally handled', the best veteran poetry is not complicit in this mediation.[71] Social memory of the war, as manifested in the Vietnam Memorial or the Welcome Home parades, has helped to tame it. Veteran poetry, however, opens up the fractures, and to write about war is not necessarily an act that domesticates its events. Apart from poets like Steve Mason, and his predecessors in *Stars and Stripes* and *DEROS*, veteran poetry represents a powerful act of witness, remembrance, and rebellion within a culture that has attempted to suppress the unpleasant aspects of Vietnam while resurrecting its soldiers as heroes.

At a literal level veteran poetry, with its 'ruthless quality of experiential truth-telling', bears witness to the actuality of war.[72] There is a problem in the absolute privileging of veteran experience, but the better poems convey a range of experiences almost entirely absent in stateside poetry. While the latter may fulminate against the napalming of children and villages in terms which are morally laudable, the former depicts the terrors of combat without, as in Komunyakaa's poems, losing sight of the moral ambiguities of the war. In fact to fight the war was to live some of the moral confusions that were articulated by stateside poets. While non-combatant poetry represents one aspect of moral and political utterance, veteran poetry presents a closer-to-the-bone sense of war. As W. D. Ehrhart writes: 'Indeed, if one wants to

---

[70] Don Ringnalda, 'Rejecting "Sweet Geometry": Komunyakaa's *Duende*', *Journal of American Culture*, 16: 3 (Fall 1993), 21–8.

[71] Jeffrey Walsh and James Aulich, 'Introduction', to Walsh and Aulich (eds.), *Vietnam Images*, 5.

[72] Philip D. Beidler, *American Literature and the Experience of Vietnam* (Athens, Ga.: The University of Georgia Press, 1982), 200.

know the essence of war, how it feels and smells and tastes, what it does to those who are scorched by its flames, one is likely to find more truth in literature than in any history ever written.'[73] The 'essence' of a war as brutal and bizarre as Vietnam may be difficult to locate, but the poetry does convey an alternative truth and history. This portrayal is rooted in experience and memory and highlights facts and emotions that are edited from public memory and discourse.

From projecting the immediacy of war, which is one type of witnessing, we can trace a movement towards more political testimonies. The veterans of VVAW who protested against the war and the poets represent 'a particular kind of moral seriousness that is unusual in America, one which is deepened and defined by the fact that it has emerged from a direct confrontation not only with the capacity of others for violence and brutality but also with their own culpability, their sense of their own capacity for error and excess'.[74] Peter Marin highlights the vital notions of 'culpability' and 'moral seriousness' in veteran poetry, which account for the political anger and commitment in some poems. Having been, as Ehrhart writes in 'A Relative Thing', 'the instruments | of your pigeon-breasted fantasies', veteran poets desire national remembrance. It is as an inscription of memory and protest that their poetry is political and disruptive. 'Remembrance of the past', as Herbert Marcuse writes, 'may give rise to dangerous insights, and the established society seems to be apprehensive of the subversive contents of memory.'[75] Poetry as inscribed memory in the public domain is not necessarily redemptive, or if it is, the path to redemption and its concomitant, historical and national responsibility, lies in the scrutiny and preservation of that memory (or memories). The often unpalatable truths articulated by the poets are feared and therefore rejected by the dominant culture. As Robert Lifton observes, 'while most Americans came to detest this humiliating and unresolvable war, and while they sensed there was much about it that was unusually ugly, they nonetheless resist the full revelations of the

---

[73] W. D. Ehrhart, 'Teaching the Vietnam War', *In the Shadow of Vietnam*, 143.
[74] Cited in Robert Emmet Long (ed.), *Vietnam Ten Years After* (New York: The H. W. Wilson Company, 1986), 73–4.
[75] Herbert Marcuse, *One-Dimensional Man: Studies in the Ideology of Advanced Industrial Society* (London: Routledge, 1964), 98.

veterans' animating guilt. For these threatened their own symbolizations around national virtue and military honor.'[76] Having fought for a set of values which the political establishment professed, and which the soldiers subsequently discovered was fraudulent, poets such as Ehrhart transcribe a classic innocence-to-disillusionment paradigm. Their protest, despite anger and outrage, is not as binary as stateside poetry. In their mature poems, simple dichotomies are replaced by a more complex desire to hold the nation to its best and professed values. Voices of anger and denunciation are often followed by, or coexistent with, articulations of responsibility and the need and hope of a better future.

Memory in the guise of post-war trauma is both personally and politically subversive. The inextricability of war memory and post-war existence is dealt with in many poems which highlight the sense of exile arising out of this double bind. Vietnam then becomes a psychological landscape of eternal nightmares totally dislocated from civilian life. Yet this poetic witnessing is not bound solely in solitude. This desire follows the classic witness paradigm indicated by Shoshana Felman: 'To bear witness is to bear *the solitude* of a responsibility, and to bear *the responsibility*, precisely, of that solitude. And yet, the *appointment* to bear witness is, paradoxically enough, an appointment to transgress the confines of that isolated stance, to speak *for* others and *to* others.'[77] Felman is referring to Holocaust survivor witnesses, but a similar pattern and motivation is discernible in some veteran poetry. The memory of war and its subsequent trauma never fades, and the poet writes that memory not only to exorcize it but 'to speak *for* others and *to* others'. The messianic tone and attitude noted in some of Ehrhart's writings draws on this deeply felt need to let others know, to teach others so that they may comprehend and be spared similar traumas. John Balaban's exhortation: 'Swear by the locust, by dragonflies on ferns, | . . . that as we grow old, we will not grow evil', is part of this desire to establish a community of hope and responsibility. Felman's observation also helps us to comprehend the relative lack of

[76] Robert Jay Lifton, *Home From the War: Vietnam Veterans, Neither Victims Nor Executioners* (London: Wildwood House, 1974), 132.

[77] Shoshana Felman, 'Education and Crisis, or the Vicissitudes of Teaching', in Caruth (ed.), *Trauma: Explorations in Memory*, 15. Italics in original text.

extreme dichotomies. As an exile and alien in his own land the veteran-poet castigates his fellow countrymen, like a prophet crying in the wilderness. Unlike some stateside poets, who often adopted a stance of poetic and prophetic infallibility, veterans often realize and accept their own complicity and counsel wisdom and patience: 'A farmer of dreams | knows what it is to be patient.' In solitude and exile, the quest for a better community and country is never relinquished.

This desire is crucial in a country that has created convenient paradigms of healing and reconciliation. Veteran poets provide a searing memory trace for events during and after the war and they believe that any healing can happen only if history, the past, and its trauma are taken into full account. This refusal to falsify the memory of war gives the poems their tentative and often tortured quality. At its worst, the pretence to truth-telling can be construed as a type of special pleading, a fulfilment of an agenda of self-exoneration. The insistence with which experiential authority is privileged substantiates this claim. Very few veteran poets deal directly with the genocidal nature of the war, and the project of a return to Vietnam in search of solidarity is often naïve and self-serving. At its best, however, veteran poetry represents gestures towards healing and comprehension that are animated by an acknowledgement of guilt and culpability. These are preliminary gestures, but they are valuable within a political climate of resurgent nationalism and ignorance about Vietnam. The poetry significantly redescribes the official language of the war (see Chapter 1 for some examples) and in that it is politically engaged as well. In its interaction with politics and culture, the poetry is often banal and self-obsessed (as in the *Stars and Stripes* poems). The better poetry forms a complex interface with history, commenting on it and moving to new perceptions and, finally, it is not limited to solipsistic, alienated outpourings. While the war remains the bedrock, the poets encompass love, family, children, and nature as a means of coping. Poems by Ehrhart and Weigl deal with a post-war self and world that is often beset by uncertainty, fear, and vulnerability. It is in the minutiae of post-war life and the hope of renewal that some of this poetry reinscribes the particularly masculinist orientation and language of war. This is perhaps the reason why recent veteran poetry is both rooted in history and intensely personal.

Frank Kermode's comments on 'good poems about historical crises' is generally apposite for veteran poetry. In its significant redescription, veteran poetry 'speak[s] a different language from historical record and historical myth. . . . They . . . protect us from the familiar; they stand apart from opinion; they are a form of knowledge'.[78] While there is an element of didacticism in some of them, the best of them gesture towards and constitute this new 'form of knowledge'.

Paul Fussell, musing on the paucity of Vietnam War poetry, attributes it to the fact that there were very few literary or highly educated people in Vietnam (in contrast to the First World War) and 'that we are now inescapably mired in a postverbal age, where neither writer nor reader possesses the layers of allusion arising from wide literary experience that make significant reading and writing possible'. He concludes his observations by dismissing the poetry: 'Whatever the reasons, it seems undeniable that no one expects interesting poetry to emerge from that sad war. All we can expect is more of what we have, a few structure-less free-verse dribbles of easy irony or easy sentiment or easy political anger.'[79] Although Vietnam was largely a working-class and poor man's war, Fussell exaggerates the absence of literary or highly educated people. There were exceptions such as Basil T. Paquet, Walter McDonald, Yusef Komunyakaa, and John Balaban, and the 'layers of allusion arising from wide literary experience' that Fussell sees as a *sine qua non* of good poetry is evident in their works, as well as in poems by Bruce Weigl and W. D. Ehrhart. Poets like Yusef Komunyakaa bring to their work allusions and rhythms from non-literary contexts such as jazz, which are shared by a significant number of African Americans.[80] Fussell's categorization of all present Vietnam poetry (and its future!) as a collection of 'a few structureless free-verse dribbles' is, on the evidence of some recent veteran poetry, an excessive criticism. His comment is apt for some of the stateside poetry discussed earlier, and for some veteran poetry, such as the ones

---

[78] Frank Kermode, 'Poetry and History', *Poetry, Narrative, History* (Oxford: Basil Blackwell, 1990), 67.

[79] Paul Fussell, 'Killing, In Verse and Prose', *Thank God For the Atom Bomb and Other Essays* (New York and London: Summit Books, 1988), 135–6.

[80] Komunyakaa refers to the influence of jazz and blues in his work when he talks of 'internaliz[ing] a kind of life rhythm'. See Vince Gotera, ' "Lines of Tempered Steel": An Interview with Yusef Komunyakaa', *Callaloo*, 13: 2 (1990), 215–29.

published in *Stars and Stripes* and *DEROS*. The exceptions to this critique are available in the poems I have discussed, ranging from the early combat poems in *Winning Hearts and Minds* to the mature and moving meditations on trauma and solidarity with the Vietnamese. There are, of course, inconsistencies and problems, as I have pointed out in my individual analyses. These problems highlight the complex position and articulations of the veteran-poets in post-war America. As accomplices in war and as 'warrior[s] for peace' they straddle an almost totally binary and incompatible divide. The best veteran poets are aware of these contradictions and try to work within and through them in their poetry. If some stateside poetry is guilty of an aesthetics of denial, veteran poets represent an aesthetics of engagement, a strenuous refusal to turn away from the horror and trauma of war memory. This aesthetic is also evident in poems expressing solidarity: there is no easy sentimentality that can transcend the barriers of culture scarred by war. Kevin Bowen's 'A Conical Hat', Bruce Weigl's 'Dialectical Materialism', and Ehrhart's 'For Mrs. Na' are examples of the poet's ability to offer new insights in the aftermath of this sad war. This new poetic is perhaps best summed up by Ehrhart in his conclusion to 'The Poet as Athlete':

> Consider poetry, how good poems
> offer us the world with eyes renewed.
> Now see the swimmer I am watching:
> all discipline, all muscle, lean and hard.
>
> (*Wreckage*, 140)

The swimmer's 'discipline' 'lean and hard' is analogous to an aesthetic that pares down language to delineate horrific events or endless trauma. There is a self-obsessive element in the focus on individual traumas, but this is counterbalanced by a commitment to witness so that the future may be less bleak than the past. It is not a comforting or beautiful picture, neither is there any sense of convenient closure. Yet their vision is not a totally nihilistic one as they address the 'moral autism' of the dominant culture.[81] The best veteran poems display a quality of 'unaccommodating stubbornness' and 'uncompromising criticism' that Edward Said

---

[81] Amos Oz, cited in Adrienne Rich, *Blood, Bread, And Poetry: Selected Prose 1979–1985* (London: Virago Press Limited, 1987), 205.

so admires in the work of Adorno.[82] They also encompass hope, possibility, and, occasionally, tenderness. The best of the poets 'offer us the world with eyes renewed', open up new moral spaces and options that will allow for rigorous remembrance and generous forgiveness. In a dominant climate of cultural amnesia, veteran poetry is often the still, clear voice of wisdom and hope, and in that lies its continuing value. As W. D. Ehrhart writes in conclusion to a recent essay:

For the nation as a whole, the Vietnam War has become only a bizarre assortment of myths and misinterpretations and is now rapidly disappearing into the fog of history. . . . These poems are the grace that's found in so much loss. And if governments and nations remain impervious to the grace of poetry, I'll still pick poetry every time.[83]

The phrase 'grace that's found in so much loss' is from Kevin Bowen's poem 'Nui Ba Den: Black Virgin Mountain', and implies regenerative energies embedded in poetry. Ehrhart's formulation encapsulates contradictions I have indicated in this chapter. Veteran poetry is both a project of self-excavation and a valuable reinscription of the war and its subsequent obliteration through mythification in American culture. '[G]overnments and nations [may] remain impervious' to its power, but that does not diminish its worth or necessity. Part of the value of literature in its engagement with politics lies in the ability

to defend language, to do battle with the twisters, precisely by entering the political arena. The writers of the Group 47 in post-war Germany, Grass, Böll and the rest, with their 'rubble literature' whose purpose and great achievement was to rebuild the German language from the rubble of Nazism are prime instances of this power.[84]

Salman Rushdie's observation on the power of language to redescribe realities is as valuable in the context of Vietnam poetry as it is with reference to post-Nazi German literature. Ehrhart echoes the 'centre–margin' paradigm noted in Nemerov's poetics and points to the paradoxical power of the poet who is not

---

[82] Edward W. Said, 'Relationship Between Endings and Beginnings', *Wolfson College Lectures*, No. 8, 1993: audio cassette, Side A.
[83] W. D. Ehrhart, ' "What Grace Is Found In So Much Loss?"', *Virginia Quarterly Review*, 73: 1 (Winter 1997), 111.
[84] Salman Rushdie, 'Outside the Whale', *Imaginary Homelands: Essays and Criticism 1981–1991* (Harmondsworth: Penguin Books Ltd., 1991), 97–8.

assimilated into mainstream jargon. There is also an echo of the instrumentalist agenda in the impotence of poetry within more powerful and influential cultural frameworks. The paradox of this position, as indicated in Chapter 2, is a type of integrity-in-marginalization, an ability to perceive and articulate perspectives seldom acknowledged and rarely expressed. Stateside poets helped to create, and functioned within, a climate of conscientious objection to Vietnam. Veteran poetry in the 1980s and 1990s has no such context to rely on. Individuals such as Chomsky maintain their incisive opposition, but there is little collective questioning of US foreign policy initiatives (the Gulf War and the parades after indicate the extent to which a national consensus has been rehabilitated). Prior to the Gulf War, Nixon in his memoirs and Reagan in public statements and actions aggressively asserted the morality of Vietnam. It is within such contexts that poetry provides 'grace' amidst 'loss' because it accepts moral responsibility, and 'keep[s] pain vocal'.[85] Just as Nixon or Guenter Lewy rewrite Vietnam, veteran poets reiterate the need for a vision that moves beyond bad faith. The collocation is a desperate one: redemption *will* or *must* come through poetry. Ehrhart also refers to the loss of innocence trope and the possibilities of reinscribing the self and nation through poetry. The latter is a tenuous goal, yet poetic inscriptions and their reading keep alive individual and collective experiences and memories. The poetic endeavour/s refuse to rewrite 'loss', pain, and brutality as acceptable and 'just', and are emblematic of integrity within contexts of cynicism and obfuscation. As John Balaban writes in 'Agua Fria Y Las Chicharras':

> Oh, the hunger for words pure as clear water
>   that shall slake the pain of our parched tongues
>   and, splashed against our brows, shall let us see.
>
> (*Locusts*, 75)

More than twenty years after the end of the Vietnam War, the best of veteran poetry is a testament to past horror and future possibility, a hope for purer words and clearer visions.

---

[85] Adrienne Rich, 'What if?', *What Is Found There: Notebooks on Poetry and Politics* (London: Virago Press Limited, 1995), 242.

6
The 'Other'
Vietnamese Poetic Representations

A study of Vietnamese poems in translation poses problems which I discuss later in the chapter. At this juncture two preliminary points are worth mentioning. The first is the rhetoric of war that is an uncanny parallel of absolutist US policy statements. Nguyen Huu Tho, presenting the National Liberation Front point of view, stated: 'Today, in spite of all kinds of double talk about "peace" and "negotiation", they [the US] have appeared under their true colors as the most cruel and bloodthirsty aggressive colonialist devil.'[1] General Tran Van Tra said of the larger political rationale behind the Tet Offensive in 1968: 'Ours was a just war against foreign aggression and a traitorous puppet regime, against brutality and injustice, for national independence and freedom, and for human dignity. The war was thus in tune with the conscience of our time.'[2] Both statements present true aspects of the conflict in that it was a war of independence for many Vietnamese, and that American attempts at negotiating peace were half-hearted at best. I have indicated the colonial aspects of US involvement in Chapter 1. Like most war rhetoric, however, Vietnamese declarations typify the desire to characterize the enemy in terms of absolute evil. The hyperbole overlooks the shortcomings of the communist party, its ruthless pursuit of power (embodied in the NLF assassinations of village chiefs in south Vietnam), and is disingenuous in defining all opponents as 'puppet[s]'. Revolutionary nationalism was capable of the type of rhetorical displacement evident in US justifications for intervention. It is a pattern that Frantz Fanon associates with the

---

[1] Cited in Marcus G. Raskin and Bernard B. Fall (eds.), *The Viet-Nam Reader: Articles and Documents on American Foreign Policy and the Viet-Nam Crisis* (New York: Random House, 1967), 393.
[2] Cited in Jayne S. Werner and Luu Doan Huynh (eds.), *The Vietnam War: Vietnamese and American Perspectives* (New York and London: M. E. Sharpe, 1993), 63.

manichaean logic of a colonial situation: 'On the logical plane, the Manichaeism of the settler produces a Manichaeism of the native. To the theory of the "absolute evil of the native" the theory of the "absolute evil of the settler" replies.'[3] Revolutionary jargon may have maintained morale and cohesion against a vastly superior enemy, but the conflict itself was more complex and multidimensional. While there is a body of indifferent poetry eulogizing the sacrifices in war, the better poems resist the heroic mode and point to the pain and fragility of human lives in war.

The second factor, implicit in the first, is the riddling complexity of the war for the Vietnamese. As David Chanoff notes: 'For the Vietnamese the war was vastly more complex—a maelstrom in which the contending tides of colonialism and liberation, communism and nationalism, reform and revolution, Northern revanchism and Southern regionalism clashed violently and mixed treacherously.'[4] The Americans were largely ignorant of these divisions and undercurrents, and created a monolithic rhetoric of saving the south from communism. Truong Nhu Tang, a former member of the NLF and minister in the Provisional Revolutionary Government of south Vietnam, comments on the American inability to perceive political nuances:

> The Eisenhower and Kennedy administrations had chosen to regard Ho Chi Minh as a tool of Chinese expansionism, ignoring the separate integrity and strength of Vietnamese national aspirations. Just so, the Johnson and Nixon administrations persisted in treating the NLF as part of a North Vietnamese monolith, casually shrugging aside the complex realities of the Vietnamese political world.[5]

Tang's memoir provides fascinating insights into a world of political manoeuvring, hope, and betrayal. The communists were also aware of these splits and their exaggerated rhetoric reflects a need to ignore differences in the quest for freedom and power. As Ho Chi Minh told Daniel Guérin, 'All those who do not follow the line which I have laid down will be broken.'[6] This melodramatic declaration provides an insight into internal party

---

[3] Frantz Fanon, *The Wretched of the Earth*, trans. Constance Farrington (1967; Harmondsworth: Penguin Books Ltd., 1976), 73.
[4] David Chanoff and Doan Van Toai, *'Vietnam' A Portrait of Its People at War* (London and New York: I. B. Tauris, 1996), p. xxi.
[5] Truong Nhu Tang, *Journal of a Vietcong* (London: Jonathan Cape, 1986), 213.
[6] Cited in Jean Lacouture, *Ho Chi Minh*, trans. Peter Wiles (Harmondsworth: Penguin Books Ltd., 1968), 130.

The 'Other'

conflicts, the difficulties of maintaining cohesion in the face of immense odds and fighting a long, brutal war. Some of the poetry delves into these confusions and contradictions, particularly the aftermath poems which share neither the triumphalism nor the moral certainties of victory.

Vietnam is a tiny country in south-east Asia with a history and cultural continuity of which most Americans were ignorant when they entered the field in the mid-1940s. American officials, such as Charles S. Reed, the consul in Saigon, viewed the capabilities of the Vietnamese in terms of racial stereotypes. 'Few of the Annamites are particularly industrious,' Reed reported, nor were they noted for their 'honesty, loyalty, or veracity'. He added that the Vietnamese national character may be 'a direct and pernicious result of decades of French maltreatment', but insisted that 'the great bulk of the population was not prepared for self government'.[7] William C. Bullitt, American ambassador to the USSR in the 1930s, was suspicious of Vietnamese communism and concurred with Reed's assessment of Vietnamese capabilities: 'The Annamese are attractive and even lovable' but 'essentially childish.'[8] Emanating from the 1930s and 1940s, these perceptions are proleptic, and were to have wide and powerful currency when the USA entered Vietnam in force. Within this dominant discourse there was an alternative that consistently, during and after the war, tried to represent the Vietnamese as a people with a credible history. There were writers in America who resisted the impulse to hate-speech and enmity. The ability to fashion an alternate description to the given structures of war is perhaps their most singular contribution. However, the counter-discourse, as manifested in the writings of Noam Chomsky, Mary McCarthy, Susan Sontag, Frances Fitzgerald, Gloria Emerson, and the stateside protest

---

[7] Cited in Werner and Luu Doan Huynh (eds.), *The Vietnam War: Vietnamese and American Perspectives*, 13. A broad framework of Annamite psychology, combined with racial and climactic theories were used to express contempt of indigenous cultural practices. 'Annam' was the term used by the Chinese during their occupation of Vietnam to signify the 'pacified south', an appellation resented by the Vietnamese.

[8] Ibid. 14. Similar value-loaded generalizations about a people, its culture, and morals are available in Stanley Karnow's history of Vietnam, which projects itself as a balanced study. Karnow writes about Thieu, the south Vietnamese leader, that 'Even in a society where scruples were scarce, he was distrusted ...', and a few pages later he refers to 'the permissive Vietnamese'. *Vietnam: A History* (London: Pimlico, 1994), 351, 355.

poets, often reiterated binary perceptions in its idealization of the 'other'.[9] Vietnam became the site for a critique of American society, and this process, as Susan Sontag points out, had a paradoxical effect in that it further distanced the reality of Vietnam:

Radical Americans have profited from the war in Vietnam, profited from having a clear-cut moral issue on which to mobilize discontent and expose the camouflaged contradictions in the system. Beyond isolated private disenchantment or despair over America's betrayal of its ideals, Vietnam offered the key to a systematic criticism of America. In this scheme of use Vietnam becomes an ideal Other. But such a status only makes Vietnam, already so alien culturally, even further removed from this country.[10]

Sontag is part of that radical America and her account is partially guilty of the type of idealization she acutely perceives in the ideological stances adopted by critics of the war. Her perception, however, is valid, and it is only in some recent poetry by veterans (see Chapter 5) that we encounter a solidarity based on both sympathy and awareness of the humanity of the 'other', with its memories, contradictions, and pain. For the Vietnam War (appropriately designated as the American War in Vietnam), as Donald Anderson remarks, was a tribulation for the Vietnamese people as well: 'And may U.S. leaders be reminded, too, that in addition to our losses—200,000 wounded, 58,000 dead—the Vietnamese suffered up to two million wounded and three million dead. And this: although Vietnam was America's longest war, the war was for Vietnam, in its longer history, its shortest.'[11] This study is primarily about American poetic responses to Vietnam, placed within a larger context of imposition of US power on a third-world country. While I have dwelt on the politics and consequences of that engagement within America, it seems appropriate to conclude with a brief discussion of Vietnamese poetic representations of that war. The idea is not only to redress the balance, as Anderson's comment implies, but to provide a glimpse of the 'other', the 'enemy' reviled, bombed, and idealized, but never quite understood. Perhaps Vietnamese poets can open

[9] See Chapter 2 for specific poetic instances of naïve idealization and overcompensation.
[10] Susan Sontag, 'Trip to Hanoi (June–July 1968)', *Styles of Radical Will* (London: Vintage, 1994), 271.
[11] Donald Anderson, 'McNamara's Makeshift Amends', *War, Literature & the Arts*, 7: 2 (Fall–Winter 1995), 57–68.

a window to the radical 'otherness' occasionally perceived by America.

The project is fraught with problems: all the poetry I discuss is in translation and most of it is translated and published in the USA; the quality of many translated poems is dubious, often marked by cliché, rhetoric, and sentimentality; to approach a literature with no knowledge of the language erases from the analysis nuances embedded in that language. Despite these caveats, I believe the study will orient us notionally towards a different culture's response to a war, which will in turn reflect on and further contextualize the American poetic response. The language of war is inherently binary and post-war bitterness in America conjoined with upheavals in Vietnam did little to ameliorate that divide. Vietnamese poetry, not surprisingly, expresses little solidarity with the 'enemy'. The designation had myriad implications: while America was the enemy for the north Vietnamese and the National Liberation Front (Vietcong for the USA), the communist north was the presumptive enemy of the south, whose 'ally' was America. The fact that in 'defending' south Vietnam, America destroyed and killed with little discrimination, complicates the designation of the enemy for the south. Further, members of the NLF such as Tang were not necessarily ardent communists. He writes that 'The South Vietnamese found themselves trapped between their loathing of the Thieu dictatorship and their fears of communism.'[12] The poems are a valuable inscription of war memory and enact experiences that were for long obliterated. Within a different context, Milan Kundera's quotation from the Czech historian Milan Hubl highlights apposite connections: '"The first step in liquidating a people is to erase its memory, its books, its culture, its history. Then have somebody write new books, manufacture a new culture, invent a new history. Before long the nation will forget what it is and what it was."'[13] This may not have been the exact pattern of the American occupation, but there are disturbing parallels. The entire engagement was mired in ignorance and contempt of Vietnamese memory, history, and culture. After the war, Vietnam was transformed into a psychological landscape for

---

[12] Truong Nhu Tang, *Journal of a Vietcong*, 192.
[13] Milan Kundera, *The Book of Laughter and Forgetting*, trans. Michael Henry Heim (London and Boston: Faber and Faber, 1980), 159.

America, while the real country reeled under an incompetent government and a US economic embargo. In dominant political and cultural memory, it was as if the Vietnamese had ceased to exist after the Americans withdrew. It is these histories and lives that are retrieved in a study of their poetry.

Before discussing some Vietnamese war poems, I will briefly examine the politics of publishing these poems in English in America. Such a study indicates a complex set of motives centred around solidarity and vestigial guilt. Most publications originate in universities and are predicated on a liberal, humanistic desire for comprehension and responsibility. Denise Levertov, in her 'Foreword' to *Writing Between the Lines*, stresses American ignorance and the need to remember and learn from the past:

> Those American readers who remember only their own wartime experiences need to be reminded of the character and actuality of the peasant people against whom they fought (often unwillingly, with pain and disgust at their own enforced actions, and, for so many, with lasting trauma) or with whom they tried to stand in solidarity as participants in the antiwar movement, yet whom they never really knew.... We need to see more of such pairings [as in the collection], such accounts of parallel experience—which are never simply mirror images, because one side was in its native land and knew what the war was about, while the other was thousands of miles from home and had only confused ideas of whom and why they were fighting.[14]

The desire to broaden perspective and knowledge is a noble one but it is based partly on the needs of America, a means to inculcate the 'lessons' of Vietnam through some salutary examples from the 'other'. While it is true that the war was fought in ignorance, it was the terrifying clarity of justifying myths and rhetoric through most of the war that allowed it to be waged. Political language and soldier recollections, from President Kennedy to PFC (later Sergeant) W. D. Ehrhart, testify to this sense of purpose. The subtext to Levertov's reference to 'confused ideas' is one that condemns the war and wishes to assuage guilt through providing the 'other' a forum for expression. *Writing Between the Lines* and *Poems From Captured Documents* are both published under the aegis of the William Joiner Center

---

[14] Kevin Bowen and Bruce Weigl (eds.), and introd., *Writing Between the Lines* (Amherst, Mass.: The University of Massachusetts Press, 1997), pp. xiv–xvi. Subsequent references are indicated as *Writing* after the quotation.

for the Study of War and Social Consequences at the University of Massachusetts. The Center invites Vietnamese writers and translates their poetry to further the process of learning outlined by Levertov. The agenda, as Bowen (the director of the Joiner Center) and Weigl point out in their 'Introduction', is 'to promote the notion of a world citizenship'.[15] It is a laudable project, but one wonders if it obscures distinctions of culture, location, and politics, while acknowledging the 'otherness' of the Vietnamese experience. The discourse of healing originates and is centred in America, reflecting a need for forgiveness and reconciliation that is evident in the return-to-Vietnam type of veteran poetry (see Chapter 5). This desire is expressed by Weigl in his 'Introduction' to *Poems From Captured Documents*:

Thanh T. Nguyen [co-translator] and I hope that these translations will serve as a bridge . . . and that by making available these intimate and deeply human glimpses from the lives of North Vietnamese and National Liberation Front soldiers during the American war, we will encourage and facilitate some kind of reconciliation—if not a political one, then an emotional and psychological one.[16]

I have tried to indicate how reconciliation as fashioned in the USA has a distinctive political quality and agenda. Similarly, the translation of the 'other' is fraught with political desires. This is evident in oral histories as well, such as David Chanoff and Doan Van Toai's '*Vietnam*' *A Portrait of Its People at War*. Although the interviews highlight Vietnamese aspects of life during the war, including some that express hatred of America, the bias of interviewees (all refugees and immigrants to the USA) seems to valorize the immigrant experience. The tragedy of the 'boat people' deserves attention, but the subtext of the recollections and Chanoff's 'Afterword' is that valiant Vietnamese fought for a corrupt revolution, and it is just that they should find refuge in America.[17] From an American perspective, the communist victory constitutes a tragedy, especially for the Vietnamese. The failures and excesses of the communists partly justify this contention,

---

[15] Ibid. p. xx.
[16] Thanh T. Nguyen and Bruce Weigl (selected and trans.), *Poems From Captured Documents* (Amherst, Mass.: The University of Massachusetts Press, 1994), p. vii. Interestingly, this is a bilingual edition. Subsequent references are indicated as *Poems* after the quotation.
[17] The term 'boat people' refers primarily to ethnic Chinese who fled the persecu-

but the exclusive attention to refugees silences the people who stayed behind. The focus of this book is on the benefits reaped by America, as Chanoff cites with approbation: '"It is perhaps terrible to say this," said a U.S. State Department Official to a former adversary, now a refugee, "but the great tragedy of your country is a great benefit for ours." He was speaking of the qualities the Vietnamese immigrants have brought along with them. I think he was right.'[18] Out of the particular travails of war, as narrated by disillusioned communists and supporters of the south, arises the enrichment of the American 'melting pot'. This scenario further diminishes the 'other' as the voices designated as significant are enclosed within a larger American identity.

The agendas of translation are not, however, all negative. As Bruce Weigl writes, there is a desire to hear and understand other experiences in order to transcend the oppositional identities created by the war:

Through their poems, these soldier-poets, many of whom are dead, are given a voice, and their poetry when embraced, provides insights nowhere else available in English. The effect of this poetry is to humanize the soldiers who fought on the side of the revolution in such a way as to dispel the stereotypes created by the United States military and the American media during and after the war in Vietnam.[19]

The translations constitute a mode of entry and comprehension for the non-Vietnamese speaker, and to these I will now turn.

A theme that recurs in poems by Vietnamese veterans is an intense love of the land, its physical presence and beauty. Of course this poetry is political for such attachment evokes a pastoral idyll undisturbed by war. The perpetrators of war, in this case the Americans, are seldom mentioned, but their presence is always implicitly challenged. Van Ky's 'My Birthplace, Nam Binh' is a typical example of the pastoral that encodes the revolutionary need to carry on fighting:

---

tions of the Vietnamese government, particularly after China invaded Vietnam in 1979. James Fenton highlights a human dimension often edited from political language: 'The boat people are not merely "obstinate elements" or Chinese comprador capitalists on their way to new markets. They are simply people without hope' (*All the Wrong Places: Adrift in the Politics of Asia* (London: Penguin Books, 1988), 106).

[18] Chanoff and Doan Van Toai, *'Vietnam' A Portrait of Its People at War*, 210.
[19] Bruce Weigl, 'Introduction', *Poems*, p. xiii.

> My village is lovely, friends.
> If you have a chance to visit Nam Dinh,
> Please do.
> Rose pink sunlight shines over fields.
> During three harvests
> The color of rice covers the village and hamlet.
> . . . .
> Walking the cool village road
> Day by day
> Deepens our love for our country.
> . . . .
> Voices of poetry and songs of peace
> Fill the air.
> . . . .
> The shade of sea pines
> Falls along the white Dragon river.
> The east ocean winds
> Inspire our heroes
> And bring many fish to our village.
> . . . .
> We must all rise up and be masters of ourselves.
> The happier our work, the freer our reunited lives.
>
> (*Poems*, 15–17)

The pastoral, as Leo Marx notes, is counter-revolutionary, and yet American radicals such as Sontag invoke the pastoral-revolutionary quality inherent in Vietnam.[20] Marx's focus is on the American left which constructed Vietnam as an idyllic counterpoint to the malaise within their own country. Ky's poem, however, inscribes this as a lived experience and attention to detail is an aspect of the 'rootedness' Kevin Bowen attributes to Vietnamese poetry:

It probably should not be all that surprising that the poetry of a people deeply uprooted by war should be a poetry of rootedness; a poetry focusing on the endurance and continuity of life in the villages, in the highlands, and along the deltas; a poetry, almost Buddhist in tone, that seeks to affirm the interconnectedness of all things. The reality of the war may intrude in Vietnamese poetry written during the American war, but

---

[20] See Leo Marx, 'Susan Sontag's "New Left" Pastoral: Notes on Revolutionary Pastoralism in America', *The Pilot and the Passenger: Essays on Literature, Technology, and Culture in the United States* (New York and Oxford: Oxford University Press, 1988), 293.

the great enduring themes remain the traditional Vietnamese ones of home and love.[21]

The language of the poem sounds translated and stilted. It also conforms to an ideal that American protest poets often projected on to Vietnam, but Bowen is accurate in his estimation of the depth of feeling. It is an emotion that conflates easily with the political as the Vietnamese, through their long history of Chinese and then French occupation, perceived their country as being under constant threat or servitude. In such a historical context, cultural memory constructs a notion of an ideal country that can and must be retrieved. As Jean Lacouture notes in his biography, part of Ho Chi Minh's intense and trans-ideological appeal was based on this idea of the nation rooted in its besieged land: 'In the minds of the Vietnamese Ho is consubstantial with the soil to which they all cling in defiance of foreign intervention.'[22] This was a potent political ideal and the last two lines of the poem indicate its power. The reference to 'reunited lives' highlights an aspect of the war often overlooked in American representations: that it was a civil war and that families were divided by ideology or misfortune. It is an idea of division and exile that would recur in different forms with the Vietnamese exodus after the war. The reference has political appeal, but it is disingenuous in suggesting a universally desired reunion, since the collaborators with America—Catholics who fled south in 1954 and non-communist nationalists—did not necessarily desire a communist reunion. In its bland inclusiveness the poem simplifies issues and is as subtly doctrinaire as stateside protest poetry was often pompously prescriptive. The ideal cultural memory referred to earlier is entwined with the politics of war and freedom. Bowen's comment on 'rootedness' is valid, but it ignores the ideological implications and uses of that ideal. Further, more sophisticated poems than Ky's reveal the extent to which war experience is enmeshed with a vision of one's country.

Nguyen Duy's 'Red Earth, Blue Water' is a concise sketch of the painful beauty of a land wracked by war:

---

[21] Kevin Bowen, 'Vietnamese Poetry: A Sense of Place', *Manoa*, 7: 2 (Winter 1995), 49–50. Subsequent references from the journal are indicated after the quotation.

[22] Lacouture, *Ho Chi Minh*, 180. It is ironic in this context that Ho initiated doctrinaire collectivization programmes in north Vietnam that led to misery and peasant revolts.

Bombs plowed into the red earth, berry red.
Scorching sunlight burned the noon air like kiln fire.
Bomb-raked funnels turned into rose water wells.
A noiseless stream of blue water gushing up.
That's our country, isn't it, friend.
The maddening agony, the honey comes from within.

(*Manoa*, 96)

Ky's poem is a one-dimensional projection of the homeland that must be defended. Duy portrays the metaphorical resilience of nature in the face of relentless devastation, a resistance akin to its human counterpart. Defoliation and bombing destroyed forests and humans without discrimination and the poem implicitly conveys some of that desperate survival. In a hellish scenario there are startlingly incongruous images of beauty and regeneration: 'rose water wells', 'blue water gushing up', and 'the honey [that] comes from within'. The last line encapsulates the 'maddening agony' of war and patriotism, and is almost ironical in its recognition of the well-springs of strength that renew the fight and the land. It is a vision of a land strangely inured to, and yet continually scarred by, war, and the lyricism evokes a desire to create a refuge for the mind battered by violence. As Keith Bosley notes:

Considering her history, it is hardly surprising that Vietnam has no body of epic or heroic poetry; instead, her greatest works are lyrical explorations of suffering. The Vietnamese sensibility reacts to horror with a poise Westerners might envy and a resignation Westerners might well deplore. There is very little blood and guts . . . that is left to the silences between the words.[23]

Vietnamese 'poise' and 'resignation', however, are not one-dimensional poses; underlying that stoicism is an amalgam of bitterness, sorrow, despair, and a desperate desire for peace. As Bao Ninh, a north Vietnamese veteran, writes in his moving novel of the war:

He [Kien, the protagonist and narrator] did not want to go north to do the course, and felt certain he would never join them, or become a seed

---

[23] Keith Bosley (trans.), 'To the Reader', in *The War Wife: Vietnamese Poetry* (London: Allison & Busby, 1972), 10.

for successive war harvests. He just wanted to be safe, to die quietly, sharing the fate of an insect or an ant in the war . . . It was clearly those same friendly, simple peasant fighters who were the ones ready to bear the catastrophic consequences of this war, yet they never had a say in deciding the course of the war. . . . war was a world with no home . . . A miserable journey of endless drifting. . . . For Kien, the most attractive, persistent echo of the past is the whisper of ordinary life . . .[24]

These patterns of 'ordinary life' were irrevocably dismantled during the war, and the idea of a calm pastoral that one could return to is severely threatened. 'Rootedness', as mentioned by Bowen, is an important trope, but it is besieged by the overwhelming presence of war. In Bao Ninh's novel and in poetry, the idyllic past seems increasingly mythical, a haunting 'echo' that makes the present an unendurable nightmare. In Bowen's formulation, the war intrudes on the poetry, but the latter can retreat to 'the great enduring themes' of 'home and love' (a variation on the American radical location of the pastoral ideal in Vietnam). There are poems, however, that can locate no literal or imaginative refuge for the war-ravaged consciousness.

Tran Da Tu's 'The new lullaby' depicts a present and a future bound by war:

> Sleep well, my child—a shadow, not mama,
> will tuck you snug in bed and help you sleep.
> A tombstone is your pillow—let the sky
> spread over you a blanket, keep you warm.
> To shield you as a curtain, there's the rain.
> A tree will be your fan, its leaves your roof.
> The stars will twinkle as your mother's eyes.
> The battlefield will be your romping ground.
> Sleep well and smile, with blood upon your lips.
> Bullets and bombs will sing your lullaby.[25]

Nature offers protection to the child in a climate of war, yet the natural world was neither benign nor invulnerable. The poem is

---

[24] Bao Ninh, *The Sorrow of War*, English version by Frank Palmos, based on the translation by Vo Bang Thanh and Phan Thanh Hao, with Katerina Pierce (London: Secker & Warburg, 1993), 15, 27, 57.

[25] Tran Da Tu, 'The new lullaby', in Huynh Sanh Thong (ed. and trans.), *An Anthology of Vietnamese Poems From the Eleventh Through the Twentieth Centuries* (New Haven and London: Yale University Press, 1996), 385. Subsequent references are indicated as *Anthology* after the quotation.

an ironic reflection on a type of revolutionary fervour, fostered by Ho, that equated the vagaries of nature (such as the terrible conditions along the Ho Chi Minh trail) and hardships of battle with patriotism. Thus Tran Van Tra, a Vietcong general, declared that 'The love one had for one's comrades and fellow fighters, for the jungles and the streams was unlimited, immense. That was the love we learned from Uncle Ho, from his vast love for the nation and for the workers and the fighters.'[26] For the child, however, this is a world of death, absence, and menace, and the future envisioned is one of eternal battle. The last two lines combine pity and terror in images of innocence and horror. The child, sleeping with blood on his lips, is akin to Macbeth's image of 'Pity like a naked new-born babe | Striding the blast'.[27] Macbeth's evocation of the child of terror is a prick to his conscience, a fear of the consequences of murder. Tu's child highlights the moral corruption inherent in war and there is no escape from its pervasive presence. While generations of Vietnamese were weaned on revolutionary ideals and died for them, Tu projects the vulnerability and terror of that continuing cycle. The child and its future are an accurate metaphor for the bloody history of Vietnam. 'The Vietnamese', Chomsky writes, 'see their history as an unending series of struggles of resistance against oppression, by the Chinese, the Mongols, the Japanese, the French, and now the Americans.'[28] While this heritage created the kind of revolutionary bonding that allowed the north Vietnamese to resist American force, it also devastated generations who lived in a perennial state of war. 'The new lullaby' thus encompasses the past and the present, and although it is couched in traditional encomiums to a close symbiosis with nature, it disrupts heroic idealizations and looks to a bleak future.

Le Thi May's 'Wind and Widow' dwells on the beauty of nature and lovemaking, only to underline the continual presence of the war:

> Wind widow willowy
> off the arms of dawn and grass

---

[26] Cited in Chanoff and Doan Van Toai, *'Vietnam' A Portrait of Its People*, 173.

[27] William Shakespeare, *Macbeth*, ed. Kenneth Muir (London: Methuen and Co. Ltd., 1963), I. vii. 21–2.

[28] Noam Chomsky, *At War With Asia* (London: William Collins Sons & Co. Ltd., 1971), 205.

> full-chested breath
> after so much lovemaking in the night
> . . . .
> wind widow after each makeup
> backward glances to another time of sadness and laughter
> . . . .
> wind elegiac-wind
> strands of hair from women who died in the bombing
> strands of hair from widows who raised orphaned children
> the war after ten years have passed—
>
> (*Manoa*, 97)

The poem begins in an anthropomorphic delight in nature as the 'willowy' wind commingles with the 'full-chested breath' of pleasure. Sensuality embodies hope and an alternative to war, but the wind is a harbinger of memory and revives the 'time of sadness and laughter'. The experience of war is deeply embedded and surfaces to dislocate the careful structure of joy. The widow in the first section is vulnerable and joyous, but in the final section women bear the brunt of sorrow and death. The particular agony of Vietnamese women during the war included not only prostitution, rape, and death, but also a commitment to the revolution (wholehearted or reluctant) that almost inevitably ended in grief and desolation.[29] The pain of loss was heightened by a barbarous practice in the north Vietnamese army: the wounded were cordoned off in special camps, and death notices were seldom dispatched to families so as to maintain morale. The trauma of war is powerfully residual in the mourning of a loss that is probably certain, but will not be believed until confirmed (a crisis reflected within different political contexts in the MIA controversy in America). As in Tu's lullaby, children are victims growing up in a country wracked by a painful history, and the strands of hair symbolize the inextinguishable memory of war. As Bao Ninh's narrator muses: 'it's hard to forget. When will I calm down?

---

[29] Recollections of the war from a Vietnamese woman's point of view are available in Wendy Wilder Larsen and Tran Thi Nga, *Shallow Graves: Two Women and Vietnam* (New York: Random House, 1986). The controlling voice is that of a shallow, patronizing American, but Nga's experiences in both halves of Vietnam, Wales, and the USA, is a moving testament of loss, courage, and exile. Burning photographs of the family at Tet, before fleeing to America, she writes: 'As the pile of ashes floated away | I felt I was burning my life' (231). Both Nga and Tran Mong Tu, whose poems I discuss, live in the USA.

When will my heart be free of the tight grip of war?'[30] The answer available in the poetry is perhaps never, for the aftermath poems turn to the ideas of loss and exile within Vietnam and in the USA.

The complex historical aftermath in Vietnam included a communist victory, elation and freedom, hatred and despair. The latter manifested itself in 're-education' camps where collaborators with the 'puppet regime' in Saigon were interned. Tang's memoir conveys a sense of bitterness at the betrayal of hope and ideals:

But peace, which they had so passionately desired, had brought with it not blessings but a new and even more insidious warfare, this time a warfare practiced by the liberators against their people. . . . Instead of national reconciliation and independence, Ho Chi Minh's successors have given us a country devouring its own and beholden once again to foreigners . . .[31]

Millions of south Vietnamese fled, and the plight of the 'boat people' underlined the terrible and ambiguous nature of victory. By 1979, unified Vietnam was embroiled in war in Cambodia, and later with China. War seemed to be the perennial state of the State, and, as Christopher Lasch observes, it inevitably affected the psyche of the nation:

As for the other side, it would be naive to think that they have not been corrupted in their own way by the bitterness generated by a very long war, by the experience of having been bombed nearly back to the Stone Age, by deprivations, the desire for revenge, and thirty years of military discipline.[32]

Vietnam had been a total war zone, and the end of the war led to a vacuum that made victory seem curiously unsatisfactory. Militarized minds were unprepared for peace and there was

---

[30] Bao Ninh, *The Sorrow of War*, 39.
[31] Truong Nhu Tang, *Journal of a Vietcong*, 289, 310. Some anti-war activists, including Daniel Ellsberg, Joan Baez, and Daniel and Philip Berrigan, perceived a similar pattern in post-war Vietnam. In a letter to Vietnam's observer at the UN, they wrote: 'We voice our protest in the hope that your Government can avoid the repetition of the tragic historical pattern in which liberators gain power only to impose a new oppression.' Cited in Bernard Gwertzman, 'Antiwar Activists Appeal to Hanoi', *New York Times*, 21 Dec. 1976, 4.
[32] In 'The Meaning of Vietnam', *New York Review of Books*, 22: 10 (June 1975), 23–33.

a paradoxical sense of deflation. Bao Ninh writes of a society almost absolutely defined by war:

> Some said they had been fighting for thirty years, if you included the Japanese and the French. He had been fighting for eleven years. War had been their whole world. So many lives, so many fates. The end of the fighting was like the deflation of an entire landscape, with fields, mountains and rivers collapsing in on themselves.[33]

It is significant that Ninh images the aftermath in terms of the landscape disintegrating, a topography, as we have seen in some poems and in political language, that constituted a vital trope of national pride and regeneration. This complex transition to peace and the totalitarian nature of the communist government was seen in America as a retrospective justification for intervention. Al Santoli, an American veteran, declared in the Asia Society Conference in 1985: 'Communism, whether it be Chinese-inspired communism or Soviet-inspired communism, does not go along with the nature of people who want to be free ... In this regard, I always feel that my involvement in Southeast Asia was the proper thing to do.'[34] The travails of post-war Vietnam enabled a defeated America to patronize the Vietnamese and reiterate the noble intentions of its own involvement. Santoli's statement is typical of a post-war consensus that, while highlighting Vietnamese problems, seemed to overlook the fact that part of those problems arose from the war imposed by America. A finer balance is necessary, and, to perceive nuances of conflict and sadness, it is the poetry to which I return.

'The dawn of a new humankind' by Du Tu Le meditates on the torturous path to and the fact of exile:

> Do you hear echoes from across
> the vast Pacific Ocean, friend?
> From all that land where darkness reigns
> my countrymen are setting out.
> . . . .

---

[33] Bao Ninh, *The Sorrow of War*, 98.

[34] Cited in Timothy Lomperis, *'Reading the Wind': The Literature of the Vietnam War* (Durham, NC: Duke University Press, 1987), 70. Nixon wrote in *No More Vietnams*: 'Today, after Communist governments have killed over a half million Vietnamese and over 2 million Cambodians, the conclusive moral judgement has been rendered on our effort to save Cambodia and South Vietnam: We have never fought in a more moral cause' ((London: W. H. Allen, 1986), 209).

> They leave because the eastern sun
> has long stopped coming up for them.
> Because they want to live as men,
> they may not choose another course.
>
> How can you ever understand?
> You've never lost and left your land.
> All peoples share the human shape,
> but human hearts don't beat alike.
>
> . . . .
>
> Last night I also had a dream.
> I saw the light of a new dawn:
> the sun was shining everywhere,
> but in the east it was pitch-dark.
>
> Do you feel joy this morning, friend,
> on finding that the world has changed?
> Because I chose to stay a man,
> I'm living now an exile's life.
>
> *(Anthology, 197–8)*

The poem's insistent, rhetorical questions are alternately addressed to America, to those left behind, and to fellow refugees. America is not only a landscape but an idea of refuge, and the attainment of that goal leads to a tenuous fulfilment overridden by sorrow. Le sees emigration in deterministic terms, something inevitable within the context of post-war Vietnam. The transfer of locale is placed within a matrix of personal integrity, and the curious phrase 'Because I chose to stay a man' makes sense in the context of a larger sorrow and isolation. Paradoxically, the alternative to exile would be a dehumanized existence. At the same time, memories of home and a land wrapped in war and failed possibilities are deeply embedded in the exiled psyche. The pain in 'How can you ever understand?' is the anguish of the exile who has had to make a choice but cannot jettison the past. It is symptomatic of the 'void' of exile that Camus portrays in another context in *The Plague*: 'that sensation of a void within which never left us, that irrational longing to hark back to the past or else to speed up the march of time, and those keen shafts of memory that stung like fire.'[35] Le's portrayal also indicates the complexity of immersion into the 'melting pot' ideal available in

---

[35] Albert Camus, *The Plague*, trans. Stuart Gilbert (Harmondsworth: Penguin Books Ltd., 1960), 60.

Chanoff's interviews, and American culture at large. It is difficult for the immigrant to adopt new cultural modes and he remains the quintessential exile in a no man's land of memory and sorrow.

Tran Mong Tu's 'The Gift in Wartime' offers a woman's perspective of the American war. Tu, a poet who worked with the Associated Press in Saigon during the war, presents a dialectical progression between an ideal of heroism and grief:

> I offer you roses
> Buried in your new grave
> I offer you my wedding gown
> To cover your tomb still green with grass
>
> You give me medals
> Together with silver stars
> . . . .
>
> I offer you my youth
> The days we were still in love
> My youth died away
> When they told me the bad news
>
> You give me the smell of blood
> From your war dress
> Your blood and your enemy's
> So that I may be moved
>
> I offer you clouds
> That linger on my eyes on summer days
> . . . .
>
> You give me your lips with no smile
> You give me your arms without tenderness
> . . . .
>
> Seriously, I apologize to you
> I promise to meet you in our next life
> I will hold this shrapnel as a token
> By which we will recognize each other.[36]

The articulation of personal loss is moving in its sense of desolation. That grief includes a simultaneous awareness of diminution of the other (death), and a constriction of the self. Thus, while

[36] Lynda van Devanter and Joan Furey (eds.), *Visions of War, Dreams of Peace: Writings of Women in the Vietnam War* (New York: Warner Books Inc., 1991), 80–1. The inclusion of 'The Gift in Wartime' in *Visions of War* is, perhaps, a sign of appropriation of 'other' experiences within American contexts. The poem is transnational and could equally refer to an American woman's trauma. 'A New Year's wish', however, is located in particular Vietnamese immigrant anxieties.

itemizing facets of life valued more than the medals and stars offered by the dead soldier-lover, the poem suggests that the 'things worth living for' are contingent on the relationship that the woman shared. However, the waste of a life in war contrasts ironically with the vibrancy and vitality of the living, even when some of the images are associated with mourning: 'roses', the green grass of the tomb, 'clouds | That linger on my eyes on summer days'. While mourning loss, the last section moves to a present lived with resilience and a token future reunion. 'Seriously, I apologize to you' is an arresting line in its ambiguous possibilities: is she apologetic for surviving her lover; for seeing through his desperate notions of heroism in war; for not being able to persuade him against the enterprise at the outset (and thereby indicating the marginality of women's discourse in war)? This poem opens up the margins of war poetry by indicating the suffering of women in and through war. Simultaneously, it inscribes a binary opposition that continually makes the writing of war experience contingent on male paradigms. Shrapnel as a token by which the parted lovers will recognize each other in a fantasized after-life articulates the contradiction: what is emblematic of violence and dismemberment becomes also a token of recognition and renewal.

In 'A new year's wish for a little refugee', Tu turns to the theme of exile in a vein not dissimilar from Le:

> Let me send you some words, a simple wish.
> On New Year's Day, alone on foreign soil,
> you feel just like a seaweed washed ashore—
> you don't know what the future holds for you.
>
> No lack of kindly hands to welcome you
> and take you home to change what's now your name.
> They'll turn you into some new human breed
> that thinks your yellow skin is cause for shame.
>
> They'll send you off to school, where you'll be taught
> their own land's history, modern ways of life.
> You will grow up denying what you are—
> you'll never hear your forebears spoken of.
> . . . .
> O little child, may you retain intact
> your past of sorrows, all your world of griefs.
>
> (*Anthology*, 198–9)

Le's poem is an adult vision of the bitterness of exile, whereas Tu projects her anxieties on to the future of a child. As adults, Le and Tu are acutely conscious of lives divided by memories, loss, and, paradoxically, freedom. It was a conception of un-freedom back home that led to their fleeing in the first place. 'Home', in a curious throwback to, and extension of, the American veteran's alienation, is a spatial and psychological goal that is unattainable. The predicament of the immigrant is compounded by the need to conform, to learn the history and 'ways of life' of the host country, and forget, if not repudiate, one's homeland. In fact, the 'otherness' of the original country is further emphasized by the repression of that matrix of culture and memory. There is a peculiar necessity and aggression involved in the process of socialization in the new country; to belong to the great 'melting pot' one must acquiesce, since there is no 'home' to turn to. Edward Said writes that 'Exile is predicated on the existence of, love for, and a real bond with one's native place; the universal truth of exile is not that one has lost that love or home, but that inherent in each is an unexpected, unwelcome loss.'[37] Said is accurate in emphasizing the exile's bond with his native country, and Tu's poem emphasizes the bond precisely through the loss of home. It may be theoretically possible to work through attachments rather than rejecting them, but the recovery of home is impossible. The repetition of 'they' in the poem underlines this sense of inexorable assimilation. The Vietnamese experience in America is further defined by the relationship between the two nations during the war. Politically and ideologically the Americans were there to 'defend' and 'save' south Vietnam. In this endeavour, however, they destroyed large areas in the south, disrupted family and village life, and treated their 'allies' with scant respect. US administrators and soldiers expressed grudging respect for the commitment and endurance of the Vietcong in contrast to the cowardice and corruption of their 'allies'. Indeed, a succession of south Vietnamese military leaders were more keen on power than on fighting the communists. As an exasperated American official asked: 'What are we doing here? We're fighting to save these people, and they're fighting each other!'[38] In defeat, these leaders and their devastated people sought refuge in America and it was

---

[37] Edward Said, *Culture & Imperialism* (London: Vintage, 1994), 407.
[38] Cited in Karnow, *Vietnam: A History*, 460.

unlikely that they would be treated with more respect there. The child in the poem may be welcomed by 'kindly hands', but those hands will mould him anew, instilling a sense of shame premised on origin and race. The poem conveys an anxiety of rootlessness very different from Bowen's notion of 'rootedness' in Vietnamese poetry. The intricate networks of family, memory, and land that sustained a meaningful community have been irrevocably disrupted, and the poet's exhortation at the end is a forlorn one. The poem articulates adult anxieties as if to prepare the child for a difficult future, and the legacy the speaker bequeaths is one of sorrow and grief. A poetry of love and hope, however stilted, culminates in one of exile and despair. 'A New Year's wish' is enmeshed in history and memory, and in its self-reflexive meditations it transcribes sad conclusions to a terrible war.

This discussion of Vietnamese poetry provides some insights into the reality and aftermath of the war for the 'other' side. It is preliminary in that it belongs to a larger body of poetry (even if one confines the study to translated poems). That corpus deals with themes of loss and parting, the struggle against foreign domination, torture, and endurance.[39] The poems are often melodramatic, and too didactic and contextualized to have the resonances and nuances available in better works. Political Vietnamese poetry is comparable to some 1960s protest poetry in its overt expression of commitment. Thich Nhat Hahn, a Buddhist peace activist and exile, offers the best example of this engaged poetry. As a tireless crusader for peace in his former homeland, he was representative of a politicized Buddhism (seen in its most extreme form in the immolation of monks in south Vietnam) that was anti-communist and anti-American. In 'Condemnation', Hahn presents a broadly humanist appeal to brotherhood:

Listen to this:
yesterday six Vietcong came through my village.
Because of this my village was bombed—completely destroyed.
. . . .

---

[39] See Thanh Hai, *Faithful Comrades* (South Vietnam: 'Liberation' Publishing House, 1962); *Eleven Poems of Political Prisoners* (Berkeley: Union of Vietnamese in the U.S., n.d.); Don Luce, John C. Schafer, and Jacqueline Chagnon (eds.), *We Promise One Another: Poems From an Asian War* (Washington: The Indochina Mobile Education Project, 1971); Nguyen Chi Thien, *Flowers From Hell*, selected and trans. Huynh Sanh Thong (New Haven: Yale Southeast Asia Studies, 1984).

> Whoever is listening, be my witness!
> I cannot accept this war.
> I never could, I never shall.
> I must say this a thousand times before I am killed.
> . . . .
> Beware! Turn around to face your real enemies—
> ambition, violence, hatred, greed.
> Men cannot be our enemies—even men called 'Vietcong!'
> If we kill men, what brothers will we have left?
> With whom shall we live then?[40]

The poem describes a situation in which most southerners were caught, particularly the ones in villages. Most hamlets were under south Vietnamese/American control during the day and the Vietcong by night. Villagers had to prove their 'loyalty' to both sides and consequently suffered at the hands of both. The politics of a civil war were further compounded by the American presence that bombed any village suspected of harbouring Vietcong.[41] In the declarative witnessing, the privileging of the personal repudiation of war, the poem veers towards the egotistical assertions found in some of Ginsberg's poems. 'I cannot accept this war. / I never could, I never shall' is reminiscent of Ginsberg's 'I here declare the end of the war', although Ginsberg goes further down the road than Hahn in his rejection. The evocation of 'real enemies' in Morality Play terminology is jarring, and although deeply felt, the words have the resonance of a harangue rather than a poem. As a south Vietnamese, however, it was courageous of Hahn to declare his affinity with the Vietcong, and what distinguishes his writings from the myriad poems of Vietnamese protest and patriotism is this quality of moral inclusiveness. He does stress the futility of the American war: that it kills and will leave no one untouched by its bitterness and hatred.[42]

---

[40] Thich Nhat Hanh, *The Cry of Vietnam*, trans. by the author and Helen Coutant (Santa Barbara, Calif.: Unicorn Press, 1968), 15.

[41] Gabriel Kolko points to the coexistence of political apathy and commitment amongst the peasantry: 'Their [the peasants] negative feelings, more in "sorrow rather than in anger," toward the NLF were often due to the fact that their presence brought bombings and that they were still too weak to win.' *Vietnam: Anatomy of a War, 1940–1975* (London and Sydney: Allen & Unwin, 1986), 243.

[42] Chi Thien's *Flowers From Hell* is an interesting variation within the genre of Vietnamese protest, since his poems perceive the communists and Western liberals as the 'enemy'. Written in highly emotive verse, they are examples of a life and memory twisted by bitterness and hate.

While discussing Vietnamese poetry in translation, the subtext and inadequacy of such a study remains, for the problems, as Kevin Bowen notes, are substantial:

> In the Vietnamese language, a line of poetry can have several literal meanings, all quite plausible, all intended by the author. That is just the start of the translator's dilemma. Monosyllabic and tonal, Vietnamese is a language of words abundant in associations and varying in meaning according to tone. Traditional poetic forms such as the *luc bat*—a form of alternating six- and eight-syllable lines—have strict requirements regarding rhyme and the alternation of rising, falling, and flat tones, resulting in a complex poetics that also draws upon a rich lexicon of symbols from the natural world. . . . All of this is so difficult to render into English . . .[43]

However, as Bowen goes on to write, there is an increasing exchange of scholars, poets, and translators between the two countries, and poetry remains an important aspect of Vietnamese cultural and political life. While the problems in translation might explain the occasionally stilted and sentimental quality of the poetry, the poems do offer a point of entry to another world. They resist the denigration of the 'other' so common during the war, and offer a salutary counterbalance to a largely solipsistic American rendition of the war. I have referred to the politics of publishing these poems in America, the possibility of translation as a liberal 'wallow[ing] by remote control in guilt'.[44] Terence Des Pres's comment refers to East European poetry, but it is applicable to the Vietnamese project. There is, however, within this politics, another perspective of solidarity that may be attributed to the enterprise. This involves, as Adrienne Rich points out, a redefinition of political perspectives: '**politics is the effort to find ways of humanely dealing with each other—as groups or as individuals—politics being simply process, the breaking down of barriers of oppression, tradition, culture, ignorance, fear, self-protectiveness.**'[45] Within this paradigm, translation is a process that enables a humane enactment of comprehension, a desire implicitly and overtly available in some of the editorial manifestos cited earlier. For this process not only reflects the 'other'

---

[43] Kevin Bowen, 'Vietnamese Poetry', 50.
[44] Terence Des Pres, 'Poetry and Politics', *TriQuarterly*, 65 (Winter 1986), 17–29.
[45] Adrienne Rich, 'Dearest Arturo', *What Is Found There: Notebooks on Poetry and Politics* (London: Virago Press Limited, 1995), 24. Bold in original text.

but also the inadequacies of the translating self, located as it is within a dominant culture that desires understanding as a means to closure. Rich's formulation does not mitigate these and other problems noted earlier, but it does provide theoretical and real avenues for hope and solidarity. The American project need not be entirely egotistical and fraught with insinuations of cultural imperialism. Such translations allow, if in a flawed and minimal way, for a resistance to the stereotypes and banalities that had led to this horrible war. It is a small beginning to a process of recovery and solidarity.

A large body of Vietnamese poetry about the war is political, in its implicit or overt concern with the sanctity, beauty, and freedom of their homeland. This, as Elizabeth Hodgkin and Mary Jameson point out, is hardly surprising: 'For a country which had lost its independence for nearly a century, political poetry aiming at the liberation of the nation and its people held an extremely important place.'[46] While some poems reflect the binarism of political language, the better ones deal with the memory and pain of war. In some ways it is a quest for identity, a groping towards life beyond war, whether in Vietnam or in exile. Nguyen Dinh Thi, novelist, poet, and playwright, muses on the aftermath in terms of ambiguity, not victory: 'The war was disembodied. It was like a ball of fire, like your napalm. It made us fight harder for survival, yes, but we also lost part of our identity. Perhaps we are still trying to recover it.'[47]

Napalm as reality and image (prominent in American poetry) signifies the omnipresence of war for the Vietnamese, so that war becomes a perpetual state of being. As a palpable and psychic reality it warped and fragmented life, and there is a profound sense of war-weariness in some of the poetry and in Bao Ninh's novel. The war was not, of course, literally 'disembodied'; it killed, maimed, and destroyed. However, as American veterans discovered, memories of war proliferated and haunted individual imaginations and the nation long after the event was over. For Vietnamese poets the end of war was not a simple matter of

[46] To Huu, *Blood and Flowers: The Path of the Poet To Huu*, trans. Elizabeth Hodgkin and Mary Jameson (Hanoi: Foreign Languages Publishing House, 1978), 17.
[47] Cited in Robert Shaplen, *Bitter Victory* (New York: Harper & Row Publishers Inc., 1986), 195.

The 'Other'

victory, it was more an attempt at meaningful recollection and recuperation. Victory, as Nhat Hanh writes in 'Our Green Garden', was mired in a complex aftermath: 'Who will be left to celebrate a victory made of blood and fire?'[48] Within this context, Tang's memoir expresses the imperative need for reconciliation: 'The first step in marshalling the people was to guide them through the infinitely delicate process of reconciling the bitter, often savage enmities that a generation of civil war had left in its wake.'[49] The aftermath was disillusioning for those who had fought for freedom and hoped for a genuine coalition between north and south. Nguyen Ba Chung's 'Nonattachment' is a profound reflection on the dilemmas of post-war existence:

> Let's gather every fragment of our memories
> It's all that we have at the end of our life
> Warring days and nights, showers of sun and rain
> What's left of love?
>
> Let's gather what remains of our memories
> It's all that we have at the close of our life
> Warring days and nights make us wonder
> Should the bundle we gather be empty or full?
>
> (*Writing*, 279)

The ambivalence arises from the incongruence between the title and the poem's articulation of a rigorous straining after dislocated recollections. This effort is not necessarily a reconstitutive one; there is no hope that healing and reconciliation with one's past will occur once the process of 'gather[ing]' memories is complete. In fact, the repetition of 'gather' followed by questions indicates the continual, perhaps futile, aspect of the endeavour. There is no alternative, however, and to discontinue the questioning is to enter a world of bad faith and amnesia. The first question, 'What's left of love?' echoes Balaban's 'After our war, how will love speak?' in its awareness of the extent to which war language dominates the imagination. From a Vietnamese perspective, the question has a further resonance in that the internecine struggle between communist north Vietnam and liberal nationalism in the south (embodied in figures such as Tang and the PRG) continued after the Americans withdrew. The bitterness

---

[48] Thich Nhat Hahn, *The Cry of Vietnam*, 35.
[49] Truong Nhu Tang, *Journal of a Vietcong*, 273.

of war was buttressed by ideological conflict that presumed moral superiority. Within a field of banal political platitudes and righteous violence, where was the space for recollection and love? The second question, 'Should the bundle we gather be empty or full?' is haunted by the futility of the struggle for independence in the context of a vicious and resentful aftermath. Above all, it is the fracturing of individual lives that dominates the poem, where 'Nonattachment' may be an ideal impossible to achieve. Underlying post-war lives is the detritus of war, 'a secret code of pain and memory'.[50] Ballard's phrase is particularly apt for this poem and for the experiences of veterans, Vietnamese and American. This is not to conflate the two, but to indicate that, despite differences of perspective, culture, and history, there are connections between politically and militarily opposed camps. Within a dominant climate of amnesia in America it is necessary to listen to the voices of the 'other'. This not only humanizes the 'enemy', but provides a valuable poetic trace for the memory of war. As To Huu writes in 'The Man From the Mountains', 'I have such pain in me, never will I forget.'[51] It is this pain that reverberates through the best poems discussed in this study, memories of a brutal and sad war that yoke together America and Vietnam.

[50] J. G. Ballard, *Empire of the Sun* (London: Victor Gollancz Ltd., 1984), 247.
[51] To Huu, *Blood and Flowers*, 75.

Bibliography

PRIMARY MATERIAL

A. Articles and Books

BAKER, Mark, *Nam: The Vietnam War in the Words of the Men and Women Who Fought There* (London: Abacus, 1981).
BAKER, RICHARD E., *Shellburst Pond* (Tacoma, Wash.: Vardaman Press, 1982).
BALABAN, JOHN, *After Our War* (Pittsburgh: University of Pittsburgh Press, 1974).
—— *Blue Mountain* (Greensboro, NC: Unicorn Press Inc., 1982).
—— *Words for My Daughter* (Port Townsend, Wash.: Copper Canyon Press, 1991).
—— *Remembering Heaven's Face: A Moral Witness in Vietnam* (New York and London: Poseidon Press, 1991).
—— *Locusts at the Edge of Summer: New and Selected Poems* (Port Townsend, Wash.: Copper Canyon Press, 1997).
—— 'Mapping Uncharted Territories: Oral Poetries From Southeast Asia', *Translation Review*, 5 (1980), 29–32.
BALLARD, J. G., *Empire of the Sun* (London: Victor Gollancz Ltd., 1984).
BAO NINH, *The Sorrow of War*, English version by Frank Palmos, based on the translation by Vo Bang Thanh and Phan Thanh Hao, with Katerina Pierce (London: Secker & Warburg, 1993).
BARDEN, THOMAS E. (ed.), *Long Time Passing: Poems, Songs & Reflections on the Vietnam War after 20 Years* (Toledo, Oh.: Radio Room Press, 1995).
BARKER, PAT, *The Ghost Road* (London: Viking, 1995).
BARR, JOHN, *The War Zone* (Easthampton, Mass.: Warwick Press, 1989).
BARRY, JAN (ed.), *Peace Is Our Profession: Poems and Passages of War Protest* (Montclair, NJ: East River Anthology, 1981).
—— and EHRHART, W. D. (eds.), *Demilitarized Zones: Veterans After Vietnam* (Perkasie, Pa.: East River Anthology, 1976).
BARTH, R. L., *Forced-Marching to the Styx: Vietnam War Poems* (Van Nuys, Calif.: Perivale Press, 1983).
—— *Looking for Peace* (Omaha: The University of Nebraska Press, 1985).

BATES, SCOTT (ed.), *Poems of War Resistance* (New York: Grossman Publishers, 1969).
BAUER, BILL, *The Eye of the Ghost* (Kansas City: BkMk Press, University of Missouri, 1986).
BERG, STEPHEN, and MEZEY, ROBERT (eds.), *Naked Poetry* (New York and Indianapolis: The Bobbs-Merrill Co. Inc., 1969).
BERRY, D. C., *saigon cemetery* (Athens, Ga.: The University of Georgia Press, 1972).
BLY, ROBERT, *The Light Around the Body* (New York, Evanston, and London: Harper & Row, Publishers, 1967).
—— *The Teeth Mother Naked at Last* (San Francisco: City Lights Books, 1970).
—— *Sleepers Joining Hands* (New York, London, Evanston and San Francisco: Harper & Row, Publishers, 1973).
—— 'Whitman's Line As a Public Form', *The American Poetry Review*, 15: 2 (Mar./Apr. 1986), 5.
—— and RAY, DAVID (eds.), *A Poetry Reading Against the War* (Madison: American Writers Against the War, 1966).
BORTON, LADY, *After Sorrow: An American Among the Vietnamese* (New York: Viking, 1995).
BOSLEY, KEITH (trans.), *The War Wife: Vietnamese Poetry* (London: Allison & Busby, 1972).
BOWEN, KEVIN, *Playing Basketball With the Vietcong* (Willimantic, Conn.: Curbstone Press, 1994).
—— 'Vietnamese Poetry: A Sense of Place', *Manoa*, 7: 2 (Winter 1995), 49–50.
—— and WEIGL, BRUCE (eds. and introd.), *Writing Between the Lines* (Amherst, Mass.: The University of Massachusetts Press, 1997).
CAMUS, ALBERT, *The Plague*, trans. Stuart Gilbert (Harmondsworth: Penguin Books Ltd., 1960).
CAPUTO, PHILIP, *A Rumor of War* (London: Arrow Books Limited, 1978).
CASEY, MICHAEL, *Obscenities* (New Haven and London: Yale University Press, 1972).
CASTAN, FRAN, *The Widow's Quilt* (New York: Canio's Editions, 1996).
CHAGNON, JACQUI, and LUCE, DON (eds.), *Of Quiet Courage: Poems From Vietnam* (Washington: The Indochina Mobile Education Project, 1974).
CHANOFF, DAVID, and DOAN VAN TOAI, *'Vietnam' A Portrait of Its People at War* (London and New York: I. B. Tauris, 1996).
COETZEE, J. M., *Dusklands* (London: Secker & Warburg, 1982).
COLEMAN, HORACE, *In the Grass* (Woodbridge, Conn.: Viet Nam Generation Inc. & Burning Cities Press, 1995).

CONNOLLY, DAVID, *Lost in America* (Woodbridge, Conn.: Viet Nam Generation Inc. & Burning Cities Press, 1994).
CROSS, FRANK A. Jr., *Reminders* (Big Timber, Mont.: Seven Buffaloes Press, 1986).
DEVANTER, LYNDA VAN, *Home Before Morning: The Story of an Army Nurse in Vietnam*, with Christopher Morgan (New York: Warner Books Inc., 1983).
—— and FUREY, JOAN (eds.), *Visions of War, Dreams of Peace: Writings of Women in the Vietnam War* (New York: Warner Books Inc., 1991).
DICKEY, JAMES, 'Spinning the Crystal Ball: Some Guesses at the Future of American Poetry', a lecture delivered at the Library of Congress (Washington: The Library of Congress, 1967).
—— *The Whole Motion: Collected Poems, 1945–1992* (Hanover, Pa., and London: Wesleyan University Press, 1992).
DUNCAN, ROBERT, *Bending the Bow* (London: Jonathan Cape, 1971).
EDELMAN, BERNARD (ed.), *Dear America: Letters Home From Vietnam* (New York and London: W. W. Norton & Company, 1985).
EHRHART, W. D., *More Recent Poems* (Imaginative Representations of the Vietnam War Archive: La Salle University, Philadelphia, 1969).
—— 'What's In a Name? The Snake', *WIN* (Nov. 1979), 13–14.
—— *Vietnam-Perkasie: A Combat Marine Memoir* (Jefferson, NC, and London: McFarland, 1983).
—— ' "Waiting for the Fire": An Essay on Vietnam War Poetry by Non-Vietnam Veterans', *Poetry East*, 9 and 10 (Winter 1982–Spring 1983), 112–17.
—— *To Those Who Have Gone Home Tired: New & Selected Poems* (New York and Chicago: Thunder's Mouth Press, 1984).
—— *The Outer Banks and Other Poems* (Easthampton, Mass.: Adastra Press, 1984).
—— (ed.), *Carrying the Darkness: American Indochina—The Poetry of the Vietnam War* (New York: Avon Books, 1985).
—— *Passing Time: Memoir of a Vietnam Veteran Against the War* (Jefferson, NC, and London: McFarland & Company Inc., Publishers, 1986).
—— *Going Back: An Ex-Marine Returns to Vietnam* (Jefferson, NC, and London: McFarland & Company Inc., Publishers, 1987).
—— 'Soldier-Poets of the Vietnam War', *The Virginia Quarterly Review*, 63: 2 (Spring 1987), 246–65.
—— 'Why Teach Vietnam?', *Social Education*, 52: 1 (Jan. 1988), 25–6.
—— *Unaccustomed Mercy: Soldier-Poets of the Vietnam War* (Lubbock, Tex.: Texas Tech University Press, 1989).
—— *Just For Laughs* (Silver Spring, Md.: Vietnam Generation Inc. and Burning Cities Press, 1990).

EHRHART, W. D., *In the Shadow of Vietnam: Essays, 1977–1991* (Jefferson, NC, and London: McFarland & Company Inc., Publishers, 1991).
—— *The Distance We Travel* (Easthampton, Mass.: Adastra Press, 1993).
—— 'The Perversion of Faith', *Long Shot*, 19 (1997), 127.
—— '"What Grace Is Found In So Much Loss?"', *The Virginia Quarterly Review*, 73: 1 (Winter 1997), 99–111.
—— *Beautiful Wreckage: New & Selected Poems* (Easthampton, Mass.: Adastra Press, 1999).
Eleven Poems of Political Prisoners (Berkeley: Union of Vietnamese in the U.S., n.d.).
ELIOT, T. S., *Murder in the Cathedral* (London: Faber and Faber Limited, 1938).
FARRELL, J. G., *The Singapore Grip* (Glasgow: William Collins Sons & Co. Ltd., 1979).
FENTON, JAMES, *The Memory of War and Children in Exile: Poems 1968–1983* (Harmondsworth: Penguin Books Ltd., 1983).
—— *All the Wrong Places: Adrift in the Politics of Asia* (London: Penguin Books, 1988).
FLOYD, BRYAN ALEC, *The Long War Dead: An Epiphany 1st Platoon USMC* (Sag Harbor, NY: The Permanent Press, 1976).
FROHMAN, BARBARA MENGHINI (ed.), *Incoming: Poems By Vietnam Veterans* (Islip, NY: Island Poets, 1993).
GETTLER, ANDREW, *Footsteps of a Ghost: Poems From Viet Nam* (New Brunswick, NJ: Iniquity Press/Vendetta Books, 1991).
GINSBERG, ALLEN, *Collected Poems 1947–1980* (New York: Viking, 1984).
—— 'Pound's Influence', *The American Poetry Review*, 15: 4 (July/Aug. 1986), 7–8.
GRAY, NIGEL (ed.), *Phoenix Country* (London: The Journeyman Press, 1980).
GREENE, GRAHAM, *The Quiet American* (Harmondsworth: Penguin Books Ltd., 1955).
GWERTZMAN, BERNARD, 'Antiwar Activists Appeal to Hanoi', *New York Times*, 21 Dec. 1976, 4.
HANSEN, VINCENT J., *Blessed are the Piecemakers* (St Cloud, Minn.: North Star Press of St Cloud, Inc., 1989).
HASFORD, GUSTAV, *The Short-Timers* (London: Century Publishing Co. Ltd., 1985).
HEINEMANN, LARRY, *Paco's Story* (London and Boston: Faber and Faber, 1986).
HELLER, JOSEPH, *Catch-22* (London: Jonathan Cape, 1962).

HEMINGWAY, ERNEST, *A Farewell to Arms* (1929; London: Everyman's Library, 1993).
HERR, MICHAEL, *Dispatches* (New York: Alfred A. Knopf, 1978).
HUYNH SANH THONG (ed. and trans.), *An Anthology of Vietnamese Poems From the Eleventh Through the Twentieth Centuries* (New Haven and London: Yale University Press, 1996).
JAEGER, LOWELL, *War on War* (Logan, Ut.: Utah State University Press, 1988).
JARRELL, MARY (ed.), *Randall Jarrell's Letters* (London: Faber and Faber, 1985).
JARRELL, RANDALL, *Selected Poems* (New York: Alfred A. Knopf, 1955).
JONES, DAVID, *In Parenthesis* (London and Boston: Faber and Faber, 1937).
KEROUAC, JACK, *On the Road* (Harmondsworth: Penguin Books Ltd., 1972).
KILEY, FRED, Lt.-Col., and DATER, TONY, Lt.-Col., *Listen. The War: A Collection of Poetry About the Viet-Nam War* (Colorado: United States Air Force Academy, 1973).
KIMLER, FOREST L. (ed. and compiler), *Boondock Bards* (APO San Francisco 96503: *Pacific Stars and Stripes*, 1968).
KIPLING, RUDYARD, *Collected Stories*, selected and introduced Robert Gottlieb (London: David Campbell Publishers Ltd., 1994).
KOMUNYAKAA, YUSEF, *Dien Cai Dau* (Middletown, Conn.: Wesleyan University Press, 1988).
——'Maps Drawn in the Dust', *Colorado Review*, NS 15: 1 (Spring–Summer 1988), 13.
KOVIC, RON, *Born on the Fourth of July* (London: Transworld Publishers Ltd., 1990).
KUNDERA, MILAN, *The Book of Laughter and Forgetting*, trans. Michael Henry Heim (London and Boston: Faber and Faber, 1980).
LANE, MCAVOY, *How Audie Murphy Died in Vietnam* (New York: Anchor Press, Doubleday, 1973).
LARSEN, WENDY WILDER, and TRAN THI NGA, *Shallow Graves: Two Women and Vietnam* (New York: Random House, 1986).
LEVERTOV, DENISE, *Light Up the Cave* (1946; New York: New Directions Publishing Corporation, 1981).
——*Footprints* (New York: New Directions Publishing Corporation, 1972).
——*The Poet in the World* (New York: New Directions Publishing Corporation, 1973).
——*The Freeing of the Dust* (New York: New Directions Publishing Corporation, 1975).

LEVERTOV, DENISE, *Poems 1960–1967* (New York: New Directions Publishing Corporation, 1975).
—— *Poems 1968–1972* (New York: New Directions Publishing Corporation, 1987).
—— *New & Collected Essays* (New York: New Directions Publishing Corporation, 1992).
—— (ed.), *1968 Peace Calendar & Appointment Book: Out of the War Shadow* (New York: War Resisters League, 1967).
LOWELL, ROBERT, *Life Studies* (London: Faber and Faber, 1959).
LOWENFELS, WALTER (ed.), *Where Is Vietnam? American Poets Respond* (Garden City, NY: Doubleday & Company Inc., 1967).
LUCE, DON, SCHAFER, JOHN C., and CHAGNON, JACQUELINE (eds.), *We Promise One Another: Poems From an Asian War* (Washington: The Indochina Mobile Education Project, 1971).
MAILER, NORMAN, *The Naked and the Dead* (1948; London: Paladin, 1992).
—— *The Armies of the Night: History as a Novel, The Novel as History* (New York: The New American Library, 1968).
—— *The Idol and the Octopus* (New York: Dell Publishing Co., Inc., 1968).
—— *Why Are We In Vietnam?* (London: Panther Books Ltd., 1970).
Manoa: A Pacific Journal of International Writing, 7: 2 (Winter 1995).
MARSHALL, KATHRYN, *In the Combat Zone: An Oral History of American Women in Vietnam, 1966–1975* (Boston and Toronto: Little, Brown and Company, 1987).
MARVELL, ANDREW, *Complete Poetry*, ed. George deF. Lord (London and Melbourne: J. M. Dent & Sons Ltd., 1984).
MASON, BOBBIE ANN, *In Country* (London: Flamingo, 1987).
MASON, STEVE, *Johnny's Song* (New York and London: Bantam Books, 1987).
—— *Warrior for Peace* (New York and London: Simon & Schuster Inc., 1988).
MCCARTHY, GERALD, *War Story: Vietnam War Poems* (New York: The Crossing Press, 1977).
—— *Shoetown* (Bristol, Ind.: Coverdale Corporation, 1992).
MCCARTHY, MARY, *Vietnam* (Harmondsworth: Penguin Books Ltd., 1967).
MCDONALD, WALTER, *Caliban in Blue* (Lubbock, Tex.: Texas Tech Press, 1976).
—— *Burning the Fence* (Lubbock, Tex.: Texas Tech Press, 1981).
—— *The Flying Dutchman* (Columbus, Oh.: Ohio State University Press, 1987).
—— *After the Noise of Saigon* (Amherst, Mass.: The University of

Massachusetts Press, 1988).
—— *Night Landings* (New York: Harper & Row Publishers, 1989).
—— *Where Skies Are Not Cloudy* (Denton, Tex.: University of North Texas Press, 1994).
—— *Counting Survivors* (Pittsburgh and London: University of Pittsburgh Press, 1995).
MCNAMARA, ROBERT S., *In Retrospect: The Tragedy and Lessons of Vietnam*, with Brian Van De Mark (New York: Times Books, 1995).
MERRILL, JAMES, *From the First Nine: Poems 1946–1976* (New York: Atheneum, 1982).
MILLER, STEPHEN P., *An Act of God* (Eureka, Calif.: Northcoast View Press, 1982).
MOK, MICHAEL, 'Reality of Vietnam', *LIFE*, 59: 22 (Nov. 1965), 50–74.
NEMEROV, HOWARD, *Poetry and Fiction: Essays* (New Brunswick, NJ: Rutgers University Press, 1963).
—— *The Collected Poems of Howard Nemerov* (Chicago and London: The University of Chicago Press, 1977).
—— *Figures of Thought: Speculations on the Meaning of Poetry and Other Essays* (Boston: David R. Godine, Publisher, 1978).
—— *Sentences* (Chicago and London: The University of Chicago Press, 1980).
—— *War Stories: Poems About Long Ago and Now* (Chicago and London: The University of Chicago Press, 1987).
—— *Trying Conclusions: New and Selected Poems, 1961–1991* (Chicago and London: The University of Chicago Press, 1991).
—— (ed.), *Poets on Poetry* (New York and London: Basic Books, Inc., Publishers, 1966).
NGUYEN CHI THIEN, *Flowers From Hell*, selected and trans. Huynh Sanh Thong (New Haven: Yale Southeast Asia Studies, 1984).
NGUYEN NGOC BICH, 'War Poems From the Vietnamese', *The Hudson Review*, 20: 3 (Autumn 1967), 361–8.
—— (ed.), *War and Exile: A Vietnamese Anthology* (East Coast, USA: Vietnamese PEN Abroad, 1989).
NIXON, RICHARD, *No More Vietnams* (London: W. H. Allen, 1986).
NYE, JIM, *After Shock* (El Paso, Tex.: Cinco Puntos Press, 1991).
O'BRIEN, TIM, *If I Die In a Combat Zone* (London: Granada Publishing Limited, 1980).
—— *Going After Cacciato* (London: Collins, 1988).
—— *The Things They Carried* (London: Harper Collins Publishers, 1990).
—— 'The Vietnam in Me', *New York Times Magazine*, (Oct. 1994), 48–57.

OLDHAM, PERRY, *Vinh Long* (Meadows of Dan, Va.: Northwoods Press, Inc., 1976).
OWEN, WILFRED, *The Complete Poems and Fragments, i. The Poems,* ed. Jon Stallworthy (London: Chatto & Windus and Oxford University Press, 1983).
PALMER, GENERAL BRUCE Jr., *The 25-Year War: America's Military Role in Vietnam* (New York: Simon & Schuster, Inc., 1984).
PALMOS, FRANK, *Ridding the Devils: Vietnam Revisited* (London: Arrow Books Limited, 1991).
PARSONS, I. M. (ed.), *Men Who March Away* (London: The Hogarth Press, 1987).
POUND, EZRA, *Personae: The Collected Poems of Ezra Pound* (New York: Liveright Publishing Corporation, 1926).
PRIMA, DIANE DI (ed.), *War Poems* (New York: The Poets Press Inc., 1968).
RICH, ADRIENNE, *The Fact of a Doorframe: Poems Selected and New, 1950–1984* (New York and London: W. W. Norton & Company, 1984).
—— *Blood, Bread and Poetry: Selected Prose 1979–1985* (London: Virago Press Limited, 1987).
—— *What Is Found There: Notebooks on Poetry and Politics* (London: Virago Press Limited, 1995).
RICH, LAURIE, *Apologia for Vietnam* (Utah: Sheepherder Woman Press, 1995).
RITTERBUSCH, DALE, *Lessons Learned: Poetry of the Vietnam War and its Aftermath* (Woodbridge, Conn.: Viet Nam Generation Inc. & Burning Cities Press, 1995).
ROBERTSSEN, LOWELL, *Remembering the Women of the Vietnam War* (Eden Prairie, Minn.: Tessera Publishing, Inc., 1990).
ROTTMANN, LARRY, *Paco's Story* (London and Boston: Faber and Faber, 1986).
—— 'A Hundred Happy Sparrows: An American Veteran Returns to Vietnam', *Vietnam Generation*, 1: 1 (Winter 1989), 113–40.
—— (ed.), *Voices From the Ho Chi Minh Trail: Poetry of America and Vietnam, 1965–1993* (California: Event Horizon Press, 1993).
ROTTMANN, LARRY, BARRY, JAN, PAQUET, BASIL T. (eds.), *Winning Hearts and Minds: War Poems by Vietnam Veterans* (New York and London: McGraw-Hill Book Company, 1972).
SASSOON, SIEGFRIED, *Collected Poems 1908–1956* (London: Faber and Faber, 1961).
SCHELL, JONATHAN, *The Village of Ben Suc* (London: Jonathan Cape, 1968).
SCHLEGEL, LEE LEE (ed.), *DEROS*, Dec. 1981–Sept. 1987.

SHAKESPEARE, WILLIAM, *Macbeth*, ed. Kenneth Muir (London: Methuen and Co. Ltd., 1963).
SHAPLEN, ROBERT, *The Road From War: Vietnam 1965–1970* (London: Andre Deutsch Limited, 1971).
—— *Bitter Victory* (New York: Harper & Row Publishers Inc., 1986).
SHIELDS, BILL, *drinking gasoline in hell* (Wichita, Kan.: Mumbles Publications, 1989).
SIMPSON, LOUIS, *People Live Here: Selected Poems 1949–1983* (London: Secker & Warburg, 1985).
SINKE, RALPH E. G. Jr., *Don't Cry For Us* (Kingsport, Tenn.: Kingsport Press, 1984).
SMITH, WINNIE, *Daughter Gone to War: The True Story of a Young Nurse in Vietnam* (London: Warner Books, 1992).
SPENCER, ERNEST, *Welcome to Vietnam, Macho Man: Reflections of a Khe Sanh Vet* (Springfield, Oh.: Corps Press, 1987).
SPENDER, STEPHEN, *Collected Poems 1928–1985* (London and Boston: Faber and Faber, 1985).
STALLWORTHY, JON, 'A poem about Poems About Vietnam', *Critical Quarterly*, 10 (1968), 57.
STOKESBURY, LEON (ed.), *Articles of War: A Collection of American Poetry About World War II* (Fayetteville, Ark.: The University of Arkansas Press, 1990).
SULLY, FRANÇOIS (ed.), *We the Vietnamese: Voices From Vietnam* (New York, Washington and London: Praeger Publishers, 1971).
SWAIN, JON, *River of Time* (London: Minerva, 1996).
TERKEL, STUDS, *'The Good War': An Oral History of World War Two* (London: Hamish Hamilton, 1985).
THANH HAI, *Faithful Comrades* (South Vietnam: 'Liberation' Publishing House, 1962).
THANH T. NGUYEN and BRUCE WEIGL (selected and trans.), *Poems From Captured Documents* (Amherst, Mass.: The University of Massachusetts Press, 1994).
THICH NHAT HAHN, *The Cry of Vietnam*, trans. by the author and Helen Coutant (Santa Barbara, Calif.: Unicorn Press, 1968).
TO HUU, *Blood and Flowers: The Path of the Poet To Huu*, trans. Elizabeth Hodgkin and Mary Jameson (Hanoi: Foreign Languages Publishing House, 1978).
TOPHAM, J. (ed.) *Vietnam Literature Anthology* (Philadelphia: American Poetry and Literature Press, 1990).
TRUONG NHU TANG, *Journal of a Vietcong* (London: Jonathan Cape, 1986).
ULISSE, PETER, *Vietnam Voices* (Lewistown, Queenstown, and Lampeter: The Edwin Mellen Press, 1990).

'Viet-Nam Veterans Speak Out', *New York Times*, sect. 4, 19 Nov. 1967, E 7.
WEBB, JAMES, *Fields of Fire* (London, Toronto, Sydney and New York: Granada Publishing Limited, 1980).
WEIGL, BRUCE, *Executioner* (Tucson, Ariz.: Ironwood Press, 1976).
―― *Song of Napalm* (New York: Atlantic Monthly Press, 1988).
―― *What Saves Us* (Evanston, Ill.: TriQuarterly Books, 1992).
WINTHROP, JOHN, *Life and Letters of John Winthrop, 1630–1649, ii.* ed. Robert C. Winthrop (Boston: Ticknor and Fields, 1867).
WOLFF, TOBIAS, *In Pharaoh's Army: Memories of a Lost War* (London: Bloomsbury Publishing, 1994).
WOOLF, VIRGINIA, *A Room of One's Own* (New York: Harcourt, Brace & World, Inc., 1929).
―― *Three Guineas* (San Diego, New York, and London: Harcourt Brace Jovanovich, 1938).
YEATS, W. B., *Essays* (London: Macmillan and Co. Limited, 1924).
―― *The Collected Poems of W. B. Yeats* (New York: The Macmillan Company, 1933).

B. Videocassettes

Facing the Darkness, Healing the Wounds: My Lai 25 Years After, My Lai Oral History Video (Tulane University, 1994).
Hearts and Minds, dir. Peter Davis (Embassy Home Entertainment, 1975).
In The Year of the Pig, dir. and prod. Emile de Antonio (MPI Home Video, 1968).
Vietnam Memorial, dir. Foster Wiley and Steve York (PBS Video, 1988).
Vietnam Requiem, dir. Jonas McCord and Bill Couturie, prod. ABC News Associates Inc. (Fox Video, 1982).
Vietnam: Time of the Locust, prod. Peter Gessner (MPI Home Video, 1986).

SECONDARY SOURCES

Criticism

'Allen Ginsberg', Obituary, *The Times*, 7 Apr. 1997, 23.
AMIDON, STEPHEN, 'Back to the Front', *The Sunday Times*, sect. 11, 18 May 1997, 2–3.
ANDERSON, DONALD, 'McNamara's Makeshift Amends', *War, Literature & the Arts*, 7: 2 (Fall–Winter 1995), 57–68.

Bibliography

ARMSTRONG, NANCY, and LEONARD TENNENHOUSE (eds.), *The Violence of Representation: Literature and the History of Violence* (London and New York: Routledge, 1989).

BATES, MILTON J., *The Wars We Took to Vietnam: Cultural Conflict and Storytelling* (Berkeley, Los Angeles, and London: University of California Press, 1996).

BAUGHMAN, RONALD (ed.), *Dictionary of Literary Biography, ix. American Writers of the Vietnam War* (Detroit and London: Gale Research Inc., 1991).

BEIDLER, PHILIP D., *American Literature and the Experience of Vietnam* (Athens, Ga.: The University of Georgia Press, 1982).

—— *Re-Writing America: Vietnam Authors in Their Generation* (Athens, Ga., and London: The University of Georgia Press, 1991).

BELLHOUSE, MARY L., and LITCHFIELD, LAWRENCE, 'Vietnam and the Loss of Innocence: An Analysis of the Political Implications of the Popular Literature of the Vietnam War', *Journal of Popular Culture*, 16: 3 (Winter 1982), 157–74.

BHABA, HOMI K. (ed.), *Nation and Narration* (London: Routledge, 1990).

BIBBY, MICHAEL, 'Fragging the Chains of Command: GI Resistance Poetry and Mutilation', *Journal of American Culture*, 16: 3 (Fall 1993), 29–38.

BLY, ROBERT, *Talking All Morning* (Ann Arbor: The University of Michigan Press, 1980).

CAPPS, WALTER (ed.), *The Vietnam Reader* (New York and London: Routledge, 1990).

CARTER, SUSANNE, 'Variations on Vietnam: Women's Innovative Interpretation of the Vietnam War Experience', *Extrapolation*, 32: 2 (Summer 1991), 170–83.

CARTON, EVAN, 'Vietnam and the Limits of Masculinity', *American Literary History*, 3: 2 (Summer 1991), 294–318.

CARUTH, CATHY (ed.), *Trauma: Explorations in Memory* (Baltimore and London: The Johns Hopkins University Press, 1995).

CHRISTOPHER, RENNY, '"I Never Really Became a Woman Veteran Until . . . I Saw the Wall": A Review of Oral Histories and Personal Narratives by Women Veterans of the Vietnam War', *Vietnam Generation*, 1: 3–4 (Summer–Fall 1989), 33–45.

COBLEY, EVELYN, *Representing War: Form and Ideology in First World War Narratives* (Toronto, Buffalo, and London: University of Toronto Press, 1993).

COHN, CAROL, 'Sex and Death in the Rational World of Defense Intellectuals', *Signs: Journal of Women in Culture and Society*, 12: 4 (Summer 1987), 687–718.

COOKE, MIRIAM, and WOOLLACOTT, ANGELA (eds.), *Gendering War Talk* (Princeton, NJ: Princeton University Press, 1993).

CRAMER, STEVEN, 'Facts and Figures', *Poetry*, 156: 2 (May 1990), 100–15.

DES PRES, TERENCE, 'Poetry and Politics', *TriQuarterly*, 65 (Winter 1986), 17–29.

DOWLING, W. C., *Jameson, Althusser, Marx: An Introduction to the Political Unconscious* (Ithaca, NY: Cornell University Press, 1984).

DURAND, MAURICE M., and NGUYEN TRAN HUAN, *An Introduction to Vietnamese Literature*, trans. D. M. Hawke (New York: Columbia University Press, 1985).

EHRHART, W. D., personal interview, 6 and 12 Feb., 1997.

ELSHTAIN, JEAN BETHKE, *Women and War* (New York: Basic Books, Inc., Publishers, 1987).

EMERSON, GLORIA, 'Writers and War', *The Writer In Our World*, highlights of *TriQuarterly* magazine's 1984 symposium, Northwestern University, audio cassette.

ENLOE, CYNTHIA, *Does Khaki Become You? The Militarization of Women's Lives* (Boston: South End Press, 1983).

FELSTINER, JOHN, 'Bearing the War in Mind', *Parnassus: Poetry in Review*, 6: 2 (Spring–Summer 1978), 30–7.

FREUD, SIGMUND, *Civilisation, War and Death*, ed. John Rickman (London: The Hogarth Press and The Institute of Psycho-Analysis, 1953).

FUSSELL, PAUL, *The Great War and Modern Memory* (New York and London: Oxford University Press, 1975).

—— *Thank God For the Atom Bomb and Other Essays* (New York and London: Summit Books, 1988).

—— *Wartime: Understanding and Behavior in the Second World War* (New York and Oxford: Oxford University Press, 1989).

—— (ed.), *The Bloody Game* (London: Abacus, 1991).

GELPI, ALBERT (ed.), *Denise Levertov: Selected Criticism* (Ann Arbor: The University of Michigan Press, 1993).

GILMAN, OWEN W. Jr., and SMITH, LORRIE (eds.), *America Rediscovered: Critical Essays on Literature and Film of the Vietnam War* (New York and London: Garland Publishing, Inc., 1990).

GINSBERG, ALLEN, *Allen Verbatim: Lectures on Poetry, Politics, Consciousness*, ed. Gordon Ball (New York and London: McGraw-Hill Book Company, 1974).

GOTERA, VINCE, '"Lines of Tempered Steel": An Interview with Yusef Komunyakaa.' *Callaloo*, 13: 2 (1990), 215–29.

—— *Radical Visions: Poetry by Vietnam Veterans* (Athens, Ga., and London: The University of Georgia Press, 1994).

GRAVES, ROBERT (intro.), *New Larousse Encyclopedia of Mythology* (London and New York: Hamlyn, 1974).

GRAY, RICHARD, *American Poetry of the Twentieth Century* (London and New York: Longman, 1990).

HAINES, HARRY, 'Disputing the Wreckage: Ideological Struggle at the Vietnam Veterans Memorial', *Vietnam Generation*, 1: 1 (Winter 1989), 141–56.

HALLBERG, ROBERT VON, *American Poetry and Culture 1945–1980* (Cambridge, Mass., and London: Harvard University Press, 1985).

HANLEY, LYNNE, *Writing War: Fiction, Gender, and Memory* (Amherst, Mass.: The University of Massachusetts Press, 1991).

HARTMAN, GEOFFREY, 'Public Memory and Its Discontents', *Raritan* 13 (Spring 1994), 24–40.

HELLMAN, JOHN, *American Myth and the Legacy of Vietnam* (New York: Columbia University Press, 1986).

HERZOG, TOBEY C., *Vietnam War Stories: Innocence Lost* (London and New York: Routledge, 1992).

HOLDEN, JONATHAN, *Style and Authenticity in Postmodern Poetry* (Columbia, Mo.: University of Missouri Press, 1986).

HYDE, LEWIS (ed.), *On the Poetry of Allen Ginsberg* (Ann Arbor: The University of Michigan Press, 1984).

JAMESON, FREDRIC, *The Political Unconscious* (London: Methuen & Co. Ltd., 1981).

——(ed.), *Aesthetics and Politics* (London and New York: Verso, 1980).

JASON, PHILIP K. (ed.), *Fourteen Landing Zones: Approaches to Vietnam War Literature* (Iowa City: University of Iowa Press, 1991).

JEFFORDS, SUSAN, '"Things Worth Dying For": Gender and the Ideology of Collectivity in Vietnam Representation', *Cultural Critique*, 8 (Winter 1987–8), 79–103.

——*The Remasculanization of America: Gender and the Vietnam War* (Bloomington and Indianapolis: Indiana University Press, 1989).

JOHNSON, MARK, '"History, the Body's Prison": American Poetry During and after Vietnam', *Publications of the Missouri Philological Association*, 8 (1983), 25–30.

KENNER, HUGH, *The Counterfeiters* (Bloomington: Indiana University Press, 1968).

KERMODE, FRANK, *Poetry, Narrative, History* (Oxford: Basil Blackwell, 1990).

KIRKPATRICK, BETTY (ed.), *Brewer's Concise Dictionary of Phrase & Fable* (Oxford: Helicon Publishing Ltd., 1995).

KLEIN, MICHAEL, *The Vietnam Era: Media and Popular Culture in the US and Vietnam* (London and Winchester, Mass.: Pluto Press, 1990).

LAKOFF, GEORGE, and JOHNSON, MARK, *Metaphors We Live By* (Chicago and London: The University of Chicago Press, 1980).
LAWSON, JACQUELINE (ed.), *Vietnam Generation*, special issue, *Gender and the War: Men, Women, and Vietnam*, 1: 3–4 (Summer–Fall 1989).
LENSE, EDWARD, 'The Assyrian Lion Above the Soybean Fields: Bly's *The Light Around the Body* as Prophecy Against the Vietnam War', *Journal of American Culture*, 16: 3 (Fall 1993), 89–95.
LENTRICCHIA, FRANK, and McLAUGHLIN, THOMAS (eds.), *Critical Terms For Literary Study* (Chicago and London: The University of Chicago Press, 1990).
LIFTON, ROBERT JAY, *Home From the War: Vietnam Veterans, Neither Victims Nor Executioners* (London: Wildwood House, 1974).
LOMPERIS, TIMOTHY, *'Reading the Wind': The Literature of the Vietnam War* (Durham, NC: Duke University Press, 1987).
LY CHANH TRUNG, *Introduction to Vietnamese Poetry* (Saigon: Directorate of Cultural Affairs, Ministry of Culture, 1970).
MACHEREY, PIERRE, *A Theory of Literary Production*, trans. Geoffrey Wall (London, Henley, and Boston: Routledge & Kegan Paul, 1978).
MARCUSE, HERBERT, *The Aesthetic Dimension: Toward a Critique of Marxist Aesthetics* (London and Basingstoke: The Macmillan Press, Ltd., 1979).
MARX, LEO, *The Pilot and the Passenger: Essays on Literature, Technology, and Culture in the United States* (New York and Oxford: Oxford University Press, 1988).
'The Meaning of Vietnam', *New York Review of Books*, 22: 10 (June 1975), 23–33.
MELLING, PHILIP, *Vietnam in American Literature* (Boston: Twayne Publishers, 1990).
MERSMANN, JAMES F., *Out of the Vietnam Vortex: A Study of Poets and Poetry Against the War* (Lawrence, Manhattan, and Wichita, Kan.: The University Press of Kansas, 1974).
MITHERS, CAROL LYNN, 'Missing in Action: Women Warriors in Vietnam', *Cultural Critique*, 3 (Spring 1986), 79–90.
MONTENEGRO, DAVID, *Points of Departure: International Writers on Writing and Politics* (Ann Arbor: The University of Michigan Press, 1991).
NELSON, CARY, 'Whitman in Vietnam: Poetry and History in Contemporary America', *The Massachusetts Review*, 16: 1 (Winter 1975), 55–71.
O'BRIEN, TIM, interview with Sheila Rogers, *Arts Week* (Canadian Broadcasting Corporation, 20 Jan. 1991).
PALEY, GRACE, 'Writers and War', *The Writer In Our World*, highlights

of *TriQuarterly* magazine's 1984 symposium, Northwestern University, audio cassette.
—— 'Of Poetry and Women and the World', *TriQuarterly*, 65 (Winter 1986), 247–53.
PINSKY, ROBERT, *Poetry and the World* (New York: The Ecco Press, 1988).
PLAIN, GILL, '"Great Expectations": Rehabilitating the Recalcitrant War Poets', *Feminist Review*, 51 (Autumn 1995), 41–65.
RINGNALDA, DON, 'Rejecting "Sweet Geometry": Komunyakaa's Duende', *Journal of American Culture*, 16: 3 (Fall 1993), 21–8.
—— *Fighting and Writing the Vietnam War* (Jackson, Miss.: University Press of Mississippi, 1994).
RORTY, RICHARD, *Contingency, irony, and solidarity* (Cambridge and New York: Cambridge University Press, 1989).
ROSENTHAL, M. L., *Our Life in Poetry: Selected Essays and Reviews* (New York: Persea Books, 1991).
ROWE, JOHN CARLOS, 'From Documentary to Docudrama: Vietnam on Television in the 1980s', *Genre*, 21: 4 (Winter 1988), 451–77.
—— and BERG, RICK (eds.), *The Vietnam War and American Culture* (New York: Columbia University Press, 1991).
RUSHDIE, SALMAN, *Imaginary Homelands: Essays and Criticism 1981–1991* (Harmondsworth: Penguin Books Ltd., 1991).
SAID, EDWARD W., *Orientalism* (Harmondsworth: Penguin Books Ltd., 1978).
—— 'Relationship Between Endings and Beginnings', *Wolfson College Lectures*, No. 8, 1993, audio cassette.
—— *Culture & Imperialism* (London: Vintage, 1994).
SARTRE, JEAN-PAUL, *Between Existentialism and Marxism* (London: Verso, 1983).
SCARRY, ELAINE, *The Body in Pain: The Making and Unmaking of the World* (New York and Oxford: Oxford University Press, 1985).
SCHROEDER, ERIC JAMES, *Vietnam, We've All Been There: Interviews With American Writers* (Westport, Conn., and London: Praeger Publishers, 1992).
SEARLE, WILLIAM J. (ed.), *Search and Clear: Critical Responses to Selected Literature and Films of the Vietnam War* (Bowling Green, Oh.: Bowling Green State University Popular Press, 1988).
SHATAN, CHAIM F., 'Happiness Is a Warm Gun: Militarized Mourning and Ceremonial Vengeance: Towards a Psychological Theory of Combat and Manhood in America, Part III', in Jacqueline Lawson (ed.), *Vietnam Generation*, special issue, *Gender and the War: Men, Women, and Vietnam*, 1: 3–4 (Summer–Fall 1989), 127–51.
SLABEY, ROBERT M. (ed.), *The United States and Vietnam From War*

to Peace: Papers From an Interdisciplinary Conference on Reconciliation (Jefferson, NC, and London: McFarland & Company Inc., Publishers, 1996).

SMITH, LORRIE, 'A Sense-Making Perspective in Recent Poetry by Vietnam Veterans', The American Poetry Review, 15: 6 (Nov./Dec. 1986), 13–18.

—— 'Back Against the Wall: Anti-Feminist Backlash in Vietnam War Literature', in Jacqueline Lawson (ed.), Vietnam Generation, special issue, Gender and the War: Men, Women, and Vietnam, 1: 3–4 (Summer–Fall 1989), 115–126.

—— 'The Subject Makes a Difference: Poetry by Women Veterans of the Vietnam War', Journal of American Culture, 16: 3 (Fall 1993), 71–9.

—— 'Against a Coming Extinction: W. D. Ehrhart and the Evolving Canon of Vietnam Veterans' Poetry', War, Literature & the Arts, W. D. Ehrhart: A Special Issue, 8: 2 (Fall–Winter 1996), 1–30.

SMITH, M. VAN WYK, Drummer Hodge: The Poetry of the Anglo-Boer War (1899–1902) (Oxford: Clarendon Press, 1978).

SONTAG, SUSAN, Styles of Radical Will (London: Vintage, 1994).

SOSSAMAN, STEPHEN, 'American Poetry From the Indochina Experience', Long Island Review, 2 (Winter 1973–4), 30–3.

SPEAR, HILDA D., Remembering We Forget (London: Davis-Poynter Limited, 1979).

SPENDER, STEPHEN, 'Poetry of the Unspeakable', New York Review of Books, 20: 1 (8 Feb. 1973), 3–6.

STALLWORTHY, JON, Wilfred Owen: A Biography (London: Oxford University Press and Chatto and Windus, 1974).

TAL, KALI, 'Feminist Criticism and the Literature of the Vietnam Combat Veteran', in Jacqueline Lawson (ed.), Vietnam Generation, special issue, Gender and the War: Men, Women, and Vietnam, 1: 3–4 (Summer–Fall 1989), 190–201.

—— Worlds of Hurt: Reading the Literatures of Trauma (New York: Cambridge University Press, 1996).

WALLACE, JENNIFER, 'Exiled by foes, silenced by friends', Times Higher Education Supplement, 17 Jan. 1997, 17.

WALSH, JEFFREY, American War Literature: 1914 to Vietnam (New York: St Martin's Press, 1982).

—— and AULICH, JAMES (eds.), Vietnam Images: War and Representation (Basingstoke and London: The Macmillan Press Ltd., 1989).

WILSON, JOHN P., HAREL, ZEV, and KAHANA, BOAZ (eds.), Human Adaptation to Extreme Stress: From the Holocaust to Vietnam (New York and London: Plenum Press, 1988).

WRIGHT, ROBERT A., '"History's Heavy Attrition": Literature,

Historical Consciousness and the Impact of Vietnam', *The Canadian Review of American Studies*, 17: 3 (Fall 1986), 301–16.

History and Politics

ADDISON, PAUL, 'East is East', *New Statesman*, 95: 2453 (24 Mar, 1978), 404–5.
BENEDETTI, CHARLES DE, *An American Ordeal: The Antiwar Movement of the Vietnam Era* (Syracuse, NY: New York University Press, 1990).
CHOMSKY, NOAM, *For Reasons of State* (New York: Pantheon Books, 1970).
—— *At War With Asia* (London: William Collins Sons & Co. Ltd., 1971).
—— *Rethinking Camelot: JFK, the Vietnam War and U.S. Political Culture* (Boston: South End Press, 1993).
DICKSTEIN, MORRIS, *Gates of Eden: American Culture in the Sixties* (New York: Basic Books, Inc., Publishers, 1977).
EMERSON, GLORIA, *Winners and Losers: Battles, Retreats, Gains, Losses and Ruins from a Long War* (New York: Random House, 1976).
FANON, FRANTZ, *The Wretched of the Earth*, trans. Constance Farrington (1967; Harmondsworth: Penguin Books Ltd., 1990).
FITZGERALD, FRANCES, *Fire in the Lake: The Vietnamese and the Americans in Vietnam* (Boston: Little, Brown and Company, 1972).
FREEDMAN, LAWRENCE (ed.), *War* (Oxford: Oxford University Press, 1994).
GETTLEMAN, MARVIN E., FRANKLIN, JANE, YOUNG, MARILYN, and FRANKLIN, H. BRUCE (eds.), *Vietnam and America: A Documented History* (New York: Grove Press Inc., 1985).
GINSBERG, ROBERT (ed.), *The Critique of War* (Chicago: Henry Regnery Company, 1969).
GITLIN, TODD, *The Sixties: Years of Hope, Days of Rage* (New York and London: Bantam Books, 1987).
GREENE, FELIX, *Vietnam! Vietnam!* (London: Jonathan Cape, 1966).
HERMAN, EDWARD S., and CHOMSKY, NOAM, *Manufacturing Consent: The Political Economy of the Mass Media* (London: Vintage, 1994).
HERRING, GEORGE C., *America's Longest War: The United States and Vietnam, 1950–1975* (New York and Toronto: John Wiley & Sons, 1979).
HOBSBAWM, ERIC, *Age of Extremes: The Short Twentieth Century 1914–1991* (London: Michael Joseph Ltd., 1994).
HOFSTADTER, RICHARD, *The Paranoid Style in American Politics and*

Other Essays (London: Jonathan Cape, 1966).
JUST, WARD, *Military Men* (London: Michael Joseph, 1972).
KARNOW, STANLEY, *Vietnam: A History* (London: Pimlico, 1994).
KEEGAN, JOHN, *The Face of Battle* (London: Jonathan Cape, 1976).
KOLKO, GABRIEL, *Vietnam: Anatomy of a War, 1940–1975* (London and Sydney: Allen & Unwin, 1986).
LACOUTURE, JEAN, *Ho Chi Minh*, trans. Peter Wiles (Harmondsworth: Penguin Books Ltd., 1968).
LASCH, CHRISTOPHER, *The Culture of Narcissism: American Life in an Age of Diminishing Expectations* (New York: W. W. Norton & Co., 1978).
LEED, ERIC J., *No Man's Land: Combat and Identity in World War I* (Cambridge: Cambridge University Press, 1979).
LEWY, GUENTER, *America in Vietnam* (New York: Oxford University Press, 1978).
LISKA, GEORGE, *Imperial America: The International Politics of Primacy* (Baltimore: The Johns Hopkins Press, 1967).
LONG, ROBERT EMMET (ed.), *Vietnam Ten Years After* (New York: The H. W. Wilson Company, 1986).
MACDONALD, DOUGLAS J., *Adventures in Chaos: American Intervention for Reform in the Third World* (Cambridge, Mass., and London: Harvard University Press, 1992).
MARCUSE, HERBERT, *One-Dimensional Man: Studies in the Ideology of Advanced Industrial Society* (London: Routledge, 1964).
—— *An Essay on Liberation* (London: Allen Lane The Penguin Press, 1969).
NAVASKY, VICTOR S., *Naming Names* (New York: The Viking Press, 1980).
O'BRIEN, WILLIAM V., *The Conduct of Just and Limited War* (New York: Praeger Publishers, 1981).
OLSON, JAMES S., and ROBERTS, RANDY, *My Lai: A Brief History With Documents* (Boston and New York: Bedford Books, 1998).
ORWELL, SONIA, and ANGUS, IAN (eds.), *The Collected Essays, Journalism and Letters of George Orwell. iv. In Front of Your Nose 1945–1950* (Harmondsworth: Penguin Books Ltd., 1970).
PECK, JAMES (ed.), *The Chomsky Reader* (London: The Serpent's Tail, 1988).
PILGER, JOHN, *Hidden Agendas* (London: Vintage, 1998).
PODHORETZ, NORMAN, *Why We Were In Vietnam* (New York: Simon and Schuster, 1982).
RASKIN, MARCUS G., and FALL, BERNARD B. (eds.), *The Viet-Nam Reader: Articles and Documents on American Foreign Policy and the Viet-Nam Crisis* (New York: Random House, 1967).

SAYRES, SOHNYA, STEPHANSON, ANDERS, ARONOWITZ, STANLEY, and JAMESON, FREDRIC (eds.), *The 60s Without Apology* (Minneapolis: University of Minnesota Press, 1984).

SCHULZINGER, ROBERT D., *American Diplomacy in the Twentieth Century* (New York and Oxford: Oxford University Press, 1994).

SLOTKIN, RICHARD, 'Dreams and Genocide: The American Myth of Regeneration Through Violence', *Journal of Popular Culture*, 5: 1 (Summer 1971), 38–59.

TALLACK, DOUGLAS, *Twentieth Century America: The Intellectual and Cultural Context* (London and New York: Longman, 1991).

THOMPSON, VIRGINIA, *French Indo-China* (London: George Allen & Unwin Ltd., 1937).

WALZER, MICHAEL, *Just and Unjust Wars: A Moral Argument With Historical Illustrations* (New York: Basic Books, 1992).

WERNER, JAYNE S., and LUU DOAN HUYNH (eds.), *The Vietnam War: Vietnamese and American Perspectives* (New York and London: M. E. Sharpe, 1993).

WILLIAM, REESE (ed.), *Unwinding the Vietnam War: From War to Peace* (Seattle: The Real Comet Press, 1987).

ZINN, HOWARD, *A People's History of the United States* (New York: Harper Collins Publishers, 1980).

Index

Adorno, Theodor 36
Agnew, Spiro 41
America and the Second World War 3, 5–6
American colonialism 1, 7, 9–10, 19–24, 83–4
American foreign policy and Vietnam 2–7
anti-war movement 38–42

Baker, Mark:
  Nam: The Vietnam War in the Words of the Men and Women Who Fought There 109, 117, 135, 142–3, 145
Baker, Richard E.:
  'Hoedown' 127–8
Balaban, John:
  'After Our War' 156–8
  'Agua Fria Y Las Chicharras' 200
  'The Book and the Lacquered Box' 166–8
  'In Celebration of Spring' 159–61
  Remembering Heaven's Face: A Moral Witness in Vietnam 155–6, 164–5
  'Saying Goodbye to Mr. and Mrs. My, Saigon, 1972' 158–9
Ball, George 16–17
Bao Ninh:
  The Sorrow of War 78, 211–12, 215, 216
Barker, Pat:
  The Ghost Road 26
Beats 42–5
Beidler, Philip 97
Bennington, Geoffrey 1
betrayal 181–2, 184
Bly, Robert 52, 62
  as prophet 56, 61
  'As the Asian War Begins' 52
  'Asian Peace Offers Rejected Without Publication' 61–2
  The Teeth Mother Naked at Last 53–6, 57
  'Turning Away From Lies' 60–1
  'War and Silence' 58–60
  'Watching Television' 57–8
boat people 207–8 n. 17, 215
Boer War 76
Boondock Bards 103–6
Bowen, Kevin 209–10, 223
  'A Conical Hat' 168–70
  'Incoming' 137–8
Broyles, William Jr.:
  'Why Men Love War' 119, 126, 144–5

Carter, Jimmy 15

Caruth, Cathy 161
Chomsky, Noam 21
Cobley, Evelyn 25, 90, 112, 140
Cohn, Carol xv
Coleman, Horace:
  'D-Day + 50; Tet + 25' 145–6
colonization 3–4, 127
Committee of Responsibility to Save War-Injured Children 155
Connolly, David:
  'After the Firefight' 121–23
  'Another Chance' 176–77
'cryptoracism' 22

DEROS 106–9, 139
Dickstein, Morris 42, 43, 71
Dowling, W. C. 191
Dürrenmatt, Friedrich 37
Du Tu Le:
  'The Dawn of a New Humankind' 216–18

Edelman, Bernard:
  Dear America: Letters Home From Vietnam 110
Ehrhart, W. D. 101, 106, 111, 123, 185, 190, 193–4, 199
  'Dancing' 151–3
  'The Distance We Travel' 182–4
  'The Farmer' 186–8
  'For Mrs Na' 165–6
  'Fragment: 5 September 1967' 112–14
  'The Invasion of Grenada' 149–51
  'Letter' 180–2
  'Loving You' 191
  'The Poet as Athlete' 198
  'A Relative Thing' 147–9
  'The Teacher' 184–6
  '"Waiting for the Fire": An Essay on Vietnam War Poetry by Non-Vietnam Veterans' 92–3
  'The Way Light Bends' 189–91
  'Why I Don't Mind Rocking Leela to Sleep' 188–90
Einstein, Albert 82
Eliot, T. S.:
  Murder in the Cathedral 29, 30
Elshtain, Jean xi, 91
Emerson, Gloria 164
exile 102, 113, 121, 170, 173, 216–17, 219–20

Fanon, Frantz 22, 50, 201–2

Index

Fitzgerald, Frances 163
Floyd, Bryan Alec:
   'Sergeant Brandon Just, U.S.M.C.' 123–5
Fussell, Paul 26, 197
   The Great War and Modern Memory 115
   Wartime: Understanding and Behavior in the Second World War 27, 29–30

General Westmoreland 21–2, 64
Ginsberg, Allen 44, 48
   as prophet 56
   'America' 46–8
   'Friday the Thirteenth' 50–1
   'Howl' 43–6
   'Iron Horse' 48–50
   'A Supermarket in California' 46
   'Wichita Vortex Sutra' 49
Gitlin, Todd 38–9, 40, 78, 90–1
Green Berets 107
Greene, Graham:
   The Quiet American 7

Haines, Harry 102
Hanoi 79, 174
Hartman, Geoffrey 18
healing 101, 102, 152, 158, 175
Hearts and Minds 68
Herr, Michael 112, 119–20
Hersh, Seymour 47
Hiroshima 26
Hobsbawm, Eric 6
Ho Chi Minh 4, 182, 202, 210, 213
   'On Reading *The Ten Thousand Poets*' 158
   see also Uncle Ho
Hofstadter, Richard 8
homecoming 141–2, 161, 170
Homer:
   The Odyssey 128
House Un-American Activities Committee (HUAC) 42, 100
Hué City 181

imperialism 142
innocence (loss of) 106, 113–14, 142

Jameson, Fredric 94, 102
Jarrell, Randall:
   'The Death of the Ball Turret Gunner' 33–6
Johnson, Lyndon 4, 9
Just, Ward 12
just war 18

Karnow, Stanley:
   Vietnam: A History 9
Kelley, Jack:
   'Flak Jacket' 120–1
Kennedy, John F. 4, 11, 107
Kenner, Hugh 66
Kermode, Frank 96
Khe Sanh 113

King, Martin Luther Jr. 59
Kipling, Rudyard:
   'The Head of the District' 10–11
Komunyakaa, Yusef:
   'A Greenness Taller Than Gods' 131–3
   'Maps Drawn in the Dust' 129–31
   'Starlight Scope Myopia' 133–4
Krohn, Herbert:
   'Can Tho' 116, 168
Kundera, Milan 205

Le Thi May:
   'Wind and Widow' 213–15
Leed, Eric J. 143
Levertov, Denise 71, 74, 75, 82, 206
   'The Distance' 77–9
   'In Thai Binh (Peace) Province' 79–80
   'An Interim' 80
   'Overheard Over S. E. Asia' 72–3
   'Scenario' 73–5
   'What Were They Like?' 75–6
Lewy, Guenter 14
Lifton, Robert Jay 121, 186
liminality 143
Lowenfels, Walter:
   Where Is Vietnam? 84

McCarthy, Gerald:
   'The Hooded Legion' 150
McCarthyism 5
McDonald, Douglas 11
McDonald, Walter:
   'Black Granite Burns Like Ice' 153–4
   'Caliban in Blue' 125–7
   'The Food Pickers of Saigon' 162–4
Macherey, Pierre 3
McNamara, Robert S. 13, 19
manifest destiny 87, 104, 158
Marcus, Morton:
   'Confession' 85–6
Marcuse, Herbert 12, 39, 94, 194
Marin, Peter 37, 194
Marvell, Andrew:
   'On a Drop of Dew' 167
Mason, Steve:
   'The Wall Within' 178–80
Merrill, James:
   '18 West Street 11th Street' 50–1
Merton, Thomas 49
My Lai 50, 108

Nagasaki 26
napalm 73, 85, 124, 154, 224
National Liberation Front (also referred to as Vietcong) 53, 76, 108, 128, 130, 132–4, 163, 168, 169–70, 183, 205, 221–2
Navasky, Victor 6, 42
Nemerov, Howard 65, 68
   'Continuous Performances' 67–8
   'The Language of the Tribe' 65–7

'On Being Asked for a Peace Poem' 68–70
'On Getting Out of Vietnam' 64–5
'Redeployment' 28–31, 85
'The War in the Air' 31–3
Ngo Dinh Diem 9, 23
Nguyen Ba Chung:
  'Nonattachment' 225–6
Nguyen Duy:
  'Red Earth, Blue Water' 211–12
Nixon, Richard 4–5, 6, 7
No More Vietnams 14
North Vietnamese Army 76
Nye, Jim:
  'Chimaera' 143–5

Oppenheimer, Joel:
  '17–18 April, 1961' 82–4
orientalism 90

Palmer, General Bruce 14–15
Paquet, Basil T.:
  'Morning—A Death' 114–16
pastoral 115, 116, 167, 171, 209
Pinsky, Robert xiii, 36–7, 51–2
Poems From Captured Documents 207, 208
politics (of publishing) 206–8
Pound, Ezra:
  'Hugh Selwyn Mauberly' 54–5
POW/MIA myths 149, 159
Puff the Magic Dragon 144

Reagan, Ronald 16, 64
reconciliation 101, 158, 175
representation 192–3
Rich, Adrienne xii, 65, 84, 86, 89, 95, 223
  'Face to Face' 87
  'North American Time' 87–9
Ritterbusch, Dale:
  'Better Dead than Boring' 146–7
Rorty, Richard 96, 139
Rowe, John Carlos 8, 95
Rushdie, Salman 199

Said, Edward xiii, 16, 82, 90, 220
Saigon 167
Santoli, Al 216
Sassoon, Siegfried 98–9
  'They' 59–60
Schultz, George P. 15
Schulzinger, Robert 2
Second World War films 67 n. 73
Select Service System 147
Serigo (Igor Bobrowsky):
  'I Hate You . . .' 116–18
Shakespeare, William:
  Macbeth 129, 213
Shoup, General David 17

Slotkin, Richard 130
soldier as victim 174
solidarity xiv, 96, 102, 164, 165, 168, 170, 176, 177, 182, 188, 192, 223
solipsism 91–2
Sontag, Susan 204
Sossaman, Stephen 105, 115, 138–9, 166

Tet Offensive 64, 80
Thich Nhat Hahn 225
  'Condemnation' 221–2
torture 167
Tran Da Tu:
  'The New Lullaby' 212–13
Tran Mong Tu:
  'The Gift in Wartime' 218–19
  'A New Year's wish for a little refugee' 219–21
translation (problems of) xiv–xv, 205, 208, 223–4
trauma 102, 148, 154, 173, 175
Truong Nhu Tang:
  Journal of a Vietcong 202, 205, 215

Uncle Ho 77–8, 127
  see also Ho Chi Minh

Van Ky:
  'My Birthplace, Nam Binh' 208–10
'*Vietnam*' *A Portrait of Its People at War* 207–8
Vietnam Memorial 68
Vietnam Memorial (Washington, DC) 101–2, 149–51, 153–4, 178
Viet-Nam Veterans Against the War (VVAW) 98–100

Weathermen 50–1
Weigl, Bruce 175
  'Burning Shit at An Khe' 135–7
  'Dialectical Materialism' 171–3
  'Her Life Runs Like a Red Silk Flag' 173–6
Whitman, Walt 46, 62–3
William Joiner Center for the Study of War and Social Consequences 207
Wilson, Woodrow 20
Winning Hearts and Minds 111–18
Winter Soldier Investigation 99–100, 125, 164
witness 42, 111–12, 155, 156, 187–8, 192–3, 195
Wolff, Tobias 142
Writing Between the Lines 206, 207

Yeats, W. B.:
  'On Being Asked for a War Poem' 68–70

Zinn, Howard 38